Policing and Public Trust

The Applied Criminology across the Globe Series

Series Editor

Kimberly A. McCabe, University of Lynchburg, mccabe@lynchburg.edu

Crime and safety continue to be among the top issues facing the global world and the discipline of applied criminology addresses those issues. *The Applied Criminology across the Globe* series, is designed to address the ever-growing need for current and accurate information on a variety of subjects as related to applied criminology. The books in this series provide the readers with monographs that are able to inform and educate individuals on crime and criminal behaviors.

Books in the Series

Policing and Public Trust: Exposing the Inner Uniform, by Eccy de Jonge

Policing and Public Trust

Exposing the Inner Uniform

Eccy de Jonge

ROWMAN & LITTLEFIELD
Lanham • Boulder • New York • London

Published by Rowman & Littlefield
An imprint of The Rowman & Littlefield Publishing Group, Inc.
4501 Forbes Boulevard, Suite 200, Lanham, Maryland 20706
www.rowman.com

6 Tinworth Street, London SE11 5AL, United Kingdom

British Library Cataloguing in Publication Information Available

Library of Congress Cataloging-in-Publication Data

Names: De Jonge, Eccy, author.
Title: Policing and public trust : exposing the inner uniform / Eccy de Jonge.
Description: Lanham : Rowman & Littlefield, [2020] | Series: Applied criminology across the globe series | Includes bibliographical references and index.
Identifiers: LCCN 2020035083 (print) | LCCN 2020035084 (ebook) | ISBN 9781538146903 (cloth) | ISBN 9781538146910 (epub)
Subjects: LCSH: Police misconduct—Great Britain—Case studies. | Police—Complaints against—Great Britain—Case studies. | Discrimination in law enforcement—Great Britain—Case studies. | Discrimination in criminal justice administration—Great Britain—Case studies. | Victims of crimes—Great Britain—Case studies. | Police ethics—Great Britain. | Police administration—Great Britain. | Government accountability—Great Britain. | Transparency in government—Great Britain.
Classification: LCC HV8195.A3 D45 2020 (print) | LCC HV8195.A3 (ebook) | DDC 363.2/3—dc23
LC record available at https://lccn.loc.gov/2020035083
LC ebook record available at https://lccn.loc.gov/2020035084

∞™ The paper used in this publication meets the minimum requirements of American National Standard for Information Sciences—Permanence of Paper for Printed Library Materials, ANSI/NISO Z39.48-1992.

To: James Connelly, Dean Jones, and John Mason

Sine qua non

Contents

Preface

Since its inception in the late nineteenth century, the prevailing ethos of the police institution in Britain has been said to rest on Sir Robert Peel's 1829 mantra that "the police are the public and the public are the police." This refrain of policing by consent has constantly been challenged and no more so than in recent years. While public views of policing in Britain maintain a constant level of trust, according to opinion polls little attention is given as to why 40 percent of the population remain mistrustful of policing services. With the police receiving thousands of complaints each year and with more than one-third falling into an undefined category, there remains an aspect of policing largely ignored by both criminologists and policing agencies: the treatment of victims and complainants.[1]

In the early 1970s, two criminologists, Steven Box and Ken Russell, revealed that complainants were being habitually discriminated against in ways that had thus far received no academic or media attention. Examples included being disbelieved, maliciously arrested, wrongly diagnosed as mentally ill, or portrayed as alcoholic or drug users.[2] In seeking to explore whether such behavior is prevalent today, a call was put out on social media for those who had been discredited by the police to get in touch with the author. No definition was provided as to what "discredit" meant. Though the number of respondents was relatively small (fifty people replied over a six-month period), interviews with thirty participants and hundreds more news stories confirmed that police agencies are still discrediting innocent members of the public by using the same methods identified by Box and Russell. There was only one disparity: Those now being discredited by the police and those coming forward to be interviewed included victims of crime, police whistleblowers, bereaved relatives of road deaths, as well as complainants. New methods of discrediting the public included covert practices, contacting a complainant's employer that led to dismissal, and using the new tools of social media.

Though much of this book is confined to police operations in the United Kingdom, especially with regard to the narratives of those whose interviews were transcribed as case studies, the extent to which the modern police service sets itself apart from the public (and is therefore nonconsensual) is shown in policing practices across the globe, from the United States to Australia.

The question why police officers discredit the innocent and how they manage to do so without consequence then became a major part of the research, including an examination of whether police investigations are biased per se in favor of particular outcomes or verdicts. It was discovered that bias in policing investigations is a major cause of miscarriages of justice and may, to some extent, explain attempts to discredit victims. Focusing on the most common but least reported of police investigations in both academic and media circles, road deaths, revealed a thin line between bias and incompetence, though research also showed how, in some circles, police officers who take a creative initiative in preventing future crime can be of great public benefit. However, it was likewise discovered that other members of the criminal justice system not only support policing agencies but also heavily rely on the police for their decisions. Several bodies, including coroners and pathologists (including US medical examiners), were shown to work so closely with the police as to become almost redundant.

These findings were surprising given the College of Policing's new Code of Ethics and the Crown Prosecution Service's Victims' Right to Review. They revealed that a major problem with policing lies not with individual officers but with the so-called "police family" being seen as a closed institution that seeks to protect itself from criticism at any cost. This dispels the cliché that poor policing is the result of a few bad apples in the barrel because several police officers admitted to being treated just as poorly as members of the public when they raised concerns about colleagues' behavior, particularly in relation to biased practices. In such cases, the police institution can be seen like a closed shop, demanding its members act, not on behalf of the greater good (the general public) but the police organization itself. This hidden dimension to policing culture, which I have termed the "inner uniform," not only reduces trust in the police, but it also removes responsibility from individual officers who are either protected by the organization or regarded as dispensable. Ironically, what therefore challenges the authority of the police is not criminal activity but the cultural bullying of the institution itself, which is usually (but not always) manipulated by opaque and ineffectual professional standards departments, which espouse a rhetoric of defensiveness toward both members of the public and its own officers.

Instead of dealing with these issues, police agencies have acted to conceal them, blaming victims and complainants for their own failures. This book argues that if policing is to gain the public trust envisaged by Peel, this can only be established through a greater transparency of policing operations and behaviors. It is hoped that this book will help to create that much needed transparency.

Eccy de Jonge, London, 2020

Acknowledgments

The ideas behind the book were initially devised as a master's thesis at the Institute of Criminal Justice Studies, University of Portsmouth in 2015. Decision to do the course was taken a year after my mother, Toni Rolls, was killed by a distracted driver on the south coast of England and I sought to understand the policing policies and procedures regarding the investigation into her death and the treatment of myself, as next-of-kin. Following an article in *The Guardian* by Rob Evans and Leila Haddou regarding the case, I was interested to discover if others had experienced similar treatment. This led me to focus on examining bias in police investigations, while contacts with bereaved families of road deaths who I met through the charity Road Peace put the area of police investigations and how these may go wrong into perspective. Though I would be the first to admit that not all investigations are biased or corrupt or what may be called simply lazy, there remains a real problem in terms of the attitudes and credence given by certain investigating officers toward victims and witnesses. A lack of redress and a failure to take the accounts of victims seriously is, I argue in the book, a major reason why policing in these areas fails to improve.

I would firstly like to thank Rob Evans and Leila Haddou for reading through the hundreds of documents linked to my case and publishing their account in *The Guardian.* Though their article only told a fraction of the story, it enabled others to come forward and tell their stories to me, and for that I remain extremely grateful. Ethics approval was sought to conduct interviews with the participants whose stories are told in *Policing and Public Trust* and who were asked to sign consent forms that permitted these interviews to be transcribed and subsequently published. Asides from a few exceptions where stories were in the public eye and participants asked to be quoted, the names of those whose stories are told within this book (including several police whistleblowers) have been kept confidential, as have the names of officers and police departments involved in these narratives. Enormous appreciation goes to all those who agreed to take part. Without them, the exposure of poor policing practices, especially the means by which police professional standards departments attempt to discredit victims and complainants, would remain largely theoretical or based on third hand accounts.

Given that a person in the United Kingdom is up to five times more likely to be killed by a motor vehicle than murdered and worldwide road death collisions remain one of the highest causes of unnatural death, I was astounded to learn that no academic work has as yet been done on road investigations and the treatment by the criminal justice system of victims' families. Thus I have sought, in some small way, to readdress the balance. I was fortunate to have the support of several people who, like myself, had recently lost close relatives on the road. I would particularly like to thank: Helga Akitt, Kate Cairns, and John Thompson. A heartfelt appreciation and gratitude also goes to Cynthia Barlow, the chair of the charity Road Peace. Cynthia's support to families of road deaths goes far beyond her role as chair of a major charity. She travels the length and breadth of the country to support the recently bereaved, regularly attends inquests as an active participant and speaks on behalf of so many of us who feel the criminal justice system fails to take death by dangerous drivers seriously.

A number of individuals supported this work and contributed articles or responded to inquiries. I would especially like to thank Tim Carlisle, Sara Howlett, Brenda Marshall, Becky Milne, Julia Simon-Kerr, Paul Gregory Mitchell, and Matt Windsor. Mike McConville was extremely generous to engage with me in discussion on plea bargaining, a concern he raised within the United States justice system and has contributed worldwide, and Daniel Marshall provided draft copies of his book *Privacy and Criminal Justice*, co-authored with Terry Thomas, for which I remain especially thankful. Likewise, I am grateful to Anna Kopec-Massey for the opportunity to read her PhD thesis on empathy and social enterprise and hope I have done her work justice in applying it to policing attitudes. Thanks also to the justice campaigner Michael Doherty for putting me in touch with participants and the journalist Russell Merryman of the London College of Communication for additional information and fruitful discussion on the topic of policing and journalism, particularly the use of Twitter by certain police officers to troll complainants.

Several experts in the field provided evidence and material, from road traffic collisions to advice on pathology. I would particularly like to thank: Benjamin Heydecker, Stephen Leadbeatter, Hayley Ash, and Mark Hooghiemestra. Rachel E. Webb of the Home Office Forensic Pathology department was exceptionally kind and supportive to early enquiries on pathology as was her manager, for which I remain extremely grateful.

I am grateful for the encouragement received from Anthony Grayling, and the help of the British library staff in social sciences (particularly Phil) as well as the support from friends, particularly Brij Palmer, Philippa Whitbread, Rose L. Smith, and Garrick Twinney during the course of writing this book. I would also like to thank Andrew Halsey for his support at my mother's inquest and Debbie Radcliffe for looking through dozens of images to find the best cover art; likewise Chris Reeves who pointed us in the right direction.

I am indebted to Professor James Connelly for his friendship over many years and for providing helpful comments as an independent reviewer in the final stages. It is hard enough for friends to know what to do when a loved one dies. James's immediate reaction was to offer to accompany me to the mortuary to identify my mother's body and then stay with me afterwards through the shock and trauma. This is surely beyond what anyone can ask of another, and I will always be grateful for his support and kindness.

This book could also not have been written—or would have been a lot less accurate—without the guidance of Dr. Dean Jones, an ex-chief superintendent and criminologist who laboriously read through and discussed every chapter as the book was in progress. Not always agreeing with the polemic but offering fair and critical advice, I will be forever grateful for his help and support in writing *Policing and Public Trust* and sincerely hope this book does him justice.

Finally, my thanks goes to John Mason for his generosity in reading draft copies of the book, for his editorial proficiency, and for many evenings by the metaphorical fire place drinking red wine and discussing policing, politics, and philosophy.

List of Abbreviations

ACPO	Association of Chief Police Officers (now National Chiefs' Police Council)
CPS	Crown Prosecution Service
CSI	Crime Scene Investigator (previously SOCO)
ECRC	Enhanced Criminal Records Check (now DBS)
FLO	Family Liaison Officer
GMC	General Medical Council
HMIC	Her Majesty's Inspectorate of Constabulary
IAT	Implicit Association Test (Harvard)
ICO	Information Commissioner's Office
IDR	Incident Data Recorder (black box recorder fitted into police cars)
IOPC	Independent Office for Police Conduct (since January 2018)
IPCC	Independent Police Complaint's Commission (now IOPC)
LR	Local Resolution
MPS	Metropolitan Police Service (London)
NFI	Netherlands Forensic Institute
NPIA	National Policing Investigation Agency (now College of Policing)
NPOIU	National Public Order Intelligence Unit
PACE	Police and Criminal Evidence Act (1984)
PLO	Police or Protest Liaison Officer
PSD	Professional Standards Department
RIPA	Regulation of Investigatory Powers Act (2000)
RDIM	Road Death Investigation Manual
RP-SIO	Roads Police-Senior Investigations Officer
SDS	Special Demonstration Squad (1968–2008)
SIO	Senior Investigations Officer

1

Discrediting Victims and Complainants

Police powers may seem fairly straightforward. Despite national differences in law, policies, and procedures, police officers throughout the world use discretion when dealing with the public.[1] Officers may abuse their discretionary powers or use them inappropriately, but the public expects police officers to be flexible and to use—for want of a better phrase—their common sense. This is particularly true of minor instances such as parking infringements or infractions caused by children. Though officers must necessarily use personal judgment "to weigh up situations,"[2] they are, however, often criticized for not knowing the law.[3] Such criticism may be misplaced as a result of police officers having to make difficult choices, or it may occur because of pressures put on individual officers by management or government to reach targets in charging offenders. Because the majority of offenses are disposed of out of court, state prosecutors rarely encounter most crimes because these are dealt with by the police. These offenses may include first-time ones for stealing, minor harassment charges, being engaged in a brawl, or making impulsive threats. Occasionally these are settled by restorative procedures (e.g., meeting the victim and offering an apology), but the majority of cases are dealt with by the police giving a caution warning to the individual.

An officer's discretion is one of the main areas of responsibility which distinguishes policing powers from the exercise of power in other occupations. As the Police Federation of England and Wales make clear, "discretion is the bedrock of policing; it allows reasoned and fair decisions based on experience to be taken by police officers without the need to take a course of action merely to satisfy targets."[4] Unfortunately, while agreeing that individual discretion is part of the job, senior officers have argued that "individual bias makes it difficult to standardise national approaches," making the notion of fairness ambiguous.[5] As such, "the discretionary powers of the constable on the street . . . can lead to subjective practices."[6]

In conducting interviews with members of the public who claimed to have been discredited by the police, and in researching stories in the mainstream media, it was possible to identify types of situations in which police discretion and the legal definition of "victim" fail to do justice to people's real experiences. Among the participants were several police officers who related being subjected to smear campaigns, leading, in certain cases, to being forced to take early retirement for having raised concerns about colleagues' behavior. Ironically, within the UK College of Policing's *Code of Ethics*, the rule against "bringing the force into disrepute" may actually encourage officers to discredit members of the public.[7]

Being discredited by the police may bear similarities to being discredited by other professionals such as an employer, but the latter is unlikely to have the same long-lasting effects. When police agencies brand individuals as mentally ill or maliciously arrest people on trumped-up charges, this may result in a person losing his or her home or job. Even though the offense of Misconduct in Public Office in UK law (which carries a life sentence) states that an officer may be prosecuted for "'an abuse of the public's trust'[8] the offense must be 'culpable to an extent worthy of criminal,' and not a civil or disciplinary matter."[9] And although some officers openly breach the Human Rights Act when discrediting members of the public, no case has ever been brought under the act for discrediting victims or complainants. This is also true of police misconduct hearings, which since May 1, 2015, must be heard in public and can lead to an officer's dismissal.[10] Abuse of power may be unethical but is not regarded as a form of police corruption. Therefore, the public has no means of redress.

DISCREDITING TACTICS

In 1975, an article appeared in the journal *Sociological Review* detailing how the police discredit complainants.[11] The authors, Steven Box and Ken Russell, set out to examine police complaints in two forces in England, which to protect the forces in question, they named Marshire and Silvershire. They obtained 172 complaint forms, 30 of which were found to be justified by the police complaints departments involved. The other complaints were dismissed. Having established that manual workers were more likely to be discriminated against than white-collar workers, Box and Russell then discovered something far more disturbing. They found that each one of the discarded complaints had been rejected, either because officers said the appellant had lied or something else was found to be "wrong" with them; they were said to be drunk, mentally ill, or otherwise incapable of making a rational decision. Box and Russell thus identified that the police departments concerned had a formal process for discrediting complainants. The means identified by Box and Russell are presented in table 1.1.

Table 1.1. Techniques by Which Police Seek to Discredit Complainants.

Means of Discreditability	*Explanation*
Neutralising the complainant (includes verballing: misrepresenting or inventing words by the complainant)	This denies the voice of the complainant by accusing him or her of fabrication; denying the incident took place or classing the complainant as "deserving injury" owing to role or stigma (prostitutes, racial group, etc.)
Arresting, threatening with arrest and/or actually prosecuting a potential or actual complainant	This attempts to turn the complainant into a criminal and, when no further charge is brought, stigmatises the complainant as being potentially suspect.
Revealing the complainant to have a stigmatizing (or previous) criminal record	This suggests the complainant may be treated as a criminal suspect: "once a criminal, always a criminal" to ensure a neutralising effect.
Showing present or past evidence of mental illness or of low intelligence (includes people with dementia and learning difficulties)	Diagnosing complainants as mentally ill is intended to show them as being incapable of knowing what really occurred (being delusional) or being unable to control their own behaviour (dehumanisation)
Under the influence of alcohol or other drugs at the time of the alleged incident	This achieves the same objective as mental illness: to show that a person is incapable of knowing what really occurred or was not in control of his or her own behaviour or decision-making.

Adapted from Box and Russell (1975), "The Politics of Discreditability," 320–21.

Box and Russell's paper, published more than forty years ago, is now a mere footnote in policing studies. There has been no attempt to reexamine the study, let alone to identify if certain complainants are still treated the same way. And yet, since the 1970s, there have been dozens of media stories revealing that these same methods not only still apply but also apply equally to victims.[12] Neutralizing the complainant has been identified as a form of implicit bias (examined in chapter 2), overwhelmingly affecting victims of rape and sexual abuse, while being threatened with suspension or maliciously arrested is a common strategy used against whistleblowers or police officers who raise concerns about colleagues.[13] Of the fifty participants who came forward to be interviewed for this study, three had previous criminal records used against them, which were historic and irrelevant to their current situation; several were targeted as being mentally ill (elucidated in chapter 3); and the consumption of alcohol (whether true or fabricated) was used in several cases against road death victims to ignore the need to conduct a comprehensive investigation (see chapter 4). Several participants faced malicious arrest, with five being taken to court.

All of this reveals that the means of discrediting innocent members of the public, as identified by Box and Russell, remain a practice of contemporary policing, though to what extent remains unknown. Mental illness (along with alcoholism or abuse of liquor) was the most common means of discrediting victims and complainants, with more than one-quarter of interviewees stating that police records commonly named them as "delusional." In such cases, officers carried out their own diagnosis or employed professional psychiatrists to confirm evidence of mental illness, without speaking to, or meeting with, the complainant. In most cases, details of the person's "state of mind" were shared with third parties, thus not only breaching the UK's Data Protection Act 2018 but ensuring that no other party would take the person's concerns seriously. This reveals a complete lack of respect and discrimination against people who do suffer from mental illness.

In addition to the work of Box and Russell, four other means by which police officers attempt to discredit people were identified. All can be said to apply equally to victims of crime and to whistleblowers.

- *Surveillance*—this included watching, observing, phone tapping, following, or tailing; taking records of a person's conversation or behavior without his or her knowledge; covertly following victims on social media; holding covert meetings (e.g., to decide if a person is mentally ill); to having illicit affairs (as undercover police officers) without the participant knowing that his or her lover was a police officer working undercover.
- *Harassment on Social Media*—this included "trolling," the practice of retweeting a person's message with a figure or dot preceding the tweet so that a personal response is sent to all followers, and haranguing a victim or complainant with constant retorts including suggestions of lying.
- *Sharing Data*—this involved police officers and investigative teams sharing data on the victim or complainant with third parties without any legitimate reason, most commonly with other policing agencies, including the College of Policing, the National Crime Agency, or the Home Office,

as well as coroners, lawyers, county councils, social service departments, and doctors.

- *Illegitimate Interference*—this was an attempt to discredit the person by taking deliberate malicious action not identified previously. In two separate cases, police officers wrote to the employer of the complainants requesting that disciplinary action be taken against them even though neither person was a suspect in a case, had no criminal record, and the concern they were raising with the police had nothing to do with the employer. To take this action, covert policing, data sharing. and targeting on social media took place to obtain the complainants' personal details.

It remains unknown how many people are targeted by police in this way, though research revealed more than a hundred different media stories since the year 2000. What is clear is that the practice of discrediting victims and complainants still occurs. With the exception of high-profile cases, such as the Hillsborough inquest in 2016 and the Macpherson Inquiry in 1999, the link among poor policing investigations, confirmation bias, and the need to conceal mistakes by discrediting victims and their families remains obscure. Examining the cases of these victims and complainants who on the surface would seem to have no reason to *be* discredited exposes an underlying flaw in police culture and ethics where the terms "complainant" and "victim" start to blur.

IDENTIFYING THE SUBJECT

Although a large body of academic research exists on police misconduct and accountability, there is little research on discrediting victims and complainants.[14] In contrast, articles in the mainstream media are full of reports of those who have been discredited by the police. For the purposes of this study they comprise:

- Victims of crime (including road death victims);
- Witnesses of crime;
- Complainants: about police misconduct and officers (whose "victim status" has otherwise been ignored);
- Bereaved family members (of those killed by police or others involved in policing investigations); and
- Police whistleblowers and complainants.

If the concept of fairness remains ambiguous in policing circles, then so does the notion of "victim." To define a victim as someone who has been harmed may be literally accurate, but police officers (as well as lawyers and other professionals) need to determine not only the level of harm committed but also the onus of proof against any assailant, particularly as victims' accounts are often treated with skepticism by members of the public.[15] Notwithstanding public opinion, the police make decisions whether to believe a victim. While harm may be a deciding factor (particularly if someone presents with bruising), the matters of when harm took place, *if* it took place (where there first appears to be no substantial evidence), and *who* is responsible are not. Police officers may decide that a so-called victim has wasted their time, is not telling the truth, or is out for revenge. And in some cases, however rare, this may well be the case.[16] However, the fact that a minority of complainants qua victims are not telling the truth should not lead to a majority being disbelieved. And yet, this seems to occur with too much frequency. Though efforts have been made in recent years to enhance the status of victims by creating a Victim's Charter, this is of limited value because it states that a victim is "a natural person who has suffered harm . . . which was directly caused by a criminal offence" or "a relative whose death was caused by a criminal offence."[17] Those who fail to fit this criterion (e.g., where no criminal offence has been proved or not as yet) may not therefore be regarded as a victim.[18] Since these are the majority of people who come into contact with the police, an immediate problem arises with reporting a crime. Even if one is a victim in the ordinary sense of the word, when no perpetrator is found guilty in a court of law, the status of "victim" remains ambiguous, with the concerned party often being referred to simply as the "complainant."[19] Therefore, until an accuser is found guilty, victims remain complainants and any harm that may have been suffered is regarded not only as unproved but also suspect.

This leaves those who report a crime and for whom no accuser has been found, or for whom the police decide there is "no case to answer," regularly being dismissed as complainants.[20] It also leaves the majority of so-called "victims" out of account because it offers rights only to those who have brought a perpetrator to trial. Just as a suspect is not a criminal until proven in a court of law, a complainant is not a victim until guilt is decided against a perpetrator. Yet there are certain types of crime where officially members of the public do count as victims. This occurs in cases of (i) residential burglary, (ii) vehicle crime (but not road deaths or accidents), (iii) violence (but not harassment, rape, or threats), and (iv) racist incidents or other hate crimes.[21] Defining a victim as a complainant, however, leaves those who do not fall into any one of the preceding criteria, open to the accusation of having made a false allegation, particularly when a crime is not believed to have occurred.[22]

No one knows how common it is for police officers to disbelieve accounts offered by alleged victims because mainstream criminologists have largely ignored this area of research. Yet as shown throughout this book, there is sufficient evidence to prove that disbelieving individuals is a worrying aspect of policing discretion that occurs with some regularity.

The vagueness evoked with classifying a victim is not inconsequential. It is up to police officers to register and investigate crimes. To do so, the officer needs to believe a crime has occurred in the first place, and arguably to do so, there needs to be a belief in the status of victim and an openness to explore the truth of the matter. In recent years, the idea that certain victims should be believed has been questioned by senior police officers, with the former Head of the Metropolitan Police Service (MPS), Bernard Hogan-Howe, calling victims of sexual abuse "complainants" who should not necessarily be believed. As he states:

> We should be rigorous, independent and sympathetic but we shouldn't believe the complainant [sic], because to believe leaves us in a difficult position when we talk to the suspect, who says: "Well hang on, you just believe the victim, what are you going to believe of my claim?"[23]

In the same article Vera Baird, the Police and Crime Commissioner for Northumbria, also refers to victims as complainants, stating:

> Police have a history of disbelieving complainants. As Thames Valley, Rotherham and other areas have shown it is very difficult to complain about intimate crime. The guidance is hard-won—it is the product of failures which have been redressed by a change of attitude.

A review of press and academic papers from 2000 to 2018 identified the following "types" of victim and complainant and the behavior meted out toward them and is detailed in table 1.2.[24]

By far the greatest number of stories remains victims of sexual abuse and rape, and all but one, of young girls or women. For this reason, emphasis is given to providing several examples.

In 2013, a seventeen-year-old girl with learning difficulties, living in Hampshire, reported to the police that she had been raped. Told she was making up stories, she was immediately arrested for perverting the course of justice. During the arrest, one detective told her, "This is what happens when you lie," upon which a detective inspector told a colleague to "fucking nick her." Six months later, another police team from the same force reinvestigated the rape claim after the girl's mother complained. At this point the girl's T-shirt, which she had provided to the police at the time of the rape, was

Table 1.2. Types of Victim Discredited by the Police Reported in Press and Academic Papers, 2000–2018

Subject: Victim/Complainant	*Type of Discreditability (Review of the Literature)*
Rape victims (NB. 1 male)	Neutralising: Not believed/lying; "asking for it," "promiscuous behaviour" or lacking morals; mentally ill/ delusional; alcohol (drunk); raging hormones (adolescents); fail to fit "ideal victim" status. Arrested for lying and/or perverting the course of justice; repressed homosexual desires (male victim)
Complainants to police	Neutralised: ignored by police or shouted at or insulted; threatened with arrest for defamation of officers; "verballing"; mentally ill; regarded as "vexatious"
Bereaved families of homicide or road death regarded as suspicious, including those of Stephen Lawrence	Placed under surveillance; covert police operations; targeted as mentally ill; sharing of data; discreditation of character (Jean Charles de Menezes)
Victims of the Hillsborough football disaster, including bereaved family members	Alcohol abuse—drunk/violent/fraud (unticketed); victims "urinating on police"; interrogation of family members
Police whistleblowers	Placed under surveillance; shielded by other force; harassment; mail and telephones tapped or intercepted; unlawful arrest; bullied, suspended, or forced to resign; smear campaign
Bereaved family member of a missing child	Smear campaign
Victim of racist abuse	Threatened with Taser, disbelieved, or unlawfully arrested
Child sexual abuse victims (female)	Neutralised: disbelieved; "promiscuous," "asking for it," or "probably prostitutes"
Political campaigners	Threatened with arrest; went into hiding from police; betrayed ("spy-cops scandal")
Victims of stalking and harassment, including honor killing, seriously assaulted, or murdered	Accused of lying; ignored; threatened with arrest or arrested; charged for wasting time; fined

Eccy de Jonge (2015) "Literature Review: Confirmation Bias in Policing Investigations." Unpublished Masters paper: Portsmouth University.

forensically examined. Seminal fluid was found on the T-shirt, and her rapist was subsequently caught and successfully prosecuted. In 2015, the victim won £20,000 in compensation for wrongful arrest. However, during the time she was on police bail, the girl was subjected to further sexual assaults, and her mental health seriously deteriorated on account of being disbelieved.[25]

A similar case occurred in the United States in 2008 when an eleven-year-old girl who reported being raped twice was charged with filing a false report, leading to a deterioration in her mental health. A police lieutenant called the girl "promiscuous," adding that "sex was consensual" and that her parents were unable to accept that their "child's promiscuous behavior caused this situation," even though the age of consent where the rape occurred was sixteen and a charge of statutory rape could have been brought against the perpetrators.[26] Rather than do so, police gave the girl an ultimatum: Either she pleaded guilty to lying or she would be sent to the equivalent of a young offenders' institution. Unable to understand the decision at such a young age, she spent the latter part of her childhood in psychiatric units, due directly to having been disbelieved. It took until 2015 for police to offer an apology during which time the girl had been raped again.[27]

Banaz Mahmod, a Kurdish Iraqi, living in London, England, was just nineteen years old when she first informed police in December 2005 that she thought her family were trying to kill her. Entered into an arranged marriage at sixteen and married a year later, she had been a victim of domestic violence and left her husband two years later, returning to the family home. Knowing that her family would not approve, she then began a secret liaison with another Iraqi Kurd. When her family subsequently discovered the relationship, they informed Banaz that her life would be at risk if she did not immediately end the relationship. Banaz went to the police to report these threats and the domestic abuse she had endured. Both were ignored. Then in late January 2006, an attempt was made on her life; Banaz was plied with alcohol by her father who then attempted to kill her.[28] Banaz managed to escape through a window, which broke as she climbed out, causing severe damage to her hands and arms. In the hospital she was interviewed by a female police sergeant who denounced her allegations as "dramatic and calculating" and little more than "an attention-seeking ploy."[29] She was also told by the same police sergeant that if she did not drop the complaint she would be arrested and charged for breaking the window. During the following weeks Banaz informed police several times that she feared for her life and provided a list of five people who she believed were trying to kill her. In all cases she was ignored, including in the last four months of her life when she visited the police no less than five times. In January 2006 she was brutally raped and murdered on order of her father and uncle.

The Independent Police Complaint's Commission (IPCC) opened an investigation into the circumstances surrounding Mahmod's death and found serious failings in the way police had dealt with Banaz, including complaints of historic sexual abuse that she had raised more than a year before she died and another case where she had been found by police in a café in a severe state of distress. Two police forces were found responsible and criticized for being poorly supervised and not following lines of inquiry.[30] As the Newham Asian Women's Project (NAWP) stated, "in the 20 years that NAWP have worked with thousands of victims of gender-based violence, we have observed that such disastrous failures in police responses are not uncommon."[31] One of the reasons provided by officers for not responding to her allegations was the fear of being seen as "culturally insensitive" to the Muslim community.[32] A similar excuse was presented to the Rotherham Inquiry which examined the activities of Asian gangs who abused and raped more than 1,400 girls between 1997 and 2013 in the North of England. Victims were ignored by officers who branded them "out of control," further stating they feared being seen as "racist" if they intervened.[33] As shall be seen in the following chapter, fear of being viewed as racist overrides overt sexism and is attributed to the fear of implicit bias.

No racial issues were involved when Shana Grice was murdered by her ex-boyfriend, Michael Lane, in August 2016 in East Sussex. Just nineteen years old, Shana reported a number of incidents to the police only months before she died. These included claims of stalking, violent assault, and an attempt to steal her mobile phone, as well as a tracking device having been placed on her car and notes she left on his car to leave her alone.

Instead of taking her concerns seriously, Sussex police charged Shana with "having caused wasteful employment of police by making a false report" because she failed to disclose that Lane was her on-off boyfriend. She was subsequently issued with a fixed-penalty notice for wasting police time. A month before she died, Grice reported to the police that Lane had stolen her keys and broken into her house. While he was then cautioned by police and told to stay away from Shana, she continued to complain of stalking and harassment, but the police simply classified this as "low risk."[34] Summing up the case against Lane, the judge, Justin Green said about Sussex Police:

> she was treated as the wrongdoer and having committed a criminal offence, and Michael Lane was treated as the victim. . . . There was seemingly no appreciation on the part of those investigating that a young woman in a sexual relationship with a man could at one and the same time be vulnerable and at risk of serious harm. . . . The police jumped to conclusions and Shana was stereotyped.

An example of "neutralizing the complainant," Shana's case is not uncommon when applied to victims of sexual abuse because, as argued, the police may not regard a person as a "victim," until or unless a criminal conviction has been brought.[35] Those suffering from antisocial behavior such as Kay, described later in this chapter, a disabled woman who was repeated targeted by her neighbors, are all too often, not regarded as victims at all.[36]

As will be seen throughout this book, the gray area between victim and complainant is all too prevalent but with far-reaching consequences for families concerned. In the case of those seriously injured by police vehicles, the treatment of victims has only been skimmed in the press (though more details are provided among participants in chapter 4).[37] It is clear however, that even here a fine line exists between victim and complainant. For instance, the model Heather Mills lost a leg after being run over by a police motorcyclist. Instead of recompense or an apology she was threatened with court action by the same officer who "claimed she had been negligent in crossing the road." Though this may sound atypical, the journalist Simon Hattenstone commented that, "it's fairly common for the Police Federation to threaten to sue the victim."[38] Sheena McDonald, a BBC presenter and journalist, was left in a coma with long-lasting brain damage when she was hit by a police van traveling on the wrong side of the road. As the van was at fault she presumed an apology would be forthcoming. Instead, the police attempted to blacken her character, saying she was an alcoholic. As McDonald said, "I used to believe in the police, and law and order, and now I feel so disappointed and angry. After all they've done, they now trash my name, . . . I feel as if I've been in court. . . . I think justice is flexible to say the least. It makes me embarrassed that it's taken me so long to realise this."[39] No officers were ever held responsible, let alone charged.

Explored in subsequent chapters, two reasons will appear paramount why police discredit victims: to conceal poor police investigations or errors on the part of police officers who blame victims as a form of damage limitation and as the result of confirmation bias. Both occurred to the victims of the Hillsborough stadium in 1989, an event which remains a blight on the British criminal justice system.

HILLSBOROUGH

The Hillsborough tragedy occurred on April 15, 1989, when police incompetence in managing crowd control at a Football Association semifinal at the Hillsborough stadium in Sheffield, England, contributed to the deaths of ninety-six football fans penned into two stands without emergency access.[40]

The full revelations of what happened that afternoon, as well as the way fans and families were treated, took more than twenty-seven years to come to light with vindication of "unlawful deaths" occurring only after an official inquiry: the Taylor Report (1989), an Independent Panel (2012), and two inquests, the second which concluded in 2016. Relevant to this chapter is not the unfurling of the events that took place that day, for which two senior police officers and several others stood trial for manslaughter,[41] but the police use of discrediting tactics to silence the "complainants."

As is now known, Chief Superintendent David Duckenfield, an inexperienced officer in crowd control, was put in charge of his first football match on April 15 and made a fatal error that led to the immediate deaths of so many, and almost immediately afterward, senior police officers decided to lay the blame on the victims.[42] They accused the deceased of having forced their way onto the grounds, of being drunk, of urinating on police officers, and behaving like hoodlums, and then asked families about the drinking habits of the deceased before bodies had even been identified.[43] Though the Taylor Inquiry (1989) and the Independent Panel (2012) both found the victims not guilty of any responsibility, at the second inquest that concluded in 2016, police officers continued holding the victims responsible for their own deaths, slurring survivors, and assassinating the characters of the bereaved.[44] The verdict of *Unlawful Killing* and the acknowledgment by a jury that the victims were in no way to blame did not stop police officers from slandering the victims in the comment pages of the online police magazine *Police Oracle*.[45] Though a jury failed to reach a verdict in the trial against Duckenfield in 2019,[46] the slurs, character assassinations, and lies told against the victims (and their families) remain largely ignored.[47] This is partly because the treatment of survivors, many of whom escaped near-death experiences, and those of families whose names were tarnished by the police and subsequently the press, may be morally indefensible but legally permissible. Other reasons include the fact that inquests deal with the deceased and are not permitted to incriminate individuals or hold them to account. Consequently, police officers remain free to tarnish members of the public regardless of the hurt this may cause. That these stories are known at all is largely thanks to the work of Professor Phil Scraton, one of the first and primary authors to focus on the treatment of the families and victims of Hillsborough.

A criminologist and the author of a number of articles on Hillsborough, including the book *Hillsborough: The Truth* (1999, 2016), Scraton was also an active member of the Hillsborough Independent Panel (2012). This officially brought to light what many of the families had known for decades: that police officers had lied to conceal mistakes.[48] Less known is how police officers were themselves manipulated. Many were forced to doctor their accounts as to what occurred, and those who refused to do so had their accounts changed for them.[49] All police officers who were working at the stadium on the day, employed by South Yorkshire police, were investigated after the event by a neighboring police force, West Midlands. The following is an example, from South Yorkshire police constable (PC Finnerty) who was unhappy about having to change his account for the West Midlands investigation. It is taken from the Hillsborough Independent Panel:

> He appeared reluctant to change any part of the statement stating that if we had not wanted opinion and comment we should have made that point early on. . . . I explained to [PC] Finnerty that we had the only copies of his report and these did not go to W/Mids [police] or anywhere else until they had been checked and signed by the officer making the statement and a supervisory [sic] checking the contents. He asked for his federation representative to be present. [The Police Federation representative] . . . accepts . . . we should not be handing ammunition to our opponents.[50]

The manner in which West Midlands is regarded as an "opponent" suggests that in certain cases, other forces tasked with investigating their colleagues can be both impartial and fair. However, with regard to Hillsborough, it is clear that West Midlands failed to do a thorough job or were perhaps satisfied with the responses given.

Aside from senior offices in South Yorkshire demanding that constables change their statements, officers were also asked to delete certain words from their reports. These included: "chaos," "fear," "panic," and "confusion."[51] If they refused to comply with this request, these words were either altered or deleted from their accounts. Other officers were told there should be no criticisms "levelled at anyone in the text" and "no mention of the word CHAOTIC or any of its derivatives." Hillsborough, more than any other single event in the history of UK policing, thus reveals how certain senior members of the police are more than happy to override the experiences of the ordinary police constable who has neither power nor recourse to argue against his or her superiors. It also shows how senior police officers act to protect their own staff, even if this requires acting deceitfully in ways that would never be permitted by the public.[52]

This is not to suggest that every junior constable remained innocent, however. Having laid the blame on fans, with the dead placed in a makeshift mortuary, many ordinary police officers were reported to have behaved with contempt toward both the victims and the bereaved (as did the ambulance service who were also severely criticized).[53] As Teri Sefton, a bereaved mother who was searching for her son, recalled to Scraton:

> one of the officers asked me which pub would he have stopped at on the way over. She replied, he wouldn't have done because he was driving and besides which he doesn't drink and, not that it makes any difference, but he doesn't smoke either. The officer turned to the other officer, asking me how old Andrew was. I told him he was 23. He said, "she'll be telling us next he's a bloody virgin!"[54]

As Scraton states, "in the immediate aftermath of the disaster a standard police procedure of identification was used to focus on the personal reputations of those who died. From [Chief Superintendent] Duckenfield's earlier lie through to questions about criminal records, alcohol consumption and violent behaviour, a prevalent theme had emerged."[55] This theme was a continuous rant against the victims; many of whom, it was later discovered, had died unnecessarily. Postmortem reports discovered by the Independent Panel revealed that forty-one of the ninety-six victims could have been resuscitated at the stadium, and therefore, regardless of the errors made by the commander Duckenfield on the day, nearly half of those victims died needlessly. Not only does it remain shocking that autopsy reports were deliberately withheld from the first inquest, but also the claim that fans had been "drunk, violent and ticketless—none of which had been true" pervaded the outcome of the police's investigations into Hillsborough (and the primary inquest which fully supported the police's accounts) for decades.[56]

ANTISOCIAL BEHAVIOR: THE STORY OF KAY

The story of Kay demonstrates how one individual can be maltreated by police officers in multiple ways that remain surprisingly legal. In a case that involves more than three forms of discreditability as identified by Box and Russell, including malicious and actual arrest and a covert diagnosis of being mentally ill, Kay remains remarkably sanguine about her experience, though her trust in the police and other authorities has been irretrievably broken.

Kay is in her midfifties. Suffering from multiple sclerosis she was medically retired from her job as a personal assistant in her late forties. Since then Kay has needed the physical aid of a walking stick for balance and relies entirely on her car to take her to the nearest shops where she uses a mobility scooter to get around. Kay lives alone and has one close relative, a sister, who lives several hundred miles away in the country. Otherwise she has a small social network, but as she finds it difficult to get out and socialize, she is quite active on social media and is a member of several online communities.

Living on a council estate in South London, Kay and her former husband purchased their council house in the late 1980s. At the time of her interview in July 2015, Kay described the community in which she lived as a mixture of home ownership and council tenants with substantially more tenants than owners. These included her neighbors on either side.

In 2008 a family were housed by the local authority next door to Kay. She described them as "extremely noisy and messy, leaving rubbish in their front garden and out the back." Kay was alarmed when the neighbors started throwing dog excrement and other rubbish over the wall into her garden. When she complained, family members turned nasty. At first they started shouting abuse as she walked up to her door, mainly targeting her disability. Then a brick was thrown through her window into her living room. This was followed by the wing mirror of her car being broken off. Kay knew the family was responsible, and she tried reasoning with them—as did other neighbors who also had complaints—but got nowhere. Nor did she understand why she was being targeted. As she states,

> There was no falling out. There was no dispute or anything; I think they targeted me because they could. I'd just had major surgery, they could see I could not walk properly and I am quite a small, petite woman, I live on my own, I don't have any male visitors and I think they just saw me as a very easy target for them.

Kay was reluctant to contact the police because of a previous conviction nearly thirty years before against her ex-husband. Although Kay did not wish to go into details, she admitted to having a historic criminal record for violence when she was in her early twenties. This involved her marriage, which she described as abusive. Though she had reported attacks by her husband several times to police officers, it was not until she retaliated in self-defense by hitting him in the face, which resulted in a cut to his lip, did the police take note—in support of her husband. Kay was charged with wounding with intent and let off with a caution after her husband refused to testify. Soon after this incident they divorced, but Kay was scared that police officers would bring up her past. She was right to fear this, as police did make insinuations about her "violent past." Though they refused to elaborate, Kay believed it must have related to this previous incident.

As the bullying from her neighbors worsened, Kay started to feel personally threatened, so in December 2009 she contacted the police—believing there were laws regarding hate crimes against disability and antisocial behavior. The police told her to report incidents to the council, who in turn told her to keep a diary. It was not until February 2010 that the police started to take any notice, informing Kay they had spoken to the neighbors, a claim disputed by a witness who said the police had merely knocked on their door and the neighbors never answered. Six months later, the police informed Kay that they would install CCTV cameras around her house linked to her TV screen. This made her feel safer. When incidents occurred she could see they were being recorded. When she next telephoned the police they told her that it was unnecessary for her to keep informing them of events because the CCTV would capture evidence which they would collect when they visited. Nevertheless, each time an incident occurred, Kay recorded the event and reported the incident to the police, either by telephone or email.

The first time the police visited Kay's address, several days after the first violent offense had been captured on screen, they said they could not find any evidence of what had occurred because the cameras must have malfunctioned. When this happened a second time, Kay decided to make a complaint to the council, and it was through doing so that she first learned that police officers had been dismissing her concerns by misrepresenting what she was saying. As Kay states:

> where I had reported the neighbours putting a heavy football though the car window causing it to smash, they had written "they leant on her car" thus completely misrepresenting the incident . . . the force of the ball had hit it so hard it just all went into little tiny slithers of glass all over the inside of my car. And the police had put that they were playing football and the ball hit my car once and there was no incident. And I had explained that they had deliberately done it.

Kay had seen the incident captured on CCTV, which was played on her television screen. An officer had even attended, watched the footage, and removed the DVD several days later as evidence. She expected that as she was reporting the incidents and that there was CCTV images that these were being lodged at the station and that as the police were being "nice and helpful" that they would recognized their previous failure to do anything about the neighbors' behavior. After the disc was removed, however, Kay heard nothing until reading in the council reports that police had reported to the council that nothing had actually occurred. It was only on their sixth visit, some several weeks later that Kay learned from a visiting Police Community Support Officer (PCSO) that the films were being overridden automatically every twenty-four hours.

In March 2011, the council promised to install an action plan to prevent the neighbors' behavior from escalating, but by August nothing had been done. By then she had suffered around sixty incidents with her car being repeatedly vandalized, items thrown through the windows of her house and into her back garden, and being threatened with violence when she sat in her garden, so she stopped doing so. In December 2013, Kay stopped reporting incidents to the police. Then in January 2014, when the police came to finally remove the CCTV cameras Kay lost her temper.

> I couldn't use my back garden all the time they were living there because of missiles coming over or abuse and threats of violence; I never had any peace from them, all the time, it was really stressful to say the least, it went on and on the frustration . . . so I complained, verbally to the council and to the police that if the Council didn't do an action plan I would do back to the people whatever they did to me. If they shouted abuse at me, I would shout abuse at them. If they threw missiles over my house, I'd throw missiles over their house. . . . I said to the PCSO, "I feel like burning them out." It was just a matter of frustration. It was all very amicable and the police said to me "oh do you mean that?" But of course I didn't. . . . Then the Police Constable in charge contacted me and said, "I know how you feel; I'll come round, I'll come and meet you" and he was going to come round and was going to do something about it. They asked me about the incident and he said, "you'll have to make a statement" . . . and then . . . "say what you said to the Police Community Support Officer that you were going to 'burn them out.'" I didn't say it because I realised that was all he was there for because he could arrest me. He said, "in my opinion, we've got two extremes here. They're extremely loud and you're extremely quiet." It was as if, I was at least half to blame because I was "extremely quiet." This went on for two hours! And then the PC said, "I'm going to arrest you now." And I knew it. I *knew*. Because it had been going on for so long. Attitudes towards me. Do you know what I mean? . . . I don't remember him saying what it was for but when we got to custody apparently it was about a threat of causing criminal damage.

Subsequently the police called a van and put Kay in the back in front of her neighbors, which she believed was a deliberate attempt to cause her further humiliation and prove that her concerns were unwarranted. She also feels the situation had been a "setup" given that the police had made an appointment to take a statement (which she felt meant that finally she was being taken seriously) but also knowing that she would be at home alone with no legal representation and no witnesses present. The fact that she was placed in a police custody van rather than taken to the station in a car—given her age, build, and disability was also regarded, by Kay, as a deliberate attempt to discredit her.

It took three months before the case came to court. Bail conditions stated that Kay was not allowed to stay in her flat nor to collect any personal items, including clothes and toiletries. In court Kay had no legal representation. The duty solicitor allocated to her at the police station was unable to represent her as he had formally represented the family on several occasions and stated this would be a conflict of interest. Kay could not afford to pay for a lawyer.

While awaiting trial Kay made a formal complaint to the IPCC, which was referred to the same police force's Professional Standards Department (PSD). While the trial was pending, she was told that the complaint could not be investigated. It was not explained that to do so would have been *sub judice*—potentially prejudicing court proceedings. With no means of legal representation, Kay represented herself at the trial. She questioned the police officer who arrested her, providing evidence of all the emails she had sent police, including photographs of every event that had taken place. When a police officer admitted that her comment to harm the neighbors had been "a throwaway remark," she asked why, if the police knew she had no intention of harming the neighbors, she had been arrested. And why had they waited several weeks before making their arrest. These questions remained unanswered. Giving his ruling, the judge said that Kay was the real victim, and there was "no case to answer." The case was dismissed.

Two days after the trial, Kay received a letter from her local mental health services. The letter stated that she had been referred to them by her local police because she "was mentally ill and suffering delusions." As a consequence she was placed on the MPS's database, Merlin, for "vulnerable persons." As Kay states of the police:

> I was letting them into my home. I was talking to them. I was being honest and open and you know, I put my trust in them. And all the time they are stringing me along with their lying; they maliciously arrested me, they threw me out of my home, they were trying to say I was mentally ill. They'd failed in the court and then they had to do that referral.

When asked why she thought the police behaved this way toward her, Kay believes there were two reasons: to intimidate her so she would not report any more incidents (she thought the family might be police informants or related to the police in some way) and to cover up their failure to take action that should have been taken.

> It wasn't a failure as in "we've made a mistake" it was deliberate. I mean, all these lies, the CCTV, arresting me, the mental health thing, no one will listen to you. I can see why they use that tactic to get at people. The thing is, it works. It's like, you've only got to say, "Oh yeah, I've been recorded as mentally ill" and no one will listen to you. No one will take anything you say to them seriously, these people in authority. They should be acting; the police should be brought to account. You can see why they do it. . . . To cover up their own refusal to carry out their duty.

Kay was the first of several interviewees who provided evidence that secret psychiatric reports had been carried out by instigation of the police, by National Health Service (NHS) doctors, without her knowledge. When it came to light that other participants had also found their names on Merlin, recorded as "delusional," the author contacted several criminologists and barristers working on human rights issues but none of them claimed to have heard of the Merlin database—a database which a Freedom of Information request to the MPS revealed held more than fifty-two thousand entries between April 2013 and March 2014 of adults coming to police notice with or without their knowledge, with the full figure being denied on account of cost.[57] While records are held for seven years, it was made clear by the MPS, that until the time relapse, a challenge to the records or proof of their falsity would make no difference to their removal. At least two reports are known to have been falsified by police, but when this information was put to senior members of the MPS, the author was told, "No officer has been found to have made a false Merlin report to date." The police create Merlin records to "safeguard vulnerable adults." However, as Kay and others believe, the police often do so not to aid the vulnerable but to deliberately dissuade officers from attending to a crime should any of those who have raised concerns ever have recourse to call the police again.

POLICE CASE STUDIES

Remarkably there has been little published on the attitudes that police officers hold toward members of the public that involve the types of behaviors mentioned. While it is easy to call the police "institutionally racist" or to say "power corrupts," this does not explain why such scandals and slurs occur even after evidence to the contrary has been presented (an issue examined in the next chapter on policing bias). Why is it that so many have been discredited by the police: either harassed, bullied, maliciously arrested, incited as mentally ill, or simply ignored when requesting police assistance, yet there has been not a single study on this behavior in more than forty years? It is no secret that the police act in this way; it is certainly recognized by the criminal justice system, human rights lawyers, and others involved in criminal justice, as the Hillsborough inquiry illustrates. Of course talk of "the police" is not talk of an individual but an institution where the practices described occur. These practices occur in workplace situations as well but an employer has limited power and acts for a specific reason—to drive someone out of his or her job. While this is not criminal, workers have rights to take employers to tribunals, and many cases have been successful even for police officers.[58] That individual members of staff may harass or bully another and get away with it through the use of clever tactics, referring, for instance, to an old job description that is no longer relevant and then declaring a person has failed to comply with these expectations is one such example. Others may be subjected to sly remarks, racist or homophobic slurs, sexist touching, and a host of accusations that leave the individual feeling devastated, betrayed, and alone.

But the employer does not follow them or write to their family doctor, let alone have the power to enter their details onto a covert database.

When a person is discredited by the police, however, there is no "place" where one can escape the institution of the state, which is why it is so much more damaging when custodians of authority are permitted to arrest others at will. This includes police officers themselves. Detective Constable Kevin Maxwell was coerced into silence after revealing that "racist and homophobic behaviour" was endemic in the MPS,[59] and Chief Inspector John Buttress was accused of "bullying and persecution" by his employers (Greater Manchester Police) as a result of attempting to change the practice of ethnic minorities being routinely stop and searched. He was subjected to surveillance and then falsely accused of money laundering and fraud, including evading paying his council tax, which on appeal was revealed not only to have been false but in fact overpaid, for which he received a refund.[60] In another case, detectives who revealed the misuse of credit cards on lavish meals and alcohol by senior police colleagues had to go into witness protection for their own safety.[61] In still another case, three chief inspectors from the British Transport Police who revealed serious breaches of the Data Protection Act, including wrong data being input on the Police National Database, were suspended from duty. As Jon Williams, one of the accused, states: "we weren't told why we were suspended. About two weeks after the suspension, I had a letter which purported to explain the reasons why. It didn't."[62]

Officers who raise serious concerns about the way suspects are treated risk being branded "liars" and "criminals." This happened to Chief Inspector Clara Williams after she raised concerns about an elderly detainee who collapsed in his cell and was prevented from being sent to hospital. Detective Superintendent Pete Jackson of Greater Manchester Police was also branded by his force for exposing investigative incompetence.[63] Jackson complained that the investigation into his son who had been the victim of a violent assault had not been properly investigated. Therefore, he decided to look at the CCTV images of the night his son was assaulted. As Head of the Forces Major Incident Team, he was perfectly entitled to do so, and having identified the attacker, the perpetrator was arrested and successfully prosecuted. Instead of receiving praise, however, he was told to take early retirement.

Aside from these cases, several police officers came forward to be interviewed for this book. This included Karl, a detective sergeant currently on suspension on full pay for complaining about members of his team not pulling their weight. As Karl says,

> I'd seen first hand police corruption throughout my service so I was aware that it took place and that it existed throughout the service—mainly the prosecution of individuals and the breaching of our CPIA [The Criminal Procedures and

> Investigations Act]. . . . If you were to challenge it all the time in the police, you'd be ostracised and you'd be out of a job. So you'd have to suck it up and just carry on with things you weren't happy with because whenever you managed to challenge something, you'd ostracise yourself from that environment.

Asked for an example, Karl said:

> Two officers used excessive force on an autistic child in a swimming pool because they didn't realise they had no training about the condition. The police were sued for that [and] their wrong doing and their lack of training was exposed but nothing was ever done over the years 2008 to 2014 until they lost the very last appeal.[64]

Another police officer, George Stapleton, a detective constable, was maliciously arrested for being seen as a "perceived threat to the organisational structure" for raising concerns about colleagues. He believed that the PSD acted against him deliberately in order to teach him a lesson, or as he put it, to "level the playing field." Without knowing any of the other participants' stories or the research already conducted for this book, George said that PSDs routinely "try to make out the complainant is deluded or seriously mentally ill." As George said, "it's really just discrediting people to the point that people give up; people will say, it's not worth the hassle."

If a detective constable knows about this practice, then discrediting complainants must be endemic in UK policing if not elsewhere. A complaint is seen as something far greater than the issue at hand; it challenges the mechanization of the institution itself, revealing a weakness and insularity in the organization, where "strength," "openness," and "self-righteousness" are the main public relations (PR) drives that cannot be challenged, not even, as George and Karl both reiterate—from within. Writing in 1970, the police historian Brian Chapman wrote:

> The role of the untouchable policeman is important in this respect not because he represents virtue by being incorruptible but because he helps to keep the police organisation in a state of equilibrium between the pressures which are exerted upon it from both sides. The untouchable policeman has to exist in order to protect the police organisation from threats of outside intervention.[65]

In reporting police malpractice, which included not investigating crimes to save budgets so officers could meet targets and manipulate crime figures, Karl found himself subject to various forms of discreditation. The way this occurred was, he says, subtle. First he was removed from leading a team of first response officers, and then he was moved away from the force's main office to a regional one. Working in a different area he came across a serious mismanagement of cases involving robbery and started questioning those cases. As a result, he was confined to a desk job and told not to have any more dealings with the public. When he was eventually suspended he says he was no longer surprised,

> The whole problem is, there is no safe facility with a police officer to address police corruption. A police officer can't complain to the IPCC because they're not allowed to. All the police can complain to is the organisation and of course it's the police who investigate the police.

Karl believes that none of his complaints were excessive, but in some cases where he "got people disciplined for breaking the rules and charged with misconduct," he knew he was risking his career. Subjected to disciplinary action, he took sick leave for depression, the first time he had been off work in seventeen years. After six months, he was fit to return but a week before he was due to return to work, his management made a set of allegations that constituted disciplinary offenses. He was suspended on full pay while these allegations were being investigated. After a year, in September 2014, he was cleared of all allegations only to be arrested, charged, and remanded a month later. As he states, "I perceive . . . that once I had stepped outside the permitted norms, I was always going out the organisation."

Karl admits that on occasions he did make mistakes as a police officer which concerned the first set of allegations under which he was charged and found innocent, none of which, he told me, could be alleged to be regarded as serious. No further charges have been brought against him, though he has now been on suspension on full pay for the last four years. During this time, he claims to have been under constant investigation that has included interception of phones, bugging of his house and car, and surveillance. He adds,

> it's not rogue officers saying "oh we are going to do this"—it's actually a normal organised procedure of discrediting officers who stand against the organisation. It's not a coincidence that everyone who whistleblows meets the same fate. I don't know how many thousands of reports there are but the police can't produce one person that has been treated fairly as a result.

This rather negative picture does seem to have been played out by the "spy-cops scandal," and its new rebranded organization, the Domestic Extremism Unit, which is still placing people under surveillance without any real explanation. This includes John Catt who, at eighty-eight, won a landmark lawsuit against the MPS after officers noted details of his banner and whether he was "clean-shaven" on an antiwar demonstration.[66] If an innocuous pensioner can find himself discredited by the police, as well as road death victims and those bereaved by the Hillsborough tragedy, the very idea of police hegemony as a moral compass is thrown into question.

CONCLUSION

The points raised by Box and Russell in their seminal paper in 1975 have revealed discreditability to be as relevant today as then: with complainants against the police risking unlawful arrest, denigration of character, and the stigma of being labeled "mentally ill" as "a routine dismissal of such citizens' complaints mean that they have few rights left to be abused."[67] Media reports have revealed that denigration of innocent members of the public who "annoy" the police, face the same outcomes as in the 1970s with "the person who suffers as a consequence of an officer's conduct, likely to experience a deep sense of 'injustice'"[68] and to be labeled "vexatious" or worse "delusional." As a report in *The Guardian* by Vaughan Bell on mental health concurs:

> Delusions, in the medical sense, are not simply a case of being mistaken, as the everyday use of the term suggests. They are profound and intensely held beliefs that seem barely swayed by evidence to the contrary—even to the point of believing in the bizarre. My heart has been replaced by steam. My thoughts are being stolen by satellites. The government communicates with me through birdsong.[69]

So common is the use of the term "delusional" to label someone who speaks out against authorities that in the United States the practice of doing so has its own name, the "Martha Mitchell Effect." This is named after the wife of the Attorney General John Mitchell who, during Richard M. Nixon's administration, sought to reveal corruption among officials working at the White House and was then labeled "mentally ill," even though her claims turned out to true. As Bell states, "claims against authorities are often dismissed by suggesting that the person has mental health problems," as was the case against the NHS whistleblower Kay Sheldon after she reported failings in the Care Quality Commission. However, this does not entirely explain the motivation of the police to discredit those who are not speaking out against authorities but simply raising their own concerns. In response, Box and Russell suggested a number of reasons why the police discredit complainants.

- Police occupy a higher-ranking position in the hierarchy than most complainants, which means that the word of a member of the public is unlikely to be believed against the word of a police officer as far as magistrates and judges are concerned. This permits the police to arrest people on spurious malicious charges, by noting their "special place" in society. It is also clear that this is the case within the police force itself.

- Police are able to fabricate evidence as there is no one to stop them doing so; there is no oversight.
- There is a strong cultural issue by way of an occupational code that demands "loyalty to colleagues," which is "a higher moral ranking than the preservation of law and order." As they state, "Calling a policeman a liar is quite different from calling say, a drug addict a liar: the former is outrageous, the latter is obviously true because 'everyone knows' that addicts, like many other social deviants, are 'pathological liars.'"
- Complaints "threaten police occupational and organisational interests." For this reason, the police "need to utilize 'common-sense' understandings of, say, 'insanity' or 'drunkenness' or 'criminality' to thwart complainants." And it should be said that this applies equally to police officers who raise complaints of poor practice.
- The complainant is attempting to preserve credibility and the plausibility of the allegations. The police attempt to prevent that, so that they can maintain power; a complainant is thus seen as threatening this hegemony.
- The police depend on public-police morale—the old adage (or cliché) of policing by consent. "The police need to prevent morale from deteriorating and preserving the credibility of the police force as 'a symbolic expression of the legal system's ultimate justice and moral superiority.'"[70]

Though Box and Russell's analysis identified working-class complainants as the main victims of police malpractice, research for this book has shown there are no class or educational boundaries when it comes to being discredited. Like miscarriages of justice caused by police bias (discussed in the next chapter), the severest implications of such practices occur when police officers are involved. There is no reason to believe that the types of practices identified after Hillsborough, including the discrediting of victims and their families, are one-off events, unlikely to occur in future. Such practices do still occur (though to what extent is impossible to say) with police officers just as likely to be targets as the unsuspecting member of the public. Perhaps most disturbing of all is that unlike any of the criteria used to process maleficence or corruption in public office (e.g., theft, fraud, physical assault), the sorts of practices meted out to silence victims and complainants are routinely ignored. As the Crown Prosecution Service state: "Dishonesty or corrupt behaviour are not essential elements of the offence of misconduct in public office," and therefore do not fulfill the criteria of being a breach of public trust.[71]

2

The Meaning of Bias in Police Investigations

There are two main categories of bias that affect police investigations. These can broadly be categorized as implicit bias and confirmation bias. Confirmation bias is often seen as an umbrella term that encompasses implicit bias (see table 2.1), but conceptually they can be separated into two distinct classes. Implicit bias is the holding of preconceived ideas about a person's personal characteristics whether race, class, age, sex, or some other criteria, to ideas categorizing types of people (e.g., the notion of the "ideal victim" or the "typical culprit"). Implicit bias is thus said to be an aspect of bias that may, though not always, lead to police officers (and others) dismissing or discrediting victims or complainants because of prejudice prior to any case being brought to their attention.[1] This may include generalizations (e.g., all "Muslims are terrorists," "all blacks are criminals," "all women are liars," and "all bad drivers are young men") or, as shown in chapter 1, may be aimed at a particular person (e.g., a rape victim regarded as "promiscuous," or simply "lying"). The reason for any particular prejudice may be complex and unknown; thus, implicit bias is explored, in some detail, in the first part of this chapter.

In contrast, confirmation bias is a conviction of being right even when faced with evidence to the contrary. This is often held to explain why a case is not investigated, why it abruptly ends, or why a miscarriage of justice occurred. In the latter case, police become convinced they have found the "guilty party"—in many cases, by forcing a confession. This is particularly worrying in the United States where the Reid Technique (a form of interrogation copyrighted to John E. Reid and Associates, Inc.) is used to garner confessions from suspects that often result in false outcomes. Use of the technique is likely to be excluded by a judge in the United Kingdom as evidence obtained unfairly under Section 76.2 of the Police and Criminal Evidence Act 1984 (PACE) requiring that a confession is not obtained by oppression.[2]

It is worth noting that until 1992, after the United Kingdom introduced the PEACE framework of investigative interviewing (developed after a series of miscarriages of justice and explained in this chapter), police officers also used methods to interview suspects not dissimilar to that ascribed to Reid.[3]

Although this chapter will mainly focus on confirmation bias, it will include a brief overview of implicit bias because the phrase has become prominent in the last few years as a means of eliminating institutional responsibilities, particularly (within policing), institutional racism. Possible solutions to bias in policing will be offered in response, including the Dutch model of contrarians (i.e., police observers who act to resolve bias in policing investigations). Whether observers can themselves be free of bias is determined by the openness in which confirmation bias, as a whole, is accepted within policing investigations.

IMPLICIT BIAS

Implicit bias has become the buzz phrase of the twenty-first century, so much so that both companies and politicians now use the term without much thought. Even the College of Policing, the professional body for those who work for the police service in England and Wales, have stated that every police officer is guilty of some form of bias.[4] Determining and examining when a person exhibits implicit bias has also become something of a cottage industry, with Harvard University selling its test for bias, the Implicit Association Test (IAT) to a host of companies, from law to business firms. Implicit bias, though characterized into distinct groups including gender and sexual orientation, has become mainly associated with one major type of prejudice: *racism*.

The IAT is an online test which purports to measure associations between concepts (e.g., "black" vs "white" with "good" vs "bad"). When performing the IAT (which is freely available to anyone with an internet connection), a participant is asked to sort terms into categories that are located on the right and left side of a computer screen and to choose a key that best describes the meaning of the word.[5] It is easy to forget that the questions asked in an IAT are appropriate to a particular subject matter (e.g., race) because confusion may readily occur. For example, a participant is asked how they relate the terms "black" and "white" to "dirty" and "clean." In doing the test on race, for instance, participants are forced to associate black faces with "bad" and white faces with "good."

Refusing to apply the terms "bad" and "good" to "black" and "white" in this way halts the program. The computer screen informs the participant that a wrong answer has been given, and until this is corrected the test cannot continue. Thus, until a negative word has been chosen for a black face (e.g., pain) and a positive word (e.g., pleasure) with a white face, the test cannot be completed. Even some of the words associated with good and bad are problematic because the reader is meant to accept the negative or positive connotations of such terms. For example, "grief" is a bad word, and "spectacular" is a good one. In many ways, therefore, the test is counterintuitive, permitting no free association of terms, let alone empathy or reflection. In this sense, the IAT is actually set up to show that people have biased tendencies or tendencies that show negative connotations to certain groups of people (e.g., gays over heterosexuals, men over women) built on a quasi-recognition that certain terms are automatically negative and others are positive. It is with regard to race, however, that the IAT has become seen as most controversial, showing that everyone (including black people) exhibit racist tendencies toward black people.[6] When during the US presidential campaign in 2016 Hillary Clinton stated that "implicit bias is a problem for everyone, not just police," she too was referring to racist implications (in particular to police shootings of black people in the United States), but the link is not without controversy. As Mitchell and Tetlock (2017) state:

> the IAT . . . has spawned a cottage industry of diversity consultants offering unproven implicit bias training programs, and it has given lawyers much to fight about (and bill for) in many lawsuits.[7]

Although implicit bias may be a lawyer's dream concept, it is extremely troubling for the rest of us. As evidence suggests, there is simply no means to equate what a person may score on an IAT (a test which arguably is actually set up to determine bias and is, therefore, itself intrinsically prejudicial) with the types of behavior that person may exhibit. Moreover, the IAT has been shown to fail, with no one person being able to replicate the same score.[8] Implicit bias, then, is an extremely problematic concept, not least because determining its actual meaning remains contentious, with some psychologists equating the term with unconscious bias (i.e., the view that even when an individual claims not to be biased he or she nevertheless exhibits biased tendencies, without being aware of doing so) and others comparing it with personal preferences.[9] In the latter case, implicit bias is based on the psychoanalytic theory of social identity, which argues that all human beings are biased because our very identities are created with bias in mind. As Howard J. Ross (2014) argues,

> We are biased towards particular kinds of television shows or movies, certain foods or kinds of foods, certain kinds of books or stories, etc. Virtually any preference we have is likely to have some bias associated with it.[10]

Seeing preference or taste as a bias assumes that expressing a liking for one thing rather than another makes us automatically prejudiced toward it. In this description, a man who prefers to date a woman of the same ethnic background could be said to always *treat* women of other backgrounds differently not because of some explicit racial prejudice that he exhibits but simply because of his preference (e.g., the same might be true of a man who prefers blondes, who may therefore be said to discriminate against brunettes and vice versa). That most people who take IATs do not recognize *any* bias in themselves and remain shocked at the results further shows a problem with recognizing implicit bias, implying that it is possible to read the minds of others by psychological testing alone because true beliefs are unable to be discerned. Though there is no scope to debate this perspective in greater detail, it clearly raises a host of philosophical problems that are both metaphysical and epistemological in content. What gets lost, however, are the practical implications of using implicit bias at all because the only reason to even talk about implicit bias is to show an undetermined causal link between one's unconscious beliefs and acts of harm—or to put it another way, to discover whether people's personal preferences lead them to treat others in ways that cause them harm because of these preferences. Translated to police officers, this simply requires that members of the public are not discriminated against because of their background, race, sex, age, or other characteristic which is listed in the Equality Act 2010 for England, Wales, and Scotland under public sector duties.[11] Targeting individuals without supporting evidence or having adequate reason to do so (e.g., stopping and searching predominantly black males where no subsequent arrests are made) may be excused as *implicit* bias, but prejudice is much more likely to be explicitly recognized as an institutional problem, as highlighted in the United Kingdom by the Macpherson report.[12] More worrying, if all police officers (indeed all people) are said to hold *implicit* biases, then bias cannot be helped, and no one can be held responsible for actions that *appear* of a racist or sexist nature because their behavior is determined by something *unconscious* and, therefore, unknowable and likely inaccessible. Ascertaining that everyone is biased, police officers included, simply lets everyone off the hook. This is not to propose that bias does not exist but rather to suggest that it is *explicit* rather than implicit.[13]

The most obvious instance of implicit bias leveled remains that of race. This cannot be ignored, given that Stop and Search powers (or similar laws in the United States) are still known to target black people up to seventeen times more than their white counterparts with less than a quarter resulting in an arrest.[14] However, because Stop and Search has been well noted in both the press and government reports for decades, it is hard to imagine that racial discrimination is *implicit.* In an English county such as Dorset, where the population of black people was recorded in 2014–2015 at slightly more than 3,000 compared to over 700,000 whites, police officers stated emphatically that the overuse of "Stop and Search" was due to "targeting gangs" and to "drugs" attracting the black population in particular.[15] If this were true, arrests followed by convictions would back up the necessity of the searches without the need for further explanation. But no such arrests followed.

The claim that "police on the lookout for criminal activity are steeped in non-conscious stereotypes that affect their decision-making,"[16] is not supported either by the Macpherson report (published in 1999) or the Race Disparity Audit in 2017, which identified *institutional* bias as problematic. It is easy to claim that bias in policing is a matter of an individual's personal implicit prejudices (e.g., holding stereotypical views of black people), except that even in a rural English county like Dorset such procedures are monitored by senior officers and government bodies such as Her Majesty's Inspectorate Constabulary (HMIC). It is thus difficult to understand why institutional bias is still being ignored.

In a research study carried out by Plant and Peruche, eighty police officers took part in a simulated shooting test to determine if they would be more likely to murder black suspects. The test found that even when clear evidence of implicit bias against black suspects was noted, police officers "were less likely to shoot unarmed Black suspects than unarmed White suspects."[17] While it is difficult, though not impossible, to prove that we all act on the basis of what we believe,[18] their study suggests that implicit bias remains a poor indicator of behavior, is completely irrelevant, or does not exist. Indeed, where reverse bias has been known to occur, as in the Rotherham child abuse inquiry in the United Kingdom in which white girls were sexually assaulted by Asian gangs, police officers deliberately ignored rape allegations on the basis that they did not wish to appear "racist." This suggests that the appearance of bias is neither unconscious nor implicit but all too well-established.[19] As shown in chapter 1, police officers have been excused for not dealing with honor killings or rape among the Asian community for fear of appearing biased—a fear undoubtedly borne out by the constant stream of debate suggesting that implicit bias is inherent, particularly in police officers.[20]

Captain Tracey G. Gove, a police commander in the United States, upholds a belief in implicit bias (i.e., unconscious prejudices that individuals are unaware of holding). She maintains that such biases are "both pervasive and powerful," driven by categorizing people into age, gender, race, and roles that "encompass the myriad fears, feelings, perceptions and stereotypes that lies deep within the subconscious" and may be "completely contradictory to an individual's stated beliefs." Holding this as "fact," Gove states that a self-awareness of bias is the only way forward and that police training in knowledge of implicit bias leads to officers being *less* biased than the general public.[21] Of course this makes sense if (i) *implicit bias* is recognized as a substantiated form of unconscious belief, (ii) that holding such prejudices leads officers (and others) to act in particular ways toward victims or others, and (iii) implicit biases can be revealed as *biases* against the views of the agent who did not believe he or she held them in the first place.

As a means of determining implicit bias with regard to race, L. Song Richardson, a legal scholar from the University of California's Irvine School of Law, conducted an experiment among four actors, two who were black and two who were white. The same script consisting of an argument was read first by the two white actors, next by the two black actors, and then by one black actor and one white actor. The purpose was to judge the reaction of observers. The experiment revealed that when two white people were engaged in an argument, only 13 percent of observers regarded their behavior as hostile, but when the actors were both black, 69 percent of observers regarded their behavior as aggressive. When the victim was black, only 17 percent regarded the white actor as aggressive, with 75 percent reversing that decision when the victim was white.[22] It was argued that the experiment offered proof of implicit bias, steadfastly linked to fundamental attribution error—the view that behavior of others can be explained by reference to their character or characteristics (with or without looking for other evidence), which was proved to be irrefutable.[23]

Putting aside the fact that individuals all act differently (with some actors being more convincing than others), it remains uncertain—even where bias does exist—whether it is implicit or confirmatory though the distinction between the two terms may be somewhat arbitrary given that what may be called "normal" bias is easy to detect. If black people in the United States are often seen as "aggressive, dangerous, violent and hostile" such that "individuals, including police officers, may be more likely to think about crime when in the presence of black Americans and more likely to focus on black Americans when they are thinking about crime," this shifts officers' "attention away from true offenders who are not Black toward Black citizens who are not violating the law."[24] But where such attitudes are regarded as one of the main reasons proffered for officers conducting "stop-and-frisk" searches on black youths in the United States, these can hardly be called "implicit."[25] On the contrary as the Black Lives Matter movement has shown, such biases are all too well-known.

In contrast, faced with rape allegations, police officers tend to fall back on the view of the "ideal victim," that is, a person with a set of defining characteristics related to what fulfills the criteria of believability.[26] This type of bias is not targeted at a particular group (e.g., all women or girls) but to particular behaviors a victim is supposed to express. As one officer is quoted as saying, "I didn't believe her because of her body language. She looks down, mumbles, crosses her arms, and twists her hands."[27] The "ideal victim" is supposed to be "consistent, rational, self-disciplined, and blameless," and excludes women with histories of mental illness, aboriginal women, childhood sexual abuse survivors, and women with disabilities who are regarded as "unrapable."[28] The "ideal victim" is also one who reports incidents immediately to police because delaying the reporting of a sexual assault is seen as reducing the victim's creditability. Likewise, a woman who has made previous complaints of rape to the police is unlikely to be believed a second time because the general consensus is "that a woman is unlikely to be raped more than once."[29] In these cases bias (implicit or not) is tantamount to discrediting victims, as elucidated in chapter 1. Nonetheless, there would seem to be more than a hint of misogyny or sex discrimination linked to these cases. A literature research on attitudes toward rape victims found that in the one instance of male rape, the victim was also disbelieved,[30] as were several children who recounted instances of sexual abuse.[31]

Another instance of possible implicit bias is premature case closure related to age. Deaths are more likely to be seen as suspicious if the deceased is young and crime scene investigators (CSIs) are less likely to be called out to a suspicious death involving an elderly person. This is also true if the deceased was known to be an alcoholic or a drug user, the assumption being that such people are more likely to die of their abuse, so suspicion related to their death is more likely overlooked.[32] As one CSI reports:

> [The police] seem to take things at face value. Example; death in a care home, they automatically think it is a natural death and might not look any further into it. They don't consider medication, abuse etc. In care homes there must be all sorts of unknowns there because they are all coming to light now. It is ridiculous.[33]

The skepticism with regard to implicit bias need not imply that police officers (like anyone else) are never biased but it questions placing emphasis on *hidden* features that people seemingly do not know they exhibit at the expense of recognizing explicit cases of prejudice. For example, the G20 International summit in 2009 led to "one of the most serious critical incidents in British Policing," the death of an innocent civilian, Ian Tomlinson, who was killed by a police officer.[34] Even though Tomlinson had not taken part in any demonstrations, as a direct result of his death, HMIC identified significant shortcomings in the police's ability to manage peaceful protests resulting from the attitude of police viewing the crowd as defensive and potentially violent rather than peaceful.[35] Two years later, on December 9, 2011, when another peaceful protest was organized by students, police officers, expecting the worst, resorted to paramilitary methods of crowd control and deployed mounted police on horseback and officers in full riot gear, resulting in officers acting unnecessarily aggressive, even pulling one protester out of a wheelchair. It subsequently resulted in the police being regarded as biased against students.[36]

Such criticisms of police bias are not new. However, implicit bias is rarely mentioned. Aside from stop and search, attitudes toward victims of rape and discrimination against peaceful protestors, the police institution has also been held responsible for overt bias against gypsies.[37] In terms of the latter, the MPS even set up its own Facebook page to virulently pour scorn on the Roma community. Thus, far from bias being "implicit" and related to an individual's unconscious (for which little can be done), it seems bias is regarded as implicit to protect the police institution from criticism.[38]

It may be that certain prejudicial thoughts are not "biases" as such but based on real experiences; after all, we all act on how we see reality through the basis of our understanding and this includes views which place people (and things) into categories (e.g., titles, social class, professions). An example may be given in the surprise expressed by the roads policing officers of the West Midlands Constabulary on discovering that the poor drivers who failed the close passing initiative in an effort to tackle cycle injuries and deaths were not their usual suspects of young males between ages eighteen and twenty-five but older, more experienced drivers (see chapter 4). However, no one would regard PCs Hudson and Hodson as being biased because their so called "prejudice" against young drivers is actually weighed up by the statistics on careless and dangerous driving.[39] That they may have had a certain expectation which could be considered a bias nevertheless had no impact on their jobs because they did not stop young drivers but only those breaching the safe distance set for cyclists. This raises yet another problem for implicit bias. While people *may* hold unconscious biases, because a causal link between thoughts and actions often fails to be decisive, proving that unconscious bias leads to poor action is tenuous. This has not stopped the College of Policing suggesting that all officers hold implicit biases toward black suspects. Whether this is true, it is convenient for a body whose charge of institutional racism has been well-recognized for decades. It is much easier to blame racism and other forms of bias on an individual's personal prejudice than to explicitly assert that the police have an overt problem with ethnic minorities, which is all too often openly known and understood, as the MPS's Facebook page overtly attacking travelers and gypsies revealed.

CONFIRMATION BIAS

Confirmation bias is an umbrella term referring to beliefs held without justification. It is regarded as the main component of prejudice in police investigations and is often used interchangeably with other terms for deeper clarification. These include tunnel vision (holding beliefs when faced with evidence to the contrary), investigator bias (the belief an investigator comes to at the end of an investigation),[40] and hindsight bias (a refusal to believe that any alternative outcome could have been achieved), also known as outcome bias. "When focusing on a 'particular conclusion' investigator bias filters out other evidence which is dismissed as irrelevant, incredible, or unreliable."[41]

These terms, while having similar attributes, do not place the emphasis on "bias" per se but on problems deemed epistemological in nature, that is, on holding limited knowledge of events, where the obtainment of further evidence is deemed unnecessary. Thus, confirmation bias comes up against epistemic gaps—gaps between facts and values—between what is the case and what is perceived as being the case, owing to a priori psychological barriers because "people sometimes see patterns they are looking for even when those patterns are not really there."[42] So while confirmation bias has been regarded by some psychologists as an innate quality (along the lines of implicit bias), it is clear that failure to keep an open mind and to desire different possible outcomes increases bias. Epistemic bias (i.e., the belief that one's own knowledge is irrefutable) may occur prior to any event taking place, that is, before an officer attends a crime scene.[43] This occurs through officers' creating hypotheses prior to collecting evidence, which can easily prejudice an investigation before it has even begun. With regard to the murders of Banaz Mahmod and Shana Grice, police officers decided from the start that neither woman was telling the truth, which led to the former being ignored (and killed by her family) and the latter accused of "wasting police time" (and then murdered by her boyfriend); see chapter 1. In the case of road death investigations (elucidated in chapter 4), where "ready-made" hypotheses are provided irrespective of evidence and before attending the scene of death, confirmation bias is termed "hypotheses bias"—a blinkered view that attempts to find evidence in favor of certain assumptions at the expense of the facts, which thus becomes a type of selective thinking.[44] Since "people tend to seek information that confirms their hypothesis and to avoid information that would disconfirm their hypothesis,"[45] information that seems to support an investigator's existing beliefs may lead officers to ignore other evidence. Hypotheses provided *prior* to an investigation taking place are thus always subject to confirmation bias. This is because hypothetical assumptions created too early in an investigation are likely to be subjected to bias *whether* these assumptions turn out to be true.

In such a case, confirmation bias can be regarded as a form of belief perseverance or persistence (holding onto one's belief regardless of any evidence to the contrary). Belief persistence is sighted in many cases of wrongful conviction, which brings into play yet another position of confirmation bias, that of "case denial."[46] Otherwise "case construction" has been used to show how an investigator will create a set of hypotheses and then identify evidence to support this view, of which "case denial" is the direct opposite.[47]

Other elements may also be involved in determining confirmation bias, which are more illustrative than descriptive, for example, a conjunction fallacy, which is the tendency of investigators to regard the overlap of two events as more important than the events themselves, and "transposing the conditional," which is equating the probability of the evidence with a guilty party and the probability of guilt given the evidence[48] leading to fundamental attribution error (where the behavior of someone—in this case a victim—is judged by reference to their character without looking for other evidence). Fundamental attribution error is given as a major reason for confirmation bias with regard to race and is often held as being synonymous to implicit bias.[49] Where an investigation is based on perception rather than evidence that results in premature case closure—where there might be a case to investigate but it has been decided not to do so—confirmation bias is termed "verification bias." Though strictly speaking, "verification" has a more complex meaning in the philosophy of language, in policing terms, it represents anything "that confirms rather than disconfirms" a person's beliefs. It is generally agreed that the main problem with confirmation bias is "the tendency of people to pay the most attention to information that confirms what they already believe to be true and ignore other evidence (the other possibilities)."[50] Table 2.1 shows the various terms associated with bias in relation to the police.

Table 2.1. Terms and Concepts Associated with Confirmation Bias

Type of Confirmation Bias	*Explanation*
Anchoring Effect	Refers to people within a group tending to agree with others' beliefs, creating an "anchor" of an original set of hypotheses that refuses to be challenged
Asymmetrical Scepticism	A preference for information that confirms, rather than disconfirms, an already existing belief
Belief Perseverance	Maintaining one's belief (e.g., that the suspect is guilty) even when strong evidence (including DNA) is presented.

Table 2.1. Terms and Concepts Associates with Confirmation Bias *(continued)*

Type of Confirmation Bias	*Explanation*
Case Closure	A case may close as result of the lack of evidence or the perceived lack of evidence; may also refer to finding a fast end to a case by believing (wrongly) in the guilt of a suspect (i.e., premature closure)
Case Denial	Refusing or failing to accept there is a case to investigate (e.g., because of prejudice toward the victim)
Cognitive Bias	Predetermined set of psychological characteristics that sets a person up to be biased in investigations (e.g., belief in racial characteristics or ones based on gender, that is, the ideal victim)
Cognitive Closure	Desire for a clear-cut conclusion; to reach closure as quickly as possible
Freeze	Maintaining a steadfast position even when evidence to the contrary comes to light
Fundamental Attribution Error	Explaining the behaviour of others (e.g., a suspect) by reference to their character or characteristics (with or without looking at other evidence)
Hindsight Bias	A "we-knew-it-all-along" belief in the guilty party (i.e., outcome bias)
Hypotheses Bias	A set of hypotheses stating possible explanations for an event by ignoring or failing to consider others to the contrary ("closed mindedness")
Implicit Bias	Judgments made on the basis of a person's ambiguous behaviour often interpreting people of different ethnicities (who exhibit the same behaviour as others) in a more negative light (e.g., racial bias)
Institutional Incompetence	Pressures from an institution to find a suspect guilty or not guilty even if insufficient evidence is gathered or other possibilities exist
Tunnel Vision	Refers to holding onto one's belief even when faced with evidence to the contrary; confirmation bias may be a symptom of tunnel vision or vice versa or regarded as equivalent (i.e., investigator bias)
Verification Bias	Any instance of creating a narrative based on "perception" rather than, or prior to, "open evidence," which considers all viewpoints; often regarded as synonymous to confirmation bias

Eccy de Jonge (2015), "Literature Review: Confirmation Bias in Policing Investigations," unpublished master's paper, Portsmouth University, England.

Probably the most illustrative and worrying form of confirmation bias remains "hypotheses bias," which, once created, may exacerbate other biases, particularly tunnel vision. Any officer arriving at the scene of a crime, potential crime, accident, or tragedy creates hypotheses as to what has occurred, which may be noted as evidence.[51] This may range from deciding that there is no case to answer (the death was not suspicious) or that the victim-cum-complainant is not telling the truth. In a case study in which people were asked to find a guilty result early on in an investigation, confirmation bias was unsurprisingly found to have a much higher incidence resulting from people making unfounded assumptions than those who waited until all the evidence had been presented.[52] Rushing to judgment combined with a lack of skill and poor leadership contribute strongly to case denial or fundamental attribution error.[53]

Hypothesis or case closure is most likely to arise at the initial scene of death, where a suspicious death may be immediately regarded as a death by natural causes.[54] This decision may stem from particular biases to do with the age or behavior of the victim (e.g., attitudes toward the elderly or drug users) or simply be a matter of error on the part of the initial officer attending the scene not recognizing that the death is or may be suspicious. Error may occur for a number of reasons from relying on paramedics or nonprofessional persons to determine cause of death to considering the financial cost of a murder investigation. The first step to investigating murder in the United Kingdom is to call a Home Office forensic pathologist. Forensic pathologists will attend a scene at the request of the police because only (Home Office) forensic pathologists are trained in "the collection of forensic medicine and physical trace evidence from the deceased."[55] However, the cost of a forensic pathologist is considerably higher than that of a hospital pathologist (approximately £3000 incurred by the police, as compared to £96.80 paid for by the coroner's office). Thus, austerity measures may account for confirmation bias in creating premature case closures. Though impossible to verify, this might also account for the significant drop in homicide rates, with no recognizable explanation, since the mid-1990s.[56] One example is the case of Ricky Reel.

In 1997, Ricky Reel, an Asian student, was reported missing after a night out with friends in London. Prior to his disappearance, his friends reported having been physically and verbally assaulted by racist youths. Almost immediately, however, police decided there was nothing to investigate, but when Reel's body was later washed up on the banks of the river Thames, police ruled that he died from suicide, asserting he must have killed himself for being gay or having to accept an arranged marriage. They closed the case.[57]

Over 20 years, Reel's family fought a tireless campaign to show that he was killed as the result of a racist attack. This seemed to be confirmed after a witness came forward claiming that Reel had been murdered by a man already in prison.[58] Police refused to pursue the matter. As Dean Jones states, "preconceived views on the part of investigators can lead to '*premature closure*' of investigations prior to all reasonable lines of inquiry being followed in accordance with Section 23a of the Criminal Procedures and Investigations Act 1996."[59]

Vulnerability should alert the police to signs of suspicion, invoking the maxim: "*the higher the vulnerability of the deceased prior to death, the higher the index of suspicion.*"[60] Instead, as in the case of Reel, it often does the opposite. This may reflect an "over reliance on the medical cause of deaths" with "less consideration as to *why* the death occurred which . . . medical evidence cannot reveal."[61] The matter is not a trivial one. There were more than 1,700 open verdicts in the coroner's courts in England and Wales alone in 2015. The majority of deaths were regarded as unproven suicides, but this is where suspicious deaths are most likely to be found. "To fail to identify a homicide thereby allowing someone to 'get away with murder' is a miscarriage of justice in its own right."[62] However, failures are inevitable where there is no established protocol for officers who attend scenes of suspicious death. In England and Wales, there is no national training procedure and, consequently, no accountability or supervisory structure.[63]

In many cases, officers simply apply Occam's razor—that the simplest hypothesis is usually the right one. Because the simplest explanation is usually death by natural causes,[64] such an approach can have serious investigative consequences. CSIs or scene of crime officers (SOCOs) have expressed frustration that by the time they get to a scene, their services are not required because the attending officer has already decided the death was not suspicious. In one example, a CSI states:

> elderly gentleman found outside of his house, paramedics had been, police officer went; oh no, he's had a heart attack. So the CSI goes and moves his arm and there is a knife sticking out of his chest and nobody had moved him or touched him.[65]

Bias is also increased by consensus. As a forensic pathologist explains:

> What happens is that the first officer attends the scene and makes up his mind what has happened. His sergeant turns up and the PC briefs him by saying, it's ok sarge, its natural causes. Then the sergeant takes on the bias and then the inspector is told the same thing and on it goes and so everyone is biased by the first officer who may not have done it properly.[66]

Setting aside scenes of death, confirmation bias also takes place in the interview room, where interviewers may make premature assumptions as to the guilt of the interviewee or fail to follow established interview techniques.[67] In the United States, this has become common practice, particularly as interrogation replaces investigative interviewing. The nine steps of interrogation, which permit questioners to openly mislead suspects into making a confession, has become so controversial that not only are there dozens of academic papers against its use and known results of miscarriage of justice, but it has even been depicted in popular television series as a known problematic.[68] This is highlighted in the Reid technique of interrogation.

THE REID TECHNIQUE

The Reid technique, devised by John E. Reid, an ex-police officer, was introduced into policing in the United States in the 1940s. As a method of interrogation its sole purpose is to gain a confession from suspects. Before questioning even begins, it suggests that officers conduct a behavioral analysis of the suspect in which nonverbal tics (e.g., rubbing one's nose during questioning) are regarded as signs that a person is lying. Once this is noted, the interrogation proper begins by making leading statements, such as suggesting that evidence by the suspect was found at the scene of the crime. The interrogation is completed with officers informing the suspect that they would be better off confessing to the crime, after which their "ordeal" (the interrogation itself) will be over.

Although the legal precedent of *corpus delicti* is intended to protect the suspect by arguing that confession alone is not sufficient to convict someone of a crime, according to Micah Schwartzbach, "any evidence that *someone* committed the crime in question will be enough—the evidence doesn't have to show that the defendant was the one to commit it. And in many places, the corroborating evidence needs only to slightly suggest that the crime was committed."[69]

It is estimated that more than 30 percent of the people exonerated by DNA in the United States falsely confessed to crimes they did not commit as the result of the Reid method, with the total number of false confessions remaining unknown.[70] Several reasons have been offered why people may readily confess to a crime they did not commit. These include, "having a mental disability, being interviewed without a lawyer or parent in the room, or suffering through hours or days in jail before questioning."[71] However, the most common reason is the Reid method itself "since it can create confirmation bias in the minds of investigators while overwhelming a suspect to such an extent that the truth no longer seems like the best option."[72]

Problems of bias attributed to the Reid technique were highlighted several decades ago with police officers knowingly "misrepresenting the nature or purpose of questioning, misrepresenting the seriousness of the offence, the use of promises, and the use of fabricated evidence," with other psychological and manipulative tools being used to persuade a suspect to confess to a crime, including deliberately befriending the suspect before later asking closed questions—which demand a simple yes or no response—and interrupting the subject as a deliberate attempt to be oppressive.[73] In the United Kingdom, PACE attempted to dispose of such methods, but it was not until a series of miscarriages of justice against Irish Republican Army (IRA) suspects came to light in the late 1990s (namely those of the Guildford Four and the Birmingham Six) that investigative interviewing was revised.[74] The PEACE model replaced techniques like those provided by Reid by creating five steps of investigative interviewing:

P—Planning and Preparation (of the questions to be asked);
E—Engaging the interviewee and Explaining the rules of the interview process;
A—gaining an Account which clarifies and challenges the interviewee;
C—Closure of the interview followed by
E—Evaluation of what was achieved during the process and how the interview fits into the whole investigation.[75]

The purpose of PEACE was to open up lines of inquiry to find physical evidence and not primarily to get a confession.[76] As such, the PEACE model incorporates a set of open-ended interview questions, known as TED. This follows the simple trajectory:

T—Tell me what happened.
E—Explain to me what happened.
D—Describe what happened.

The failure of police officers to conduct open-ended interviews along the TED model (required under PEACE in the United Kingdom) may occur when investigators fail to follow established interview techniques.[77] And although the PEACE model is, unlike the Reid method, not concerned with analyzing nonverbal tics or behaviors, this does not prevent officers from looking for behaviors that they believe indicate deception (such as fidgeting or lack of eye contact) but which "may be more indicative of nervousness unrelated to deception and/or of a reaction to the interviewer's own behaviour."[78] Furthermore, while a shift from oppressive questioning has supposedly improved matters in British policing, it remains questionable whether it has become fully embedded.[79] Witnesses, for instance, are not subject to the same rigor as suspects under questioning; they do not need to be formally interviewed nor have their interview recorded, which may lead to "inconsistencies and signs of deception" in their testaments.[80] By the same token, eyewitness testaments are highly malleable because "people not only *seek* confirming information, they also tend to *recall* information in a biased way . . . preferring information that tends to confirm a presented hypothesis or belief."[81] In the United States, however, the Reid technique is not so much "accidentally" biased but deliberately so because police officers are trained to adopt tunnel vision as a matter of course. In this scenario "tunnel vision is not inadvertent, but deliberate; police are taught that this is the way to advance their investigation. Cognitive biases are openly encouraged."[82]

Research shows how police evidence which confirms investigators' original hypotheses is more readily believed than evidence to the contrary.[83] Studies also confirm that people prefer to test a hypothesis or rule "by choosing only examples that would be classified as instances of the sought-for concept if the hypothesis were correct. People disfavour choices that would disprove the hypothesis," thus showing that whatever decisions one makes can be verified as the *right* decision based simply on focusing on one set of circumstances at the expense of openness and, thus, the truth.[84]

Within the criminal justice system, it would be naïve to suggest that only police officers express bias. As will be seen in chapter 5, coroners, pathologists, and lawyers may also make unjustified claims tantamount to confirmation bias (or support thereof) and analysis in forensic science, which is sold to the public as irrefutable, is often interpreted in a subjective way. This is particularly true of fingerprint analysis, which remains open to a varying degree of subjective interpretation and a high degree of error.[85] Miscarriages of justice determined by DNA have shown "that evidence we once thought to be hard proof of guilt—confessions, eyewitness identifications, bite marks, ballistics—lack reliability."[86] DNA alone does not itself prove guilt of course, any more than evidence that a particular suspect was in the public house near the time of the murder proves that he "did it" when hundreds of unidentified persons were also present. Thus, confirmation bias may be inevitable given the need to close a case quickly and for investigations to fulfill targets and measurements as well as human fallibility.[87] Police may also believe that their responsibility ends with the arrest of a suspect and that nothing more needs to be done because once a decision of guilt has been made, no other evidence is sought, even where doubts exist or alternative evidence is provided by data.[88] This is recognized as a major problem in policing culture,[89] with "case construction" or "case denial" seen as "a root factor in many cases of miscarriages of justice."[90]

MISCARRIAGES OF JUSTICE AND WRONGFUL ARREST

Confirmation bias is not merely a set of theoretical aspersions which fail to see justice addressed but has dire consequences, both for victims of justice and for their families. This is particularly true in cases of miscarriages of justice.

After DNA testing was carried out on Marvin Anderson in 2002, he became the ninety-ninth person in the United States to become exonerated for a crime he did not commit. He had been sentenced to 210 years in prison for two accounts of rape, robbery, and sodomy in 1982 and served 20 years. The only evidence against him had been the testament of a rape victim who reported to police that her attacker had said he had a white girl at home. Because the only black man that local police investigators knew who lived with a white woman was Anderson, he was immediately arrested. Even though forensic tests of blood and semen failed to reveal any connection between Anderson and the victim, with the photo circulated of the attacker bearing little relation to Anderson except that both men were black, investigators refused to consider Anderson as innocent.[91] When the real culprit, a known sex offender, John Otis Lincoln, confessed to the rapes in 1988, and evidence proved Lincoln's guilt, Anderson was still not released. Anderson's exoneration occurred 14 years later after the Innocence Project demanded that DNA testing be carried out. This proved that Anderson was innocent, and he was finally exonerated. "The police ignored the evidence because they thought they already had their culprit."[92]

David Camm was a former police officer who was sentenced in 2000 for the murder of his wife and daughters. Set free on appeal, he was tried again, successfully appealed, and was tried a third time. After spending a total of thirteen years in prison, he was exonerated in 2013. The reasons given for his conviction included a poor investigation, witness and evidence tampering, and the testament from Charles Boney (a suspect with a history of attacks on women) who was later found guilty of the murders. DNA not only exonerated Camm, it also identified Boney as the perpetrator.[93] At the trial, Kim Rossmo, a Canadian criminologist specializing in geographic profiling, and a leading criminologist at Texas State University, argued that the police came to the conclusion that Camm was guilty before evidence had even been collected and were therefore unwilling to consider any other suspect. According to

Rossmo, confirmation bias caused the police to ignore the DNA on Boney's sweatshirt and even when Boney was finally identified, "they downplayed the significance and attempted to make it fit within their established theory of the crime."[94]

In 2014, five men (Antron McCray, Kevin Richardson, Raymond Santana, Kharey Wise, and Yusef Salaam) were awarded more than $40 million for a miscarriage of justice that had occurred in the late 1980s. Released from prison over a decade before, the men, known as the Central Park Five, had been wrongly convicted of the rape and murder of a woman in Central Park, New York, in 1989. Between the ages of fourteen and sixteen at the time of the crime, each of the five had been interrogated by police for between fourteen and thirty hours until full confessions were obtained, even though no adults were present.[95] Each confession had contradicted that of the next boy, with none confessing to rape or even getting the location of the attack correct. Although there was no physical evidence linking any of the boys to the crime, the court held that the confessions were sufficient to find all five guilty.[96]

In 2002 Matias Reyes confessed to the crime. DNA corroborated that he had acted alone.[97] Though Reyes had been identified by police as a suspect at the time, officers working for the sex crime department had been unable to find him and closed the case. It was only when the homicide department decided to carry out their own investigations that the five teenagers were arrested, subjected to interrogation, and charged. Thirteen years after conviction, the boys were freed. However police investigators refused to believe in the boys' innocence, doubted the confession of Reyes, and were willing to disbelieve the DNA evidence linking the crime to Reyes, even though it was irrefutable.[98]

Since 1973 confirmation bias has been linked to more than 159 people on death row in the United States who were later exonerated, with 58 having been imprisoned for over ten years, 22 for over twenty, and 10 for more than thirty years. Of those whose sentences have lasted more than three decades, these include three men, who each served thirty-nine years for murder based on the testament of a twelve-year-old boy who later recanted his confession with witnesses stating the boy was somewhere else entirely at the time of the crime.[99] Twenty of those wrongly convicted were exonerated due to DNA, one of whom, Frank Lee Smith, died in prison.[100]

The United States is not the only country with miscarriages of justice linked to confirmation bias. In Sweden, Joy Rahman was released from prison in 2002 having been sentenced to life imprisonment for murdering an elderly woman in Stockholm in 1994. The evidence against him was slim: He had bought coffee from the same place as lighting fuel used to torch the woman's apartment. He served eight years in prison. When Rahman was released, the main reason for the investigator's bias was given as the desire to arrive at "definite conclusions" ("cognitive closure").[101] In the United Kingdom, recent exonerations for miscarriages of justice have included Victor Nealon, Sean Hodson, Eddie Gilfoyle, Sam Hallam, Barry George, and Paul Blackburn. Victor Nealon spent seventeen years in prison for attempted sexual assault. He was released in 2013 and denied compensation even though his wrongful conviction was a result of police officers failing to test the victim's clothes for DNA, which revealed that another person had been responsible for the rape. The reason for his lengthy sentence was the rule in British law that only an admission of guilt can herald parole and, thus, an early release. Because Nealon always declared his innocence, his sentence was indefinite.[102] At seventeen, Sam Hallam was sentenced to life imprisonment for the murder of a chef in a street fight in 2005. Although, like Nealon, no forensic evidence linked him to the murder scene, and the police interviewed more than thirty-seven witnesses (none of whom identified Nealon as being present), he was convicted on the basis of one witness who contradicted herself in court by admitting that she was "just looking for someone to blame." After serving eight years in prison, the Court of Appeal quashed Hallam's sentence after another police force reviewed the original evidence against him. They noticed that photos on Hallam's mobile phone showed he had been with his father in a pub at the time of the murder and, therefore, could not have committed the crime.[103] Crucially, "police did not investigate his alibi—and he was convicted after a failure to disclose crucial evidence including mobile phone data and CCTV footage."[104]

Confirmation bias may not always lead to miscarriages of justice but still be responsible for harmful effects against the innocent. This is particularly true in cases of wrongful or malicious arrests, which not only shut down further investigation but may cause untold harm to the innocent victim. In a case that reeks of racial bias, Brandon Mayfield was arrested by the FBI for the Madrid train bombings in 2004 after fingerprints were found by Spanish police on the detonating devices. When these fingerprints were shared through INTERPOL, the FBI arrested Mayfield, even though his prints were not identical to those found on the detonators and the Spanish authorities disagreed with the evidence. The case against him was built entirely on FBI investigators being convinced that Mayfield, a qualified lawyer, was guilty because he was a convert to Islam, was willing to work for low-income clients, and had represented the Portland Seven—"a group of men who tried to travel to Afghanistan to fight for Al Qaeda and the Taliban against U.S. and coalition forces, in a child custody case."[105] Even when Spanish police informed the FBI that they had other terrorist suspects in custody with strong links to the case, the FBI detained Mayfield under the Patriot Act without charge. Eventually Mayfield was freed and successfully sued for damages.

Christopher Jefferies was not so fortunate, gaining little more than a begrudging apology from police officers after being wrongly arrested for murder. In December 2011, a young landscape architect, Joanna Yeates, went missing from her flat in Bristol. Her body was found several miles away on the side of a road on Christmas Day. In a classic example of hypotheses bias, the police arrested her landlord, Jefferies, before collating any evidence against him, telling press, that "Mr Jefferies was their man."[106] After gaining an extension for questioning, Jefferies was released on bail but was not permitted to return home to his flat for several months. Jefferies was subsequently vilified in the mainstream media after police provided the press with his name. Even when DNA convicted the real killer, Vincent Tabak, a neighbor of Yeates who had been ruled out by the investigative team early on, police continued to claim they had been right to arrest Jefferies, even after a government inquiry (the Leveson report into press standards) called the actions of the police "unbalanced, prejudicial and wildly inaccurate."[107] Jefferies described his ordeal by the police, his arrest, and bail conditions, which prevented him being able to go home to even get a change of clothes, "a form of psychological torture."[108]

While the Jefferies's case could be seen as one of hypotheses bias and tunnel vision, that of Georgina Halford-Hall is one of case construction linked to case closure. Halford-Hall was interviewed in 2015, a year after being maliciously arrested for theft and a breach of the UK's Data Protection Act, which holds a maximum penalty of fourteen years in prison. Although her case involves several UK police forces and thus suggests a complexity of internal policing politics, for the sake of brevity (and clarity), this will not be discussed.

In 2013 Halford-Hall, a company director, became increasingly concerned about the treatment of her son at his private boarding school, the Duke of York's Royal Military School in Dover, Kent.[109] After several other parents and staff members raised allegations of abuse, both sexual and physical (including punishing children by subjecting them to hours of solitary confinement), she wrote to the school to make a formal complaint. In response, the school's child protection officer asked her to withdraw the complaint, accusing her of "bringing the school into disrepute," even though she "let slip that they'd had quite a lot of problems at the school." Getting nowhere with the school's complaint system but concerned that the activities were serious enough to be illegal, she contacted her local police, with whom she was on good terms as a member of her local neighborhood watch committee. Her local police advised her to gather evidence, which she passed on to nurses and other parents who had children at the school.

In September 2013, an anonymous correspondent sent Halford-Hall the school's medical facility logbook. This provided evidence that children were being held in solitary confinement for several hours as a form of punishment. In response to receiving this book, Halford-Hall sent it to Ofsted, a ministerial department of the UK government responsible for standards in education and children's services. Her concerns were ignored.[110]

Then on June 6, 2014, seven police officers arrived at her house in three cars; these included five officers from her local police station and two detectives from the police force in Kent where her son's school was located. Thinking the police had turned up to discuss the allegations of abuse at the school, Halford-Hall welcomed them into her house and was immediately arrested for handling stolen goods and breaching the Data Protection Act 1998 (now DPA 2018). Having entered her home, Halford-Hall was arrested and served with a Section 18 notification. Under the Police and Criminal Evidence Act, Section 18, "a constable may enter and search any premises occupied or controlled by a person who is under arrest for an indictable offence, if he has reasonable grounds for suspecting that there is on the premises evidence, other than items subject to legal privilege, that relates to that offence."[111] Asked why she believed the police acted in this way, Halford-Hall stated that "the local magistrate would never have given them a search warrant, they would have said, 'just make an appointment for her to come down to the station, I'm sure she'll come and chat to you, if not, then you can go and arrest her.'" However, magistrates do not advise the police and serving a Section 18 notification is normal procedure; thus, no such warrant was required. Officers then searched her house and took away hundreds of documents, during which time a call to her lawyer prevented them taking away computers and other equipment.

Halford-Hall was extremely ill on the day the police called at her house and was, by her own account, treated extremely badly, watched by officers as she dressed and went to the toilet, and then, according to her account, thrown into the back of a police car, even though she had a high fever.

At her local police station, after being strip-searched, she was interviewed by the two detectives from Kent and though unwell (at one point she "slipped off the chair and fainted"), they took no notice, presenting her with "loads of documents" including "all of the private communications" between the family "and the army who were in charge of the school," as well as "the chairman of governors at the school, the local authority, and Ofsted." As Halford-Hall states, "you'd have thought [after] a quick read through they would have realised, we weren't the bad guys, we were actually trying to do the best for those children that were left at that school." Eventually she was permitted to return home pending criminal charges.

In June 2015, a year after her arrest and three court appearances later, the Crown Prosecution Service (CPS) dropped all charges against her as "not being in the public interest." Tracey Austin "who had resigned from her position as deputy child protection officer in protest at the way the school dealt with concerns about sexual abuse of a teenage girl, was also arrested and faced similar charges. She was later told no further action would be taken against her."[112] Even though Detective Chief Inspector Emma Banks of Kent Police said she was "completely satisfied" with the investigation into Halford-Hall, calling her officers' behavior "entirely justified and proportionate," two years later, Kent police were forced "to launch a review into their alleged failure to investigate dozens of criminal allegations at The Duke of York's Royal Military School," leading to a detective inspector being disciplined after it came to light that police records showed more than thirty-eight crime reports against the school in the last two decades.[113] "Of these, 12 were sexual offences and 11 were 'child protection incidents,' according to police records obtained through freedom of information requests."

Halford-Hall's story is an obvious one of case construction against her on one hand and case closure on the other, with regard to an investigation of child abuse that was ignored and with officers having tunnel vision which lasted for several years. Under the description of discreditability, outlined in chapter 1, the way Halford-Hall was treated was also a clear case of attempting to "neutralize the complainant."

AVOIDING BIAS: RESOLUTIONS AND SUGGESTIONS

In 2000, two children, a ten-year-old girl and an eleven-year-old boy, were attacked in the Beatrix Park in Schiedam, a town four miles west of Rotterdam in the Netherlands.[114] The girl was killed and the boy badly injured. Stumbling out of the park where his friend had been killed, the boy, Maikel Willebrand, approached a passing cyclist, Kees Borsboom, who telephoned police. Although Willebrand gave an accurate description of the killer, which the police circulated to the press, and a police woman recognized the description as that of an infamous sex attacker (who years later confessed to the crime and was corroborated with DNA), detectives believed the boy had done the killing. Then they arrested Borsboom. Though Borsboom did not fit the description Maikel had provided and had a strong alibi for the time the killing took place (he was at work), and no forensic evidence tied him to the crime, he was a known pedophile who the main detective disliked.[115] At that time, Dutch police did not routinely record interviews with adult suspects and were not required to write accurate statements by witnesses. Instead, police provided brief summaries in the dossier which were presented to the prosecution as evidence. In Borsboom's case, he was said to have confessed to the crime in a nonrecorded interview, even though he had no legal support, and his "confession" was inconsistent with the facts. No other statements or witnesses were recorded. Subsequently, Borsboom was sentenced to eighteen years in prison, followed by a compulsory stay in a forensic state hospital, meaning he would never be released. Although his conviction was questioned two years later, it was not quashed until 2004 when DNA discovered on the body of the girl by the Netherlands Forensic Institute (NFI) was presented on television in a news program as not belonging to Borsboom. Having raised awareness of the case, Borsboom was released and subsequently exonerated, and the NFI forced to introduce "contrarians" to oversee criminal investigations, specifically with the aim of avoiding the type of confirmation bias that had led to Borsboom's wrongful conviction.[116]

Though the job of the contrarians is not unique,[117] and the case of Sam Hallam shows how another police force overseeing original evidence is able to pinpoint fundamental errors, the Dutch model of using independent crime analysts to systematically code evidence to explicitly counter confirmation bias remains original in its approach.[118] Analysts ("contrarians") are required to look for alternative explanations to identify missing evidence and to question the data presented to them. Unlike the Hallam case that only reviewed the murder inquiry on suspicion of a miscarriage of justice, the role of contrarians is to oversee the "first phase of the criminal investigation, which focuses on identifying the suspect."[119]

The Netherlands' system of using contrarians to rule out tunnel vision does not come without its own set of problems, however. Either the contrarians are too close to the investigative team, which raises problems of institutional bias, or they enter the investigation too late, by which time their usefulness is questionable.[120] One way of avoiding these issues is to ensure that investigations do not take place until contrarians are involved, but this can delay the vital gathering of evidence. Furthermore, like forces in England and Wales, "the police family" are a close-knit group, and thus, true independence may not be possible. "Contrarians also have the task of preventing tunnel vision in themselves," a matter which has proved difficult because "the members of the team are their colleagues"; furthermore, many contrarians like to get involved in the investigation process and "solve the case," thus, risking being "caught in the same 'tunnel' as the team members."[121] While some officers in the Netherlands resent the role of contrarians, leading researchers to doubt whether their role makes any real difference, it has been proposed that contrarians be extended to less serious cases.[122]

The need for some kind of independent evaluator has been suggested outside the Netherlands, with commentators pointing out that simply being aware of potential bias is not sufficient to avoid bias altogether.[123] Research has shown that even when evidence is provided contrary to the so-called "facts," police officers will stick to the evidence that supports their initial hypotheses even if this is less reliable or points to the opposite.[124] One of the ways contrarians work is to ask individuals "to consider the opposite of their position and to articulate the reasons why the results at issue could have been different."[125] This idea, which stems from Socrates's *elenchus* (i.e., self-examination for the purposes of refutation), has been shown to be more successful than any other method because people who are asked to consider evidence from various positions show less bias than those who do not.[126] Failure to pursue all investigative leads or "requiring police to consider alternate suspects' may simply lead officers to become biased against other innocent people."[127]

The problems associated with confirmation bias are well-known and recorded in British policing with resolutions on bias avoidance provided in the *Core Investigative Doctrine* of the Association of Chief Police Officers (ACPO). The main forms of bias, which an investigator is asked to consider, include:

- Making sweeping statements;
- Oversimplifying the facts;
- Making inferences from the particular to the general;
- Begging the question (e.g., taking things for granted which have not yet been proven);
- Potted thinking (i.e., using simplistic assertions in an unwarrantable fashion);
- Making early assumptions about material, causing relevant material to be overlooked;
- Building unlikely hypotheses that do not reflect the known facts; and
- Underestimating the importance of victims or witnesses.

As the manual states: "All of the above limitations can have a detrimental effect on the quality of the decisions made by investigators but by being conscious of them, investigators can adopt a disciplined approach to decision making."[128] This applies particularly to hypotheses and what the manual terms "availability error," which is "the danger that an investigator might base their decision on material that is 'psychologically compelling' because it appears to be familiar or is linked to a memory, but it may not necessarily reflect the material at the investigator's disposal."[129] For example, "an investigator attends the scene of a domestic burglary and decides not to conduct house-to-house enquiries in the vicinity because of an assumption that no one will tell them anything worthwhile," or "investigators develop an early view as to what has occurred or who is responsible for a crime," which "can result in a situation where they only gather material that supports their view, thus reinforcing their opinion that their view is correct."[130] This often occurs with making inferences based on a previous case or a statistic that bears no relevance to the present situation. The way to deal with bias is therefore for investigators to "continually challenge both the meaning and the reliability of any material they gather." This is summed up by the ABC approach:

A—Assume nothing.
B—Believe nothing.
C—Challenge everything.[131]

Unfortunately, while the theoretical recognition of bias exists, there is no means of upholding what actions, if any, have been taken to undermine confirmation bias in practice. Without full accountability, including full disclosure of police files, and transparency of how any particular investigation is carried out, bias will continue, however positive the incentive is to get things right. Case dismissal occurs in many incidents but is nowhere more worrying than when a death fails to be regarded as suspicious whereupon the process of who should be informed and what should be done determines the entire process of investigation. As one Home Office Pathologist remarks:

> In my opinion everybody at the scene (if there is one) needs an experienced detective and/or crime scene investigator to attend before it is deemed non-suspicious. The police and some coroners have a misplaced faith in the ability of non-forensic pathologists to spot any homicide that slips through the investigative net. These pathologists on the whole assume that if a case is referred to them it is not suspicious or a homicide. They do not have the appropriate suspicious mind-set and they are not trained to deal with such cases. If the wrong call is made by the police/coroner the chances of things being retrieved are slim.[132]

Because it is the least experienced officers that usually arrive at a crime scene, training is cited as another means to avoid bias.[133] While police guidelines in England and Wales on murder investigations do state that all cases of suspicious death should be treated as homicides unless proven otherwise, there is "little guidance on decision making" because the document is not written for those officers most likely to attend the scene.[134] As Dean Jones, the current Senior Manager at the Home Office for Forensics, states:

> The police themselves have recognised the need for professionalising and have introduced many measures to safeguard against the failings of the past; such as

> the introduction of reviews for homicide cases, and the writing of the Murder Investigation Manual (MIM) the first version of which was published in 1998. . . . The MIM sets out the process of a murder investigation but only at the point a death is deemed to be suspicious. It does not create policy in respect of the process prior to that, namely the initial stage of the police attending a sudden and unexplained death.[135]

While "it should not be assumed that police investigation is driven by simple malice or a wilful disregard for the 'truth,' it is also important to have some sense of the pressures placed on the police to get results."[136] It is easy to see how confirmation bias can occur, particularly in the United States where the overreliance on confession without material substantiation is a known factor in causing miscarriages of justice. In the Netherlands, where suspect interviews were formally not recorded, following the Borsboom case, not only has this been reversed but more detailed interview notes are also now required to be taken. However, this still does not apply (in any of the countries examined) to all but *significant* witnesses (e.g., those regarded as potential suspects).

Aside from the police, the public needs to be educated not to accept presented evidence as incontrovertible. Because "expertise does not eliminate confirmation bias" with even "fingerprint experts" being "influenced to interpret fingerprints consistently with other information provided to them prior to their forensic analysis," it would seem that simply offering additional training or warning officers of the dangers of bias will not be sufficient. "In the end, greater transparency at all stages of the criminal process might be the most powerful way to counter tunnel vision" because "transparency also helps to modify the effects of biases on decision-makers. Research shows that when people know their actions are being observed and that they will be held publicly accountable, they tend to exhibit less bias in their hypothesis testing strategies," so that the more that decisions "are made in open an observable ways, the more likely they will be to resist biasing pressures and tendencies."[137] Thus, "remaining impartial and open minded" may be the best means to "accurately assess new information" and avoid confirmation bias but no less difficult to enforce because of that.[138] In cases of premature closure of rape victim cases, where the victim is often blamed or not taken seriously, it is clear that only a cultural shift will do; a view which, as seen in chapter 1, remains deeply problematic, with senior officers still insisting that skepticism should be brought to mind when women make claims of being raped or sexually assaulted. Though the general culture toward female victims may now be changing, the implicit or overt bias toward such victims should always favor the victim's narrative until after an investigation has concluded. To force police officers to challenge their own assumptions, however, may well be a step too far because policing culture dictates that police "never can admit a mistake."[139]

In relation to implicit bias, which may exist (it is just as likely that such biases are simply not admitted), Richardson has argued that "the most effective way to reduce the effects of psychological biases on policing is through institutional reform. Examining the institutional environment in which officers operate is critically important, including exploring how existing department incentives and culture influence officer motivation and information processing."[140] This would seem crucial because it shines a spotlight on (i) incentives and (ii) the effects of culture on motivation and information processing (discussed in chapter 6).

Hiring workers from diverse backgrounds and ensuring positive interactions between police officers and groups outside one's race or ethnicity would reduce implicit bias or bias associated with referencing some individuals over others.[141] However, a high proportion of bias is against victims of sexual abuse, mainly women, who are neither a select nor a minority group and are targeted equally by ethnic minorities (indeed may even be singled out as in the case of Rotherham as one of reverse racism). Thus, it would seem that simply "mixing with others" is not sufficient to turn over deeply misogynistic or racist attitudes. In fact, given the evidence about sexual abuse victims, none of the so-called "suggestions" would seem to work alone, unless a cultural shift forces police officers to take the complaints of women seriously. With the Me Too movement leading women to become more outspoken with regard to abuse (the Harvey Weinstein scandal is a contemporary example), police officers may be forced to change their attitudes as such behaviors become less tolerated by society as a whole. However, it may be that police culture is confined by other members of the criminal justice system less able to keep up with societal changes, which up until now has maintained an aggressive stance on women who "cry rape" with little sympathy for rape victims. For instance, the New York police did take seriously the account of a woman who accused Weinstein of sexual assault, equipping her with a wire to carry out a sting operation. However, in that case it was the local district attorney (equivalent in the United Kingdom to a crown prosecutor), Cyrus Vance, who decided not to take matters further. As a New York Police detective stated, "We had the evidence. It's a case that made me angrier than I thought possible, and I have been on the force a long time."[142] As for cases where people are maliciously arrested as suspects, a start might be to follow the Dutch model of not publishing names in the press until a formal charge has been brought. This may have spared Jefferies some of the worst humiliation after police officers released his name.[143]

CONCLUSION

It may be that the means of ridding the system of bias in policing altogether lies outside that which policing investigators can challenge.[144] This would seem particularly the case when it is the criminal justice system which is at fault or when a particular method (e.g., the Reid technique or the nonrecording of witness statements) makes bias more likely. And yet, given some of the absurd reasons for conviction, and the fact we would not accept such bias from other professionals such as doctors (or at least, not without a challenge), the need to review policing decisions is imperative.

Unfortunately, unlike the accounts of eventual freedom recounted under miscarriages of justice, the saving grace of DNA or the new light of evidence, "reversals in criminal cases are quite rare,"[145] and thus, there is no way of knowing how many miscarriages of justice exist or exist as a result of confirmation bias. The problem of "fixing" the issue is vast and as the discussion herein suggests, it is not merely critical reasoning or ethics that might hope to change matters but the need to revise the whole policing culture, including the reason people become detectives.

No one has ever said that policing was an easy job, and confirmation bias or one of its various forms is likely to be intrinsic to human judgments and affect other professions. Indeed, far from being a "problem" confined to policing investigations, confirmation bias is regarded as a common psychological tendency found in other professions, including doctors, bankers, jurors, prosecutors, and expert witnesses.[146] One of the reasons given is that "people seek information in ways that increase their confidence in prior beliefs or hypotheses and disfavour choices that would disprove their hypotheses."[147]

It should be part of the job of investigators to be committed to truth seeking, to being open minded, to having critical reasoning skills, and to seeing various sides of an argument because literally anyone can form hypothetical assumptions of a case and assign blame or guilt or even innocence to a guilty party. As for resolutions, it seems clear that merely considering a hypothesis affirms the truth of that hypothesis, leaving confirmation bias open to a variety of interpretations.[148] In the United Kingdom and the Netherlands, giant leaps have been taken in the last twenty years to avoid confirmation bias as a result of several miscarriages of justice, including the need to oversee policing investigations. Nevertheless, the recent Hallam case and evidence that has come to light regarding the convicted killer Jeremy Bamber (serving a whole life sentence for killing his family, when evidence remains undisclosed) suggests that improvement and a general will for transparency is still required.[149]

3

Covert Policing

Covert policing is a term used to describe all forms of police operations in which one or several police officers monitor individuals or groups without their knowledge. This may include direct observations, phone tapping or tailing, carrying out investigative checks, or holding data on a police database without the person's knowledge.[1] Though a major tool in crime fighting, problems occur when the intention of such practices is ambiguous. This chapter focuses on such ambiguities, from the uncovering of the "spy-cops scandal," revealed in 2010, to the holding of information on innocent people on police databases, the practices of police and family liaison officers, and the testaments of those who have been diagnosed by police officers as mentally ill, without any formal diagnosis or interview with the subject. With this in mind, "covert policing" may mean different things to the police and the criminal justice system than it does to the public or human rights organizations.[2]

A distinction can be drawn between two types of covert policing: (1) deliberate or *essential* covert practice and (2) normal duties based on "information sharing and communication."[3] In the former case, officers work in divisions as undercover officers, whereas in the latter, covert practices are seen as part of ordinary police duties of which the subject remains unaware (e.g., where surveillance is adopted as part of routine information gathering). In these cases, officers may not regard their activities as covert, though the only difference to the unsuspecting individual may be one of degree. An example of both distinctions can be seen in the changing deployment of officers attending a political demonstration. At the G20 protests that took place in 2009, for instance, undercover officers mingled with the crowd without making their presence known in order to gather information.[4] In subsequent protests, police liaison officers have been deployed. Although they also mingle with the crowd, they wear police uniforms with a distinguished light blue bib and are therefore clearly visible as police officers. However, while not employed in any clandestine mission, they too are deployed to gather evidence on protestors by documenting everything told to them and may also be monitoring particular individuals.[5] In this sense police liaison officers fill exactly the same role as their undercover counterparts. In both cases and in that of *family* police liaison officers assigned to families where a police investigation is required (usually but not exclusively, homicides), the "innocent victim" qua bystander is led to believe that the officer is there to "offer support" or keep the family informed of the progression of the investigation, never knowing that they are being investigated. Where "covert techniques are those used to gather information about a person who is unaware that such an attempt may be taking place,"[6] there is no doubt that both police liaison and family liaison officers are engaged in covert practices in this sense.

The introduction of the UK Human Rights Act (1998) at the end of the twentieth century left undercover policing with a problem because Sections 8.1 and 8.2 seemed to contradict much policing practice. Article 8 of the Human Rights Act states:

> 8.1 Everyone has the right to respect for his private and family life, his home and his correspondence.
> 8.2 There shall be no interference by a public authority with the exercise of this right except such as is in accordance with the law and is necessary in a democratic society in the interests of national security, public safety or the economic well-being of the country, for the prevention of disorder or crime, for the protection of health or morals, or for the protection of the rights and freedoms of others.[7]

Because Section 8.2 stipulates that there should be no interference in a person's private life *except in* accordance with the law, the Regulation of Investigatory Powers Act 2000 (RIPA), also known as Part III of the Police Act 1997, was instigated to offer interpretation of the phrase "accordance with the law." RIPA listed the reasons when authorization may be given and regarded as necessary to be able to protect officers from seemingly overriding Section 8. These include cases in which police act for the benefit of national security or public safety or for preventing or detecting crime.[8]

RIPA focuses on those charged with *criminal* offences. Yet, as we shall see, many innocent people have been subject to covert operations, which fall outside RIPA and may breach the Human Rights Act. As a UK Operational Handbook published by the Serious Fraud Squad in 2012 states:

> Covert techniques are those used to gather information about a person who is unaware that such an attempt may be taking place. . . . This breaches Convention Rights under Article 8 of the Human Rights Act to respect for private and

> family life. . . . Watching the everyday activities of an individual in the course of conventional covert surveillance, for example, clearly engages with their right to respect for private and family life (and that of their associates and passers by).[9]

The MPS define covert policing in a more generalized way:

> Policing tactics are covert if they relate to investigative and intelligence gathering operations that are carried out in a manner calculated to ensure that the persons subject to such activity and the general public are unaware that it is, or may be, taking place. This includes safeguarding methodologies, intelligence/evidence gathered and equipment used for covert policing purposes.[10]

In what follows, practices not usually associated with covert policing will be examined. These include the covert recording of information on the Police National Database in the United Kingdom, the use of Family Liaison Officers to gather information on family members suffering from bereavement, and the use made of covert psychiatric diagnoses either by police officers themselves or by psychiatrists acting on their behalf. In recent years in the United Kingdom, the disclosure of one of the more shocking aspects of covert policing used in the orthodox sense has been the action of the MPS's Special Demonstration Squad (SDS). Euphemistically regarded as the "spy-cops scandal," it shows how covert tactics may be both ambiguous and amoral even for the officers under deployment.

"SPY-COPS"

More than half of all press stories regarding covert policing focus on the activities of the SDS. In an undercover operation set up by the MPS from 1968 until 2008, officers were recruited from London's MPS's Special Branch to target individuals and political groups around the country. Given false identities, many officers lived double lives, having sexual relationships and children with political activists while continuing to live with their own families. This has become known as the "spy-cops scandal" currently under investigation by the UK government as the Undercover Policing Inquiry by Sir John Mitting (following the illness and withdrawal of the previous incumbent Lord Justice Pitchford).[11] The Inquiry's remit is "to investigate and report on undercover police operations conducted by English and Welsh police forces in England and Wales since 1968," examining "the contribution undercover policing has made to tackling crime, how it was and is supervised and regulated, and its effect on individuals involved—both police officers and others who came into contact with them."[12]

The SDS are reputed to have focused on a number of grieving families, including that of the black teenager, Stephen Lawrence, killed in a racist attack in 1993.[13] Among those placed under surveillance was Lawrence's friend and witness to his death, Duwayne Brooks, who was maliciously arrested under a false charge of rape. Others include the family of Jean Charles de Menezes, shot dead by police in 2005, having been mistaken as a terrorist and later defamed as a drug dealer; Harry Stanley, shot dead by police in 1999 for carrying a gun (which was actually a table leg); the family of Ricky Reel, an Asian man whose murder in 1997 police dismissed as suicide; and Cherry Croce who was accidentally shot and left paralyzed by police in 1985 after police raided her home looking for her son, Michael.[14] All these cases (except for de Menezes) took decades to come to light with full details of the surveillance on the Lawrence family remaining unknown until 2015.[15]

Pivotal to the disclosure of the SDS were the activities of five environmental activists who hatched a plan to break into Ratcliffe-on-Soar electrical power station in 2009 to turn off the electrical supply. This involved abseiling inside the vast chimneys to force the electrical company E.On "to turn off the coal-burning furnaces for health and safety reasons, [forcing E.On] to switch to an emergency supply of gas-produced energy, thereby leading to a huge reduction in carbon emissions for the period during which the plant was occupied."[16] In an unprecedented move, police used undercover agents not only to attend meetings but also to play an active role in helping to harbor their activities; upon which, so the plan aimed to show, the environmentalists would be arrested before any illegal activity took place. According to the work of two *Guardian* journalists, Rob Evans and Paul Lewis, who worked extensively to expose the activities of the SDS in various articles and a book, *Undercover*, the plan was scuppered as the result of the covert activities of one undercover officer, Mark Kennedy, who the organizers recruited as their driver.

> Kennedy knew about the plan to break into the power station even before he was asked to drive [the activists] to the plant. Two months before Kennedy was approached by the activists, his superiors had authorised a surveillance operation, stating in internal NPOIU [National Public Order Intelligence Unit] documents that they were aware there was a protest that could "damage" a power station and could cause a "severe economic loss to the United Kingdom and have an adverse effect on the public's feeling of safety and security." Kennedy was the undercover officer tasked with finding out as much as he could.[17]

Kennedy, it seems, had other ideas. Having become obsessed with the plan, he reported to his superiors that he had agreed to be one of the abseilers. In response, his handler, Detective Inspector David Hutcheson, became concerned with Kennedy's involvement and reminded him that his role was that of an observer. "He only had permission to hire a van and drive activists to the gates of the power station. He was prohibited from entering the site and barred from taking part in the demonstration."[18] Well before the protest got underway, police raided the school where more than one hundred activists were staying and arrested everyone in the room. As Evans and Lewis point out:

> The police raid was unprecedented. Throughout the history of the SDS and NPOIU, police always waited for a protest to happen before arresting the suspects. . . . This was the birth of a new strategy: wait for activists to gather in one place and then pre-emptively arrest them on charges of "conspiracy."[19]

In July 2010, a year after the events at Ratcliffe, Kennedy was deployed as an undercover agent under the alias Mark Stone. Carelessly leaving his real passport in the campervan he shared with his unsuspecting girlfriend, she discovered the document and told various friends. A group of activists then confronted Kennedy who admitted being an undercover police officer. After this revelation, the Crown Prosecution Service (CPS), who were in the process of taking several protestors to court for conspiring to break into Ratcliffe-on-Soar power station, dropped the case, while others, who had already been convicted, had their convictions overturned. Kennedy's involvement had jeopardized the Crown's attempts to prosecute activists because doubt was raised that Kennedy had been acting as an agent provocateur. As the appeal judge against those accused stated, "By 2009 Kennedy, apparently convincingly, purported to be a supporter of the beliefs of those who later became involved in the plot with which we are now concerned."[20]

Kennedy's involvement with the Ratcliffe environmentalists became widely publicized in *The Guardian*, leading Peter Francis, another member of the SDS, to come forward as a police whistleblower. Dozens of stories emerged about undercover policing in the United Kingdom, most of them from women whose lovers and partners, some who fathered children, had mysteriously disappeared decades previously and who, it turned out, had all been members of the SDS.[21]

Disbanded in 2008, it seems that many SDS officers transferred to the National Public Order Intelligence Unit (NPOIU) set up in 1999 to run the National Domestic Extremism Unit, a unit still in operation and so secretive that even its precise location is unknown.[22] Thus, although the SDS was disbanded in 2008, it remains unclear whether the activities of the NPOIU differ, in any great respect, from the former SDS or if the National Domestic Extremism Unit (NDEU; now called the National Domestic Extremism and Disorder Intelligence Unit) has taken its place. Finally exposed in 2010 and publicly recognized in 2017, members of the SDS are known to have infiltrated thousands of political groups with its operatives using false identities while living double lives.

An interim report on behalf of the MPS by Durham Chief Constable Mick Creedon published in 2013 states that the SDS "infiltrated and reported on groups concerned in violent protest."[23] This claim was omitted in the 2015 edition because police infiltration scuppered any potential violence. However, it left open the role of the police in helping to plan (if not incite) direct action.[24] After the revelation that SDS officers used the details of forty-two dead children as part of their cover identity, the police received inquiries from fourteen families regarding the identities of seventeen children. The MPS's stance of "neither confirming nor denying" the facts has continued to block details being verified to the families concerned. It has thus been left to police whistleblowers, in particular Kennedy and Francis who gave evidence to the official inquiry in 2014, to reveal details of how the SDS operated.

When Channel 4 raised issues about the SDS, Creedon ordered the TV station to hand over all its documentation and correspondence with Francis, along with notes and unseen video footage.[25] Channel 4 refused. To date, therefore, there are two simultaneous inquiries, the government Undercover Police Inquiry in which victims and police whistleblowers (as well as invited police officers) have been presenting evidence, and Creedon's Police Inquiry (run on behalf of the MPS), which does not seek to hear the voices of victims but to exonerate the workings of the SDS/NPIOU. It remains unclear whether the MPS or Chief Constable Creedon are in denial over the devastating effects of what has become known on social media as the "spy-cops scandal." The "scandal" aspect has focused on those officers engaged in long-term sexual relationships with women, none of whom were ever prosecuted for a crime but who left their former partners devastated when they suddenly disappeared. In the first case of its kind, in 2014 the MPS paid a woman, identified only as "Jacqui" £425,000 in compensation for having brought up a son, the father of whom, Bob Lambert, had once run the SDS. Facing a court case for assault, negligence, deceit, and misconduct of senior officers, the MPS settled out of court, but would neither "confirm nor deny" that the man in question had been Lambert, the former head of the SDS.[26] Jacqui searched for more than two decades to find the father of her son who had suddenly disappeared—a man she'd known as Bob Robinson—a name that Lambert had taken from the grave of a child who died in 1959.[27] The payment was the first concrete admission of police duplicity, after dozens of women had complained of being duped into relationships with men who were undercover officers tasked with spying on them—the benefit of which has never been made clear but which the Undercover Policing Inquiry seeks to discover.

Though the "spy-cops scandal," first revealed in 2010, has caused major anxiety for the British establishment, it is nothing new. Before the SDS existed, Scotland Yard ran the "ghost squad." This comprised a group of detectives assigned "to infiltrate the criminal underworld, maintain contacts with informants, and in complete secrecy to gather information that would lead to the arrest and conviction of criminals."[28] As Brian Chapman pointed out in the 1970s,

> [Undercover] work . . . touches people who have little intention of engaging in illegal activities and have no subversive ends. The police simply argue that it takes time to know, and that the price of security is eternal vigilance. The crux of the matter is that certain police intelligence work is justified, and some is not.[29]

The use of undercover officers taking on false identities is not unique to Great Britain, however. In his book on policing ethics focusing on the United States, Tom Barker mentions officers who worked as gang members within organizations such as the Mafia.[30] Even within organizational criminal activity—"entrapment"—trying to make an innocent person commit a crime (the "dirty Harry" problem), "some officers believe that the end justifies the means," with one officer in the United States actually manufacturing his own crack cocaine to arrest people for buying the product.[31] With this in mind it is understandable why the MPS would use and repeat its "never confirm nor deny" mantra because when the prosecutions against those accused of planning to attack the station at Ratcliffe-on-Soar were quashed, it became clear that Kennedy had been an integral part of operations. As police intelligence already knew of the plot to raid the power station, had Kennedy not been involved, the outcome would likely have been different. As for Lambert, a darker shadow hangs over his deployment, with the question of whether he also coordinated planned attacks, most notably, planting an incendiary device in a department store in the late 1980s, remaining currently unanswered.[32] Aside from this speculation, in 2017 it came to light that senior politicians in the Labour Party, including the former party leader, Jeremy Corbyn, MP, had been under police surveillance for more than two decades for "undermining democracy,"[33] while others were placed on the covert database run by the NPOIU for being domestic extremists.[34]

COVERT RECORDS AND DATABASES

Police services worldwide hold information on individuals that they suspect of being engaged in criminal activity without them necessarily ever having been convicted of any crime.[35] These databases differ from those containing information on actual criminal convictions. In the United Kingdom, information held on convicted individuals is maintained on the Police National Computer (PNC), whereas records of would-be suspects, would-be terrorists, peaceful demonstrators, and others are held (among other places) on a database called the Police National Database (PND).[36]

The PND was set up in 2011 on recommendation of the Bichard Inquiry that took place in 2004. The inquiry followed the conviction of Ian Huntley, a school caretaker who had been convicted in December 2003 of the murders of two ten-year-old girls, Jessica Chapman and Holly Wells, on August 4, 2002, in his house in Soham, Cambridgeshire. Following Huntley's conviction, the then Home Secretary, David Blunkett, ordered a public inquiry into the police investigation, which revealed previous accusations against Huntley by Humberside police for rape and sexual assault. Though the actual records had been destroyed (Humberside police wrongly believing that holding onto them breached the Data Protection Act 1998), concern was raised that Huntley had been given a clear safety check when he had applied to work at the local school, which would have been refused had these accusations been known. Huntley had one previous conviction for burglary, registered on the PNC, which the school later testified, would have disqualified him anyway from being employed at the school, but this had not come up on his criminal records check.[37]

Among Bichard's recommendations was a national police registration scheme for everyone working with children or vulnerable adults, which employers could request the police to access to discover if there was any reason why someone should be barred from working with children. The resulting PND, which aimed to collect local police "intelligence" into one IT system for police forces covering Great Britain, was thus established, and soon the data collected moved beyond this remit. By 2013, the PND was said to contain more than 1.8 billion records,[38] including those of peaceful protestors at antiwar demonstrations and speculatively, any other allegations made to the police.

Records on the PND do not constitute a criminal record but contain information treated as "intelligence," though it is unclear what information is held. Prior to the instigation of the PND, local police forces had Force Intelligence Bureaus to record police "intelligence" on their local files. Known as "collators," these files contained "every possible information source within a police station—officer's daily reports, crime investigations, cases before the courts, information from police files elsewhere, hearsay from any kind of source, stop checks and vehicle checks and so on." Indiscriminately, it seems, "in one collator's office . . . there was a file marked 'cows, queers and flashers.'"[39]

While most local police records are kept for a maximum of seven years, records held on the PND and PNC are kept until the person reaches one hundred years of age. As the campaign group *GeneWatch* note:

> In the past, PNC records used to be deleted after 42 days if a person was not convicted. People with cautions had their records deleted after 5 years, and those with single convictions for minor offences after ten. People with multiple convictions or convictions for serious offences could have their records kept for life. There were some exceptions e.g. records from people arrested but not convicted of sexual offences could be kept for five years with the authorisation of a superintendent. By 2006, these guidelines had been abandoned in favour of retention of all PNC records, from everyone arrested for any recordable offence, to age 100. The change was made as a matter of Association of Chief Police Officer (ACPO) policy and never debated by parliament. The justification provided at the time was that the police needed to retain PNC records to see whether or not they had already taken a DNA sample from an arrested individual, and to help them track an individual down in the event of a DNA match. This justification no longer applies because new legislation requires a person's record on the DNA database to be deleted. . . . This affects both innocent people and people convicted of a minor offence, including children.[40]

Though a person has a right to see information held on them by making subject access requests to the relevant authorities, the MPS have stated that "there may be instances where this information wouldn't be released."[41] What instances these might be (since they contain one's own personal information) is anyone's guess. Worryingly because such records can contain mere allegations, it cannot be ruled out that accounts may be malicious, exaggerated, or have no basis in fact. While DNA can no longer be held on innocent people, following a landmark ruling in the European Court of Human Rights that required police to remove 1.7 million DNA profiles from innocent members of the public and to destroy more than 7.5 million actual samples,[42] details of arrest and *potential* future suspects will be kept seemingly forever. This will include people such as Kay, who, as we saw in chapter 1, was maliciously arrested by the police, bailed, and then taken to court only to have all charges dropped. As has been noted, "the digitalisation of police records on a centralised database does not necessarily equate to a more efficient and effective organization."[43]

The "PND does not create any records of its own but serves to house those records created by police forces in accordance with MOPI [Management of Policing Information]." This means that potentially millions of people have a police record. This is not the same as having a criminal record but may nevertheless prevent a person from passing an Employment Check and gaining a job, without their knowledge. The quality of information supplied to PND from forces therefore has a direct consequence on PND's ability to match and identify critical intelligence links. Since the PND is simply a collection point for very different types of information from local forces, it has no real function in deciding what is unimportant, since allegations may not have been investigated. Furthermore, "the prompt and regular download of forces material on to PND underpins its effectiveness."[44] This had led Her Majesty's Inspectorate of Constabulary (HMIC), which oversees police efficiency in the United Kingdom, to criticize the PND in both form and content, stating: "Nationally inconsistent and locally based information management practices potentially frustrate the integrity of the collective information picture."[45] While at present the PND remains separate from the PNC, which holds criminal records, the British government plans to create a centralized intelligence system that will host records now contained on both the PNC and the PND, as well as records of Automatic Number Plate Recognition (ANPR) taken from roads policing and speed cameras which can read and check vehicle registration numbers against police databases (storing up to 30 billion scans a year).[46] Known as Law Enforcement Data System (LEDS), this mega database will be one of the largest intelligence-gathering information systems in the world.

While those wrongly accused of crimes such as rape may campaign for anonymity,[47] details of potential or false suspects will nevertheless remain on police records, with the provision that should a rape occur in their area, the person can be considered a suspect. Thus, the PND, by its very creation, permits the potential harassment of innocent people who have never been investigated but have nevertheless had allegations made against them without any charges having been made. Even if charged and found not guilty, police records will forever shackle individuals with an element of suspicion. Similarly, as seen in chapter 1, it remains a mystery why the eighty-eight-year-old artist and peace campaigner, John Catt, should have discovered that he was on the National Domestic Extremist Database (NDED), with notes filed against his name that he was not "clean-shaven" and "drawing pictures." Unsurprisingly, in 2013 the keeping of such records was judged by three Court of Appeal judges to be unlawful. However, the Supreme Court ruled, inexplicably, in 2015, "that whilst Catt's right to privacy had been interfered with, that interference had been justified."[48] In 2016, Catt won the right to take his case to the European Court of Human Rights. Now age ninety-three, his case is still pending.

What is problematic is not merely that records are covert but that their intended use is highly speculative, with one *Guardian* journalist being told that a record on him is being kept in case he ever becomes a victim (of what or whom has never been made clear).[49] In addition, the NDED holds records on peaceful demonstrators and left-wing politicians who may remain completely unaware that police are creating, holding, and maintaining such records or remain puzzled as to who benefits from keeping these files.[50]

The PND which was intended to hold details of potential sex abusers now holds data on individuals well outside that remit, while the MPS's Merlin database, advertised "to record missing people, and children and adults coming to police notice," is led by a Detective Inspector from a unit known as the Mental Health Team Territorial Policing Command and maintains allegations of those the police have decided are "delusional." In 2014 Detective Inspector Frankie Westoby stated that:

> The number of adults recorded on the Merlin from April 2013–March 2014 was in excess of 52,000. This is the figure for both those with and without the adult's knowledge. The search required to give the exact figure would exceed the allowed 18 hours stipulated by the Act. Officers and staff do record the interaction and record opinion when they have identified potential vulnerability [*sic*], recording comments relating to the health of an individual.[51]

In more than one case identified on the Merlin database by the author, records included speculative insinuations by officers that the person they had been dealing with was "delusional" when otherwise there was no evidence of "vulnerability" or mental ill health.

Intelligence gathering and processing can of course be used for legitimate ends (e.g., as inculpatory evidence, intended to show a person's involvement in a crime or evidence of guilt) or indeed for illegitimate purposes. But "illegitimate" in policing terms refers to officers accessing information for some private end (e.g., to find out the details of a love interest or to engage in criminal activity).[52] It does not refer to the millions of records held on innocent private individuals, which, even when incorrect, are virtually impossible to challenge.[53] Yet police officers keep records of *everyone* they meet or interview without individuals necessarily being aware of it, and this may include in-depth information on victims as well as witnesses and suspects. Because in most cases people have no idea that information is being recorded, they will have no knowledge that it is being kept, so the reason for information being retained remains ambiguous while its accuracy is unchallenged. Since there is no means of checking the information, or changing information once it becomes known (many who have challenged police records discovered in subject access requests have received short change from both the police forces concerned and from the Information Commissioners Office), it would seem that Section 8 of the Human Rights Act—the right to privacy—is being breached with impunity. Officers need only claim, under RIPA, that such a right is not absolute and can be overridden to, for example, "safeguard" victims (even where the victim has no idea they are in need of safeguarding) for a record to be created and maintained. As safeguarding is defined as a means of "protecting people's health, well-being and human rights, and enabling them to live free from harm, abuse and neglect,"[54] it makes no sense why a so-called "vulnerable" person should have information created and retained without their knowledge. Police guidance, however, makes clear that "intelligence of any grading" can be kept and that even where retention of records shows the perpetrator to be innocent (e.g., where someone was previously arrested for a crime and subsequently found that it was a malicious accusation or another person was convicted), no records will be deleted.[55] This is particularly worrying given that in 2015 the Chief Constable of the British Transport Police admitted to a UK Parliamentary Home Affairs Committee that there was no means of telling from a PND nominal record whether the person named had been input for a serious violent or sexual crime or for a minor traffic offense.[56]

The information kept on police files may not seem particularly serious or unique. After all, when it comes to covert record keeping, we know, thanks to the former US National Security Agency (NSA) whistleblower Edward Snowden, that billions of people's personal data, including Google and Yahoo email accounts, browsing records, and phone records, are being regularly recorded (and illegally) obtained by government agencies in five countries (including Government Communications Headquarters [GCHQ] in the United Kingdom) and that there is little anyone can do about it. However, arguably, obtaining billions of records for its own sake, regardless of suspicion, is not on the same remit as police records. These may have a worse effect on the lives of individuals, owing to records being flagged up on police databases (including the PND) stating that the individual concerned has been accused of the most heinous crime albeit without proof. Several implications of this are given in the European Court of Human Rights Case of *MM v. the United Kingdom* (application 24029/07). This concerned a woman from Northern Ireland, known only as MM, who brought a case against the government questioning why a caution she had received was being retained indefinitely on the PNC. At the time of her caution (for which she admitted guilt), the woman in question had been told that her police record would be held for five years, until November17, 2005. In 2006 she was offered employment as a health-care worker and was asked to disclose details of prior convictions and cautions. When she did so, her offer of employment was withdrawn. Two years later she applied for another position, but this was also unsuccessful and she was never given a reason. In the wake of this case, other illustrations of the dire effects of police records were revealed.

In 2004 the Court of Appeal considered the compatibility with Article 8 of the Human Rights Act in the context of an Enhanced Criminal Records Check (ECRC; now called a DBS), which is required in the United Kingdom for those working with minors and vulnerable people. The case concerned a man who had once been charged by police with indecent exposure but had all charges against him dropped when the alleged victim failed to identify him as the culprit. Several years later, he applied to become a social worker and his potential employer requested an ECRC. Though he had no criminal record, the chief constable of the force where the certificate was being issued provided full details of the historic allegation of indecent exposure under the heading "other relevant information." Subsequently he did not get the job, even though he had never been found guilty of any crime.[57]

In another judgment, the Court considered an appeal regarding a person who had secured a job as a playground assistant, which also required an ECRC to be carried out and for which the prospective employee consented. Although "the ECRC disclosed that the appellant had been suspected of child neglect and non-cooperation with social services . . . [she] had not been charged with, or convicted of, any offence, nor had she received a caution." As the Court thereby stated:

> This line of authority from Strasbourg shows that information about an applicant's convictions which is collected and stored in central records can fall within the scope of private life within the meaning of article 8(1), with the result that it will interfere with the applicant's private life when it is released. It is, in one sense, public information because the convictions took place in public. But the systematic storing of this information in central records means that it is available for disclosure . . . long after the event when everyone other than the person concerned is likely to have forgotten about it. As it recedes into the past, it becomes a part of the person's private life which must be respected. Moreover, much of the other information that may find its way into an ECRC relates to things that happen behind closed doors. A caution takes place in private, and the police gather and record information from a variety of sources which would not otherwise be made public. It may include allegations of criminal behaviour for which there was insufficient evidence to prosecute. . . . It may even disclose something that could not be described as criminal behaviour at all. The information that was disclosed on the appellant's ECRC was of that kind.[58]

The court thus directed that following the previous ruling by the European Court of Human Rights, "the retention and disclosure of the applicant's caution data accordingly cannot be regarded as being in accordance with the law. There has therefore been a violation of Article 8 of the Convention in the present case."[59] However, police ignored the Court's judgment to remove unnecessary data on innocent people (therefore not abiding with the law) and continue to do so.[60]

The maintaining of records for their own sake paves the way for further abuse in which innocent victims and complainants may be discredited at the police's discretion. Furthermore, "the erosion of trust between police and other police, and between police and the public that they serve, ultimately undermines the ends of law enforcement itself. For, at the end of the day, individual police rely on one another to enforce the law, and they also rely on the community."[61]

When arrested "a person has a right to silence in order to protect himself or herself from self-incrimination."[62] But no such right exists for those who find themselves on a police database, despite a 2016 High Court ruling that it is unlawful for police to disclose information to potential employers for minor criminal convictions.[63] There may of course be many reasons why a person does not get a job. However, where the reason lies in information held on the PNC or PND, there is very little that anyone, in the United Kingdom at least, can do about it. One in four UK citizens are named on the PND, including victims, suspects, and others defined as "vulnerable." In addition, the PND holds more than twenty million photographs of members of the public, including 19 million images that are searchable by facial recognition technology.[64]

In 2012, at the same time as the European Court ruled that police had breached Article 8 of the Human Rights Act by continuing to keep and disclose records of people not convicted of any crime, the UK High Court ruled that this also applied to police keeping photographs on the PND, with the Equality and Human Rights Commission confirming that this would apply to "photographs of anyone who is innocent of any crime."[65] In February 2017, the British Home Secretary, Amber Rudd, stated that people who were innocent could now request their image be removed but added that "it was impractical to insist police forces go through all 19m images and delete those of people who were not convicted of an offence." This prompted Bella Sankey, the civil liberty group Liberty's policy director, to state:

> The Home Office has been knowingly breaching the law for years—and all they've finally managed to come up with is a cop-out. Police hold thousands of pictures of activists and bystanders who were never even taken into custody and may not know their photo was taken. That was ruled unlawful. . . . those who have been arrested but are no longer suspected should not have to ask for their images to be deleted—it should happen automatically.[66]

A month later, in March 2017, the House of Lords continued to debate whether the storing of these nineteen million facial images was lawful (in light of the 2012 ruling), with Baroness Jenny Jones raising the question of how an innocent member of the public "will know that their image is on the database," suggesting that "it would be easier for the police just to delete those innocent people without putting them to the trouble of applying."[67] Baronness Jones, a member of the UK's Green party, had particular cause for concern. In 2014, she discovered through a Subject Access Request to the MPS that a record on her was maintained on the NDED. The MPS had kept her and a colleague under surveillance for more than a decade. Her "crime" had been to sit on an official committee run by the mayor of London, set up to scrutinize the MPS.[68]

POLICE AND FAMILY LIAISON OFFICERS

In UK policing, there are two types of liaison officers associated with the police: Police or Protest Liaison Officers (PLOs) and Family Liaison Officers (FLOs).[69] The two perform different roles: PLOs cover demonstrations and protest marches and FLOs are assigned to bereaved families. While PLOs mingle with the crowd as a way of officially providing a "link between the police, protest organisers and protestors by focusing on negotiation, mediation, initiation, communication and sensing,"[70] FLOs are assigned to families of homicide, road deaths, other fatal catastrophes, and missing persons and act as a link between the family and the investigative team. To peaceful protestors, families, and even to many academics—in other words, to those who are not clear as to the role of PLOs or FLOs—the job of the former is to keep the peace and maintain good relations with the crowd, while the role of the latter is to offer "emotional support" to the families involved.[71]

In both cases, however, liaison officers are part of investigative teams tasked with discovering as much information as possible. PLOs for example may observe particular demonstrators on a march or gather general intelligence from among a crowd. In the case of FLOs, intelligence is gathered from the bereaved families of people whose death or disappearance the police are investigating. PLOs rarely have intimate communications with those they encounter, while FLOs, given the nature of their job, are given a detailed strategy of dealing with families, which includes having an "exit policy," as soon as their task is over. For many bereaved families who are assigned a FLO, the majority have no idea that they are under investigation, but see the FLO as a sympathetic addition to the police team. The sudden departure of a FLO may thus be emotionally upsetting to the family but is often deliberate on the part of the officer.[72] The role of the FLO and how their behavior may constitute covert practices will be discussed in more detail.

Police liaison officers (PLOs) were introduced as a result of poor policing practices after the G20 summit in London in 2009, in which Ian Tomlinson, an innocent bystander, was beaten by a police officer as he walked home and subsequently died. Seen by the police as a threat, the public were kettled for several hours (a practice which had become common in UK policing in the past few years, whereby police cordon off crowds and protestors), a tactic that was ruled lawful by the European Court of Human Rights in 2012 but had previously been condemned in the UK High Court.[73] As a result of the G20 protests, the HMIC made several recommendations with regard to changing the way public order policing was supervised. These included: (1) communication to be made between police officers and organizers and protestors before, during, and after an event; (2) a "no surprises" approach to demonstrations so that organizers and protesters alike have prior knowledge of the types of policing methods that may be used and clear instructions on the use of containment; and (3) the introduction of the Swedish model of "dialogue policing" known as PLOs to be deployed in different contexts including, demonstrations, music festivals, and football matches (table 3.1).[74] The official appointment of PLOs is to work with organizers and protesters adopting a community style method of policing.

Table 3.1. The Core Functions of (Sweden's) Dialogue Police (Police Liaison Officers)

Function	*Definition*
Negotiation	To facilitate compromises and agreements between police commanders' interest in getting the best tactical conditions, and the protesters' interest to get best terms for their goal
Mediation	To explain the police point of view to groups of demonstrators and the demonstrators' view to the police in order to increase mutual understanding and avoid stereotyping
Initiation	To come up with possible solutions to avoid or minimise the risk for conflicts and confrontations
Communication	To function as a link between demonstrators and commanders in their exchange of information
Sensing	To read moods and preparedness for action in the group of demonstrators and how that is affected by police activities and to inform commanders of consequences of different courses of actions in a short- and long-term perspective

Source: HMIC (2009), *Adapting to Protest: Nurturing the British Model of Policing*. Reproduced with kind permission from the HMICFRS (August 2019).

While some might argue that the introduction of PLOs leads to "reduced tension" between protesters and police, enabling the police "to retain proportionality,"[75] for others, PLOs are seen as no better than "police spies."[76]

The Network for Police Monitoring (Netpol), for instance, warns of "the danger" of speaking to PLOs, adding that:

> The collection and retention of personal data relating to protesters forms part of police strategy. It has been well established that the police have retained personal data relating to thousands of protesters, regardless of whether or not they have ever been arrested or convicted of a criminal offence. . . . Regular participation in protest activity is, in itself, seen as sufficient justification for the police retaining personal information on databases which are searchable to provide a pattern of individual protest activity over time.[77]

In a documentary made by *Guardian* journalist Jason N. Parkinson in 2012, PLOs are seen visiting a woman at her home after having identified her on a protest march. The video shows a PLO demanding to know if she is a member of the campaign group UK-Uncut and if she intends to attend any future protests.[78] The officers fail to state how they gained information on where she lived or why they turned up at her house because officially the police are supposed to negotiate with organizers. Netpol suggests that this behavior is indicative of a strong link between PLOs and the previous police units known as Forward Intelligence Teams (FITs), whose role it had been to gather information from unsuspecting individuals. The role of PLOs might therefore be seen as one which combines the "intelligence-gathering" roles of FITs with the new "dialogue-friendly" role of PLOs. However, most campaign groups have disputed that PLOs are anything *other* than intelligence officers, and as Parkinson's video shows, it is clear that naming and locating demonstrators is part of their role. Furthermore, the covert function of PLOs is not something that when questioned, police have denied,[79] though their role within or on protests and marches may remain unknown to members of the public.

While the role and performance of PLOs has come under scrutiny, most people will never have contact with a police family liaison officer or FLO because they are only assigned when the police are investigating a suspicious murder, disappearance, or road death. There is therefore no collective information on the effect of FLOs from family perspectives because these are isolated cases. On one internet site, HealthTalk.org, run from the University of Oxford, interviewers put together a number of people's responses on their experience of FLOs. These are some of the comments posted:

> Misunderstandings may occur if people don't realise the liaison officer is an intermediary between the family and the investigation team. Ann thinks the police should have made this clear.

> The liaison officers called at the house for three months and then suddenly disappeared. This distressed Erykah; she realised that the police had not been there to support her but to build a case.
>
> Alison cried when the liaison officers left. She had first thought they were there to support her but decided that they had only called at the house to get as much information as possible.[80]

The formal training of police family liaison officers came as a result of the Macpherson Inquiry into the death of the black teenager Stephen Lawrence on April 22, 1993. Macpherson showed that despite prolonged police investigations into Lawrence's death, the failure of police to prosecute several prime suspects was largely the result of institutional racism. Officers failed to acknowledge that Lawrence's death had been racially motivated, even though the key witness had informed police that his attackers had shouted, "*what, nigger*?"[81] Macpherson also noted that from the beginning of the police investigation, relations between the Lawrence family and liaison officers went badly wrong.[82] While FLOs had been in operation before the Macpherson Inquiry, these roles had been assigned to any officer available willing to deal with the family. As one ex-assistant chief constable informed the author, "no one ever wanted to do this job as families too often interfere with the investigation."

After the Macpherson Inquiry, it was accepted that the role of FLOs needed to be made official, so officers were provided with training (albeit, this lasts only five days). Though the role of FLO remains a volunteer one away from an officer's normal duties, police departments now have dedicated officers on hand to deal with families in the case of deaths and missing persons which require police investigation. The Association of Chief Police Officers (now, National Police Chiefs' Council [NPCC]), provided the first formal guidelines into the role with the publication of *Family Liaison Strategy Manual* in 2003, which was followed in 2008 by *Family Liaison Officer Guidance*. In both manuals, the *investigative* nature of FLO work is clearly outlined. The primary objective of FLOs is "to gather material from the family in a manner which contributes to the investigation and preserves its integrity" and "to secure the confidence and trust of the family, thereby enhancing their contribution to the investigation."[83] Both versions call for risk assessments to be carried out on the family with the 2003 version stating that this should include "a thorough search of databases . . . to establish as much information as possible about the premises and occupants,"[84] while the 2008 version states that "where the deployment of FLOs takes place outside the scope of this guidance, the SIO/SIM is expected to detail the decision-making process within their policy file."[85]

Those assigned FLOs, however, are rarely informed that all communications with family members (including descriptions of their behavior) are being recorded and gathered into the Family Liaison Log. The log, which families do not have access to and can never correct—though it is simply the opinion of one officer—may however be discovered through making a formal subject access request to the police force concerned. As William Middleton, who was wrongly arrested and accused of murdering his daughter, stated:

> Clearly if there is a suspect there is a need to gather information which either confirms or refutes that position. Which is where the stream of information comes into play, the family is befriended by the Liaison Officer who is considered by them to be in a position of trust and providing nothing more than a supportive role. However . . . if a member of the family is a suspect for whatever reason, their role includes covertly obtaining information to return to the investigative team which they themselves are part of. This can in no way be considered anything other than a conflict of interests which gives rise to the questionable use of any information obtained as a result if it is indeed passed on.[86]

In 2014, more than twenty years after Lawrence had been killed in South London, the House of Commons ordered an Independent Review into the role of undercover policing after the police whistleblower and "spy-cop" Peter Francis told the press that PLOs in the Lawrence investigation had been ordered to spy on the family, passing details on to Special Branch. However both FLOs denied this. As stated in *The Stephen Lawrence Independent Review*:

> Both family liaison officers concerned, Detective Sergeant John Bevan and Detective Constable Linda Holden, maintain that no such request was made of them. They say that the taking down of names of those in the house was their own idea as detectives involved in the murder investigation. It was unfortunate that the two family liaison officers failed to inform the family clearly that they were also active detectives on the investigation, and that they would report back any information they could glean. We believe that even in 1993 it should have been recognised that a family might not realise that such officers had a dual role. However, we also accept that it has only been in more modern times that the role of family liaison officers has been clarified, and they have been instructed to make this dual role clear to a family.[87]

Unfortunately, none of the families that formed part of this research had *any idea* that their communications were being monitored, although one was told—(to her surprise given that it was a road death case) that police were monitoring her Facebook account, while another was informed that her "social media platforms were being monitored," including Twitter and YouTube accounts that held nothing but music videos. At no point was any family member made aware that liaison officers would be taking down the names of those in their house, monitoring their phone calls (as later became apparent), and taking extensive notes, including the bereaved persons, reaction to seeing their loved one in the mortuary. The most likely explanation for not providing this information would seem simple: once families know this is the purpose of the FLO's presence, they usually decline to have such officers in their company. However, when Janet Alder, the sister of Christopher Alder who died in police custody, dismissed her FLO, she was placed under surveillance and followed.[88] Though tarnished as a fantasist when she complained of police behavior, an IPCC report found evidence that local police had indeed been following her for years.[89]

Inexplicably, the British press have failed to reveal the extent to which FLOs are involved in covert practices. Instead the "spy-cops scandal" has been singled out without referring to the normal function of FLOs even when highlighted in official publications. This is particularly true of FLOs involved with the Lawrence family. The failure to reveal the full extent of FLOs' behavior means that for many, the targeting of Doreen Lawrence and other family members remains an isolated incident. However, FLOs post-Macpherson conduct their investigations in precisely the same way as occurred with the Lawrences, by making notes of all communications and names of people entering and leaving a property. Even though a main police textbook on family liaison has stated that "openness and accountability sit at the heart of family liaison work,"[90] it is doubtful how many individuals would accept police officers keeping a log on their speech and everyday behavior if they knew this was occurring. Doreen Lawrence has expressed rightful outrage at the knowledge that FLOs "spied" on the family—according to the whistleblower Peter Francis—to discredit the family's campaign to bring justice for Stephen—by passing material gained by the FLOs on to members of the SDS (the "spy-cops"). However, even this is not unique. Documents from a bereaved family member involved with Sussex police reveal that information from FLOs was passed on to no less than three other UK policing agencies, including the MPS (who placed information about the individual onto their Merlin database), the College of Policing (where the UK lead for FLOs was based), and South Yorkshire Police, who had a vested interest in information presented to one of their colleagues—the same lead person at the College of Policing who was acting on secondment but never revealed to the individual concerned that he was an acting police officer.

The College of Policing insist that "before attending the family home a risk assessment is carried out."[91] However, in one case, this "risk assessment" occurred only *after* the individual had informed police officers that she never wanted to see any FLO ever again. This resulted in police officers ordering a check on the PND for "any information with regards to previous mental ill health or anti-police feeling." When the PND failed to reveal any records, intelligence checks were ordered which noted her political views (including letters published in the *Independent* and *The Guardian*).[92] The reason for the "risk assessment" was thus illegitimate and could have had nothing to do with officers' safety because at the time it was carried out, the individual no longer met with any of these officers.

It may be understandable why FLOs would carry out risk assessments before deployment, but the role of the FLO is a double-edged sword—families who admire the kindness of their liaison officer remain unaware that their reactions and words are being taken down in every detail, without explanation, and others who do become aware of the practice (and this is the crux) usually readily dismiss their FLOs without a moment's hesitation, feeling this to be an insult to their loss or bereavement. As one FLO comments in a police magazine:

> I'm still involved as the Family Liaison Officer for the first murder this year [four months earlier] and I interviewed on a second one. So what has now landed on my desk are all the tapes and transcripts to read through and check. I am going to have to find time to do it because the job will have to be done, and quickly, as all of them are subject to time restraints. Those are the sorts of things that keep coming in, yet you're expected to do your normal job at the same time.[93]

The police would argue that in cases of homicide, the FLO plays a vital role because a high percentage of homicide victims, at least in England and Wales, are acquainted with the principal suspect (68 percent for women and 52 percent for men).[94] However, where the family are ruled out of playing any active role in an investigation (either because the suspect is known to have no link to a family or the death is not suspicious), the role of the FLO is simply intrusive. As one FLO wrote about the next-of-kin of a road death victim:

> the NOK [next-of-kin] went into the viewing room. . . . Almost immediately [she] walked straight back out in tears. She explained that she was not prepared for what she had seen. There were comments about her mother's hair and that she was not sleeping she was a corpse. There were comments about her facial injuries. She then went back in. Prior to this [redacted] was asked to have a look at her mother which s/he did. [The Coroner's Officer] then went into the viewing room with [her]. There was discussion in the room. . . . As [she] was visibly upset with everything including the surroundings [her friend] became a very important person.[95]

There follows half a dozen pages of redactions in the Family Liaison Log about the same person, followed by details of a telephone conversation:

> [The next-of-kin] stated that she was very upset and again started to rant about what happened at the viewing. The call was ended by me telling her to have a think about things and get the important matters in hand. She explained that her diet at the moment is coffee and whisky [*sic*].

The log, which takes words and meanings out of context, paints a picture of the participant as someone unable to cope, who is turning to alcohol for emotional support, while the word "rant" is used to belittle the person's concerns with regard to the identification of a dead relative only days after the event. Steve Woodward, a Traffic Police FLO, had this to say on the keeping of the log:

> Every meeting with the family, every phone call made or received, all dealings with the press, the SIO/PIO [Senior Investigations Office/Police Investigations Office], with any other outside organisation, in fact anything and everything connected with that case was to go into the FLO log. It could mean hours of writing but everything needed to be recorded on a daily basis to protect me, the family and others in the event of any complications or complaints.[96]

While families remain unaware of the log, as Woodward clarifies, information from the log is kept in the case of any complaint. This seems to be the overriding factor when collating information on family members, perhaps more important than gaining intelligence from the family. As John Thompson, whose son Jake was killed by a speeding lorry hundreds of miles away from the family home, conveyed:

> When introducing themselves FLOs give the impression they are there to help and support relatives, giving guidance and advise on the process of the investigation and the inquest. We now know their primary function is to protect the police from any criticism, gathering any information which they consider may help them should a civil action be brought against them. Making notes on the emotional state and behaviour of people who are grieving is both callous and devious in the extreme. Deceit and deception are difficult to cope with at any time let alone when you are trying to come to terms with the unexpected death of someone you have loved and shared your life with.[97]

Even though *Police Family Liaison Guidance* states that the log should be shown to families, none of those interviewed were aware that such a log even existed until long after the event. The knowledge that details of telephone calls, conversations, and other meetings were being recorded, caused not only distress but a breakdown in police relations, with one person quoted as saying, "Now I know how they operate, I'll never trust the police again."

COVERT DIAGNOSES: CASE STUDIES

Slightly more than a quarter of participants that were interviewed expressed serious concern with the way the police used mental health as a weapon to discredit them. From Kay in chapter 1 to Melanie, a bereaved next-of-kin who, like Kay, also found herself on the MPS's Merlin database, declaring a person mentally ill seems to be a common practice. The undercover methods used to determine a person as "mentally ill," usually without the person's knowledge, are spurious and rarely, if ever, rely on medical records or actual diagnosis. There are no police documents suggesting that should suspicion fall on a person being declared "mentally ill" that the person themselves should be ignored. Instead it seems the individual concerned is the last person to hear that they have been defined as "mentally ill" and even less able to prove their sanity once a record has been created by police officers (sometimes with the help of psychiatrists) and thereafter impossible to challenge, let alone delete. When one participant attempted to take the police to court, under the system of Judicial Review for breaching the Data Protection Act, they were informed they would need to remortgage their home and provide the solicitor with more than £80,000 upfront. Such means of redress are not open for most people.

While mental health may provide police with specific issues, the added concern is that officers not only decide that someone *is* mentally ill (the term "delusional" is the preferred term) but choose not to convey this information to the individual concerned. In such cases, police officers seek to take this action as a means of covering up their own incompetence or as a mean of revenge. In another case, police officers (one a coroner's officer) attempted to access the complainant's medical records from their doctor. When this was refused, the officers created their own records and entered them on a police database. Instead of addressing the issue of obtaining medical records covertly, according to one chief constable, these are "needed to help police cope with growing numbers of vulnerable people" even "without an individual's consent."[98] It is difficult to understand why such records would be needed. In cases where people do suffer mental health issues, these are usually known by the individuals and certainly their family members. There is thus no reason or justification why anyone *suspected* of being mentally ill should not be directly asked whether they suffer from a mental illness. If this is not possible to obtain, then it would seem obvious to ask their next-of-kin. By its nature, a person with a mental disability is no more a criminal or likely to be one than a person with a physical illness. Yet it is clear that police officers regard mental illness as a dangerous disease which can readily be used to stigmatize individuals.

The following two narratives, though extremely personal to the subject concerned, are by no means unique. They reveal how officers, with the full support of third parties (often social services and other times psychiatrists) have discredited members of the public through carrying out covert mental health assessments—of which the participant, whether regarded as victim or complainant, remained unaware but was unable to get the data changed. The first case concerns Theodore whose complaint of heavy goods vehicles (HGVs) illegally using his quiet street led to officers contacting social services stating that he was "seeing buses" and was therefore delusional. The second case concerns an ex-farmer, Alec, who, as a result of being a witness in a previous case of police malpractice, had two covert psychiatric reports carried out on him, which though disputed by his local doctor, he was unable to challenge and had to eventually abandon the family business.

Theodore: A Mental Health Referral

Theodore never had any reason to distrust the police or to believe they would try to use a previous mental health condition against him. Prior to the incident that led officers to discredit him by informing several agencies that he was "delusional," Theodore had only praise for his local constabulary. He had suffered from hepatic encephalopathy (a form of reversible dementia linked to liver disease) prior to having a liver transplant. One day, unable to gain entry to his house after dismantling a faulty alarm, he decided to walk to the house of his ex-wife (with whom he was still close friends) around twelve miles away. After several miles he stopped to rest at the roadside and was approached by several police officers. As a result of the illness, Theodore could not remember his name or where he lived, but he did manage to recall the medication he was taking and the name of his medical consultant. Within a short space of time his family were contacted, his home checked, and he was taken to accident and emergency (A&E). As Theodore comments,

> Two or three officers remained around the corner from me. . . . They were obviously amused by the situation but were plainly affected in a very human and sympathetic way. Before leaving with my wife and son these officers shook hands, expressed good wishes for my recovery and said they would inform the other shifts of my condition should something similar occur.

Theodore lives on the edge of a small town in the southwest of England. Backing onto a road that has restricted access to HGVs, he and several neighbors started raising concerns when HGVs started making illegal detours through his narrow street from which they were banned. "It was through traffic, illegally passing throughout the day and night on route to various transport depots causing inconsiderable nuisance—using [my road] as a short cut."

When a manhole cover broke, the noise of the HGVs started to wake Theodore at around 4 a.m. every morning. He contacted the local council who informed him that while their job was to maintain the road, it was the duty of the police to ensure no unwelcomed vehicles were driving through. Theodore contacted the police who said it was the council's responsibility. Theodore then went back to the council.

Feeling he had been ignored by police and worried that this might be attributable to bias surrounding his former illness, Theodore bought CCTV and audio equipment and made a 24-hour recording of the traffic outside his property to gather evidence and "prove" his sanity. At the same time, several neighbors had been making representations to the police and the council in parallel with his own, with a local councillor commenting on record that he had forgotten how many times he had reported incidents to the council and police and nothing had been done. Eventually, Theodore wrote to his MP who wrote to both the council and the police on his behalf. While the police replied to the MP, dismissing Theodore's complaints, the council repaired the road surface after several residents complained to the local government ombudsman, but this did not halt the constant flow of HGVs nor resolve the issue of who was responsible, with the police and the council still blaming each other.

Several months later, the council conducted a formal traffic survey. The survey revealed that more than a hundred HGVs each day were making illegitimate use of a road with restricted access. "The council asked the police to enforce these traffic rules but after several months the police did absolutely nothing." Theodore then telephoned the police to ask if they had seen the survey and if they were going to do anything about it. A few weeks later he was visited by a sergeant and another officer from the local road's policing unit (RPU). The sergeant informed him that the survey revealed there were forty-six vehicles driving down his road in a fortnight period, and they could not really do anything about this. Theodore was astounded: "That's not what the survey says," Theodore reported, "the survey says there were fourteen hundred vehicles in that period, over a hundred a day." Unable to find the survey in his home when a police officer was present, he discovered his copy later that day and visited the police station the next morning where he gave the same sergeant a copy of the council's survey with the qualifying definitions of the vehicle categories to confirm what he had been saying. "The sergeant looked at the figures and said 'Oh, I rely for my information on my officers.'"

Since his liver transplant, Theodore regularly attended his general practitioner's (GP's) surgery every few months for a "competency test" to ensure that the symptoms of hepatic encephalopathy had not returned. He was used to the regular checkups and, as he had been well since his transplant, had no concerns. The last test had also gone without concern. To his surprise, ten days after passing his latest test, he was called into his GP's office for a "reality check," but he was unconcerned, stating, "I thought they had just slipped up on the paperwork." Having carried out another test, which Theodore passed without issue, his doctor then asked, "'so you haven't got any problems with heavy goods vehicles or buses?' I said 'What? Where's that come from?' I thought, there's only one place where that could have come from and was astounded when she said, 'we had a referral from the mental health team.'"

Theodore explained to his GP the problems he had been having concerning HGVs illegally using his road, which the police had failed to act on and thought this information could only have come from the police. His GP assured him that she had been contacted by the mental health team but added, "'nothing you've said surprises me, I used to be married to a police officer.'" On exploring how his doctor had received this information, Theodore visited the mental health team who referred him to social services. Social services confirmed that they had received an email from the police traffic unit, alerting them to the fact that Theodore was "delusional," repeatedly complaining of buses and other vehicles speeding in his street. Not allowed to see the email, Theodore was forced to make a subject access request to the police. As he states, "When I received it I was absolutely distraught—the police officer who actually made the report repeats quite provable many lies regarding the whole situation and I just didn't know what to do, I was beside myself."

Theodore took his concerns up with a local councillor and magistrate who he had known for several years. He then made a formal complaint to the police. "My wife is a retired senior nurse, my daughter is a mental health social worker and deals with special needs—I think, between them, if there had been any mental health problems they would have noted this with my medical team. I was also carefully monitored by my medical team, post transplant; they [the police] have shown no concern whatsoever for my mental health."

Theodore's formal complaint was investigated by the same force's PSD, standard practice in England and Wales for any offense not involving death in police custody (which is investigated by the Independent Office for Police Conduct [IOPC]). The officer in charge ignored his complaint but stated that Theodore was suffering delusions by imagining a bus route in his road and that he hallucinated seeing buses. Because there *is* a bus route in Theodore's road, this claim was easily refuted and was done so with confirmation by two bus companies and by the provision of bus timetables. Since the original issue (of HGVs passing through a restricted road) had now reached the level of fiction, Theodore appealed to the Head of the PSD, a Chief Superintendent (CS), but the CS simply repeated verbatim what the investigator had said.

Theodore then wrote to his MP who took up his case, writing a personal letter of complaint to the Chief Constable. Though the Chief Constable agreed to do a review, he informed the MP that he could not find anything wrong with the way his officers had behaved. Theodore felt devastated: "Basically it was an arse covering exercise; they had been treating me appallingly . . . they could have suggested I was mentally ill through having suffered from hepatic encephalopathy i.e. liver failure and raised concerns at any time but they didn't; they only raised them a week after I confronted them with evidence of their own wrong doing." As Theodore later commented:

> That mental health labelling continues to be used as a convenient cop out for accountability avoidance by police management can only harm public trust and confidence. The hard won reputation achieved with simple common sense and humanity by everyday plod inevitably suffers as a result. I don't think either of the originating officers had the integrity to admit their mistakes. Had they done so I would have dropped the complaint there and then, with the confirmation that "Ok, they cocked up in a big way and I hate it but there you go, that's life." I can deal with that but to continue the torment as they have—and it was torment—I think that's absolutely outrageous and I think they're prepared to do that to anybody.

Alec's Story: Covert Psychiatric Reports

Until the end of the twentieth century, Alec and his father ran a family farm in Scotland going back several generations. Alec had no particular qualms against the police, believing "they were okay and honest" though some years before, in 1992, he had been a witness against two police officers who had both been disciplined as a result. Having bought two firearms at an auction, Alec had come home to find two firearms' licensing officers on his doorstep. Both refused to show any identification, one appeared drunk and the other "flipped his jacket back and put his hand on a Glock handgun." Alec had been terrified (and later suffered from posttraumatic stress disorder as a result), but the two officers were eventually disciplined, and Alec received a formal apology.

A decade later, the incident behind him, Alec made a successful application for a firearm certificate. His father had just renewed his own gun license and Alec had recently gained a new license when he received a notification from the police that he had to renew his license. As Alec said: "my name is Alec Harris and my father's name is Alec Harris. It was clear the police confused the two." Thinking the matter a simple administrative error, Alec had no real concern, believing the matter would be sorted without much ado. When he made inquiries, however, Alec was suddenly informed that he was not eligible for a shotgun license because of issues affecting his suitability. Asked what they were, he was informed they concerned matters to do with his mental health. Confused, he sought to take this up with the licensing manager, only to discover it was the same officer who had drawn a gun against him more than a decade before against whom he had testified.

His application turned down and shocked to discover that (according to police) he now had to contend with psychiatric reports against him (though he had never seen a psychiatrist or had any sort of psychiatric evaluation), Alec visited his GP who was also a family friend. His GP wrote to the police that Alec had no history of mental illness and that he would confirm his well-being. In response the police said that two psychiatrists had independently verified that Alec's "mental health" affected his suitability to hold a shotgun license, as a result of which there was nothing they could do. As Alec comments, "my doctor said, 'there's nothing wrong with you.' I did have post traumatic stress disorder after the officer in the house drew his gun against me, as that was quite stressful but it was a long time ago."

Unable to get a license, and with his guns confiscated, Alec went through several years of campaigning and court cases spending his life savings, eventually resulting in the High Court ruling in his favor. However, the police refused to comply with the court's request to revoke their decision, leading Alec to eventually abandon the farm altogether, to move out of the country, and to take up another profession. He continues trying to clear his name from police files but believes that the situation is hopeless: "there's a two-tier law system: there's one for you and me and there's another for them, the police and government, so you'll discover if you go to court you have no rights at all . . . and that can't be okay."

As P. Duff reported more than twenty years ago, in the Scottish criminal justice system, the prosecution case rests almost entirely on the police report submitted to the prosecutor fiscal (the Scottish term for public prosecutor), and in a large number of cases, the police will decide if a person suffers from mental illness and will write this in their report, regardless of whether a psychiatrist has been present. The police can also recommend that someone receive psychiatric treatment which would divert the offender from receiving a prison sentence.[99]

> It was generally accepted by fiscals that they have to rely upon the police to inform them whether the offender's actions were a result of psychiatric problems . . . the police were the most important source of information about the psychiatric state of accused persons . . . it is purely within the discretion of the

> police whether to comment upon the offender's behaviour or include details about his or her mental state.[100]

Regardless that police officers are not medically trained, they still commonly determine people to be mentally ill. It has also been widely reported that *victims* who *are* mentally ill are rarely served well by the police, in one case resulting in a victim not receiving any attention when he was attacked owing to prior knowledge that he suffered from a mental illness.[101] The denigration of those as being "mentally ill," "delusional," or whatever term is used to discredit a person is thus not a light one. It has real repercussions for the person concerned who risks being left without any legal or policing support should the need arise. Given the use of covert databases and that many people will not even be aware they have been branded this way (inappropriately, given that under RIPA, a vulnerable person is one in need of community care services),[102] the branding of a victim or complainant as "vulnerable" or "mentally ill," as in the cases highlighted here, is clearly meant to stick. Thus, it is right that the public should be wary if or when police officers seek "to access medical records and other confidential data without an individual's consent."[103]

CONCLUSION

As this chapter has shown, there seems scant justification for many of the types of covert practices and procedures that currently exist in modern-day policing. Yet even with the Undercover Policing Inquiry, hearing testaments from both covert officers and victims of surveillance, it is hard to see how most practices carried out against noncriminals can be justified and what purpose such covert tactics have served. While the police are given authority by laws to prevent crime, this should not exclude any officer from stepping outside the boundaries of the law, but in the case of covert operations, where this boundary lies is extremely hazy. The "spy-cops scandal," for instance, is a long cry from the familiar patrol officer or detective that most members of the public associate with the police or even with the aggressive riot squad whose presence is at least known. The fact that any one of us may be a suspect, without us even knowing that suspicion has fallen on us, and that the only means of finding out may be to conduct one's own investigation or subject access requests and then hope that the governing body will comply with one's request, is extremely worrying. No less are those who find themselves on covert databases, sanctioned as "delusional," and made *voiceless* without any right to reply forever branded by a word that is so abused that literally any one of us may be or become *delusional* simply because a police officer has decided as much. Yet the reason for such branding seems to have little to do with concern for an individual's mental health because how could concern for a person's state of health lead to a covert record on some database or a mental health referral without the individual's knowledge?

While Liberty, the Human Rights charity, may have a point in calling for politics to be kept out of policing, the surveillance and condemnation of political figures and the "naming and shaming" of who is or is not to be regarded as "subversive" is worrying for us all.[104] There seems to be something fundamentally askew with a society that has decided it is perfectly legitimate to hold secret records on one in four of the population, to photograph any person who attends even the most prosaic demonstration, to call out those who question the status quo (and even those who do not), and to portray anyone with political views left of center as a potential "domestic extremist." As Brian Chapman wrote on the history of the police in the eighteenth century, "the traditional police state combined paternalism, autocracy and enlightenment on the one hand, with secret police, constant surveillance and paid informers on the other."[105] We may be forgiven for thinking that little has changed.

4

Road Deaths

Books on the police generally ignore the issue of police investigations into road deaths. This is surprising since every year in Britain around 2,000 people die in road traffic collisions. Of this number, approximately 400 are pedestrians and 100 are cyclists. In 2015, to be precise, there were 1,732 reported road death incidents on Britain's roads and 22,137 serious injuries. The statistics are difficult to interpret because "serious injuries" also refer to those involved in road traffic collisions who later die in hospital. However, for those who died at the scene or within a month of being in collision with a motor vehicle, the reported incidents for 2015 show there were 409 pedestrian deaths and 100 killed while cycling.[1]

Worldwide there are around 1.25 million road deaths a year with road traffic injuries being the leading cause of death for those aged fifteen to twenty-nine. Of these approximately 387,500 are pedestrians and 50,000 are cycle casualties. The World Health Organization (WHO) estimates that where motorized traffic mixes with pedestrians and cyclists, an adult pedestrian has less than a 20 percent chance of dying if struck by a car at less than thirty miles per hour but almost a 60 percent risk of dying if hit by a vehicle at fifty miles per hour (figure 4.1). The WHO reports that "the type of crash that is likely in a particular situation is also an indicator for determining a safe speed."[2]

While statistics are useful in helping to understand the extent of the problem, in Europe, including the United Kingdom, casualty figures are fairly low compared to road deaths that occur in African counties or even the United States. Nevertheless it is useful to compare pedestrian and cycling deaths in the United Kingdom with statistics for murder. In 2015, 574 pedestrians were killed on British roads compared to 509 homicides. Although the real figure for homicide may be much higher (and a recent spate of violent crime

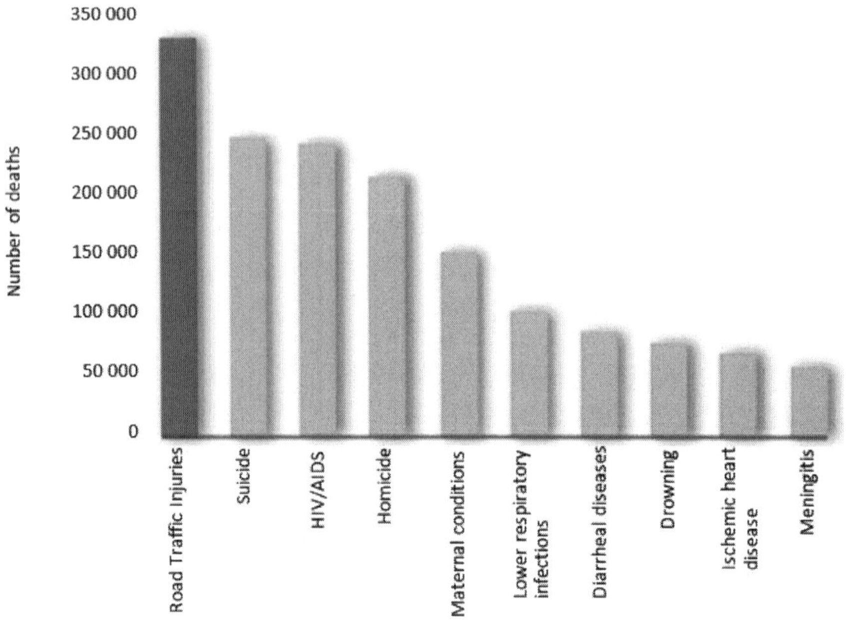

Figure 4.1. World Health Organization (WHO) Global Status Report on Road Safety, 2015.

in 2018 has raised the figure considerably), for reasons discussed in chapter 2, it remains the case that a person is more likely to die as a result of a road traffic collision than as a result of violent assault.

Though guidelines do exist for road death investigations and for homicides and other crimes, there is no obligation, at present, for officers to adhere to published instructions. This reveals a deep malaise within many investigations. These include the deaths of Toni Rolls, eighty-three, a woman killed on a pedestrian walkway near Seaford, East Sussex; Eilidh Cairns, thirty, a proficient cyclist killed by a tipper truck lorry in Notting Hill Gate, London; Jake Thompson, twenty-seven, killed by a speeding lorry on a pedestrian crossing in Bristol; and James Sutton, forty-seven, killed by a police vehicle on pursuit of a suspected disqualified driver. When the inspector in charge of family liaison officers (FLOs) in Sussex was shown that the police had failed to adhere to guidelines stated in ACPO's *Road Death Investigation Manual* and *Family Liaison Officer Guidance*, the inspector tapped the hard copy of the road death manual presented before him and said, "Read that? It says *Guidelines*. It means, we don't have to adhere to them."

This cavalier attitude gives rise to a suspicion that in the absence of a comprehensive investigation, there is a bias against victims, particularly where death has resulted. Not only does this leave families feeling betrayed and without redress when things go wrong, it also blocks the introduction of improvements. At present, the failure to make guidelines obligatory fails both police officers who seek to follow due process and members of the public, particularly victims, who have no course for redress when things go wrong.

POLICE INVESTIGATIONS INTO ROAD DEATHS

Changes to the governance structure of UK policing in recent years mean that policing recommendations and guidelines are constantly changing ownership, though content remains largely unchanged. The main document for road deaths remains that published by the National Police Improvement Agency (NPIA) in 2007 on behalf of ACPO, now reformed as the National Police Chiefs Council (NPCC).[3] When the announcement was made in December 2011 that the function of the NPIA would be transferred to other organizations, its guidance was published (and became known) as Authorised Professional Practice. Its existing documents, published under the ACPO banner, were transferred to the College of Policing (established 2013) with the NPCC taking over publication of the former *Road Death Investigation Manual*. There are now two documents in operation that are, or may be, used as guidance for road death investigations.

1. *The Road Death Investigation Manual* (2007), written by the NPIA/ACPO, and
2. *Road Policing: Investigation of fatal and serious injury road collisions* (2014), published by the College of Policing.

Both documents are freely available online.[4]

In general, the *Road Death Investigation Manual* (RDIM) offers commonsense approaches to what should occur at the scene of a collision, forming the basis of good practice. It is a comprehensive manual which refers to other documents that should be read in conjunction and should be used to determine where investigations fail. As a foundation for investigative practice, it could be a basis for raising concerns if those guidelines are ignored or for examining deviations in practice from set procedures. However, this is where the term "guidance" exposes a major flaw in modern British policing: No individual officers (let alone forces) are under any obligation, legal or otherwise, to follow the advice of any manuals published as good practice. Therefore, it simply becomes a bureaucratic representation with little or no effect. Victims of road deaths and their families thus have no justified means of determining how an investigation took place, why it failed to take place, or how it might have been accomplished. Instead of police investigations being transparent, as they would be if these documentations formed legal protocols, policing of road deaths remains idiosyncratic and opaque to anyone outside the current operation, including other investigative teams (e.g., those who deal with homicides).

One of the first points made in the RDIM is the claim that "all fatal collisions should be investigated as 'unlawful killings' until the contrary is proved."[5] Though encouraging, this first precept has been and continues to be ignored, as "unlawful killings" are reported and investigated in distinct ways from road deaths and involve different third parties. For instance, on arriving at the scene of a road death, the police are legally required to call the coroner. In England and Wales (which has different rules than the rest of the United Kingdom), a coroner is called where a person has died and not been certified dead by a doctor (or not been seen by their GP in the fourteen days preceding death). This does not mean that the death is regarded as "suspicious" or as an "unlawful killing." If it were treated as an unlawful killing, a forensic Home Office pathologist would be invited to attend the scene to carry out careful and detailed examination of the body and SOCOs, also known as CSIs, would make detailed examinations of the scene. In the case of a road death, neither a forensic pathologist nor a CSI is required to attend. Instead, road traffic police attend the scene with their own forensic collisions expert, an expertise that falls far short of the qualifications and expectations of CSIs where a SOCO is expected to have a degree in forensic science as a minimum requirement. There is no degree qualification requirement for collisions experts who may operate without formal qualifications (e.g., policing experience and some evening courses being deemed satisfactory) or at most hold a Level 4, City & Guilds Certificate in Forensic Collisions, equivalent to a predegree foundation course taken by distance learning.

Arguably, CSIs are not required to attend a road death scene because their job is to determine trace elements left on surfaces (e.g., fingerprints, fibers, DNA, flecks of paint, etc.) to help the police investigation team gather evidence for a conviction. The forensic collisions investigator aims to determine the fault, if any, of the vehicle(s) involved and, thus, conducts mathematical equations to determine skid marks, speed of travel, pedestrian throw (if appropriate), and so forth. The collisions investigator is not trained in more detailed analysis (e.g., where the pedestrian may have been standing in relation to the vehicle, which might be determined by CSIs if they were to attend). The lack of training and forensic detail given by collisions investigators may, as a result, cause controversy and is often criticized by families (as will be shown).

A major discrepancy exists in England and Wales between forensic pathologists and hospital pathologists. Forensic pathologists are largely paid for by the police (£2600) with an additional cost paid by the coroner (£260). They attend scenes of crime, isolate the body, ensure that DNA is captured on the scene, and that corpses are kept in a sterilized environment. In the United Kingdom, they are fully regulated by the Home Office. In contrast, hospital pathologists work for the NHS but when conducting a postmortem, they work for the coroner on a self-employed basis and are paid a standard fee of £96.80. Though hospital pathologists are members of the Royal College of Pathology, who set minimum guidance, the quality of the autopsies they perform is not assessed. In fact, the United Kingdom remains one of the few countries in the world where nonforensic autopsies remain unregulated. Hospital pathologists do not attend scenes of crime and, in many cases, only supervise the postmortem examination. The financial differentiation may play a large part in determining when and if a forensic pathologist is required. As with the distinction between CSIs and collision investigators, where forensic pathologists are highly qualified and specialized in their field, hospital pathologists, when acting as self-employed pathologists on behalf of the coroner, are not regulated by anybody in the United Kingdom, and thus the quality of the autopsies that they carry out is unknown.

A legal distinction exists between unlawful killing and road deaths. Prior to 1991, the offense of Reckless Driving and Causing Death by Reckless Driving had to prove the state of mind of the driver (*mens rea*, the central concept of criminal intentionality), but the Road Traffic Act (1991) rejected this principle. Road deaths were then separated from the rest of criminal law, with the Road Traffic Act focusing attention on the standard of driving rather than the mental state of the driver.[6] There is therefore little incentive for road police investigators to treat road deaths as a detective might do when arriving at the scene of a suspected homicide. Thus, road death victims and their families may well feel, with some justification, that their cases are not being treated with the same care that they would be if their loved ones had died as the result of an "unlawful killing" because the quality of the investigations bear little resemblance. This is not to suggest that the RDIM is misguided. By stating that road deaths *should* be treated as unlawful killings, it is insisting that the same rigor with which unlawful killings are investigated is applied to road deaths. In practice, however, emphasis is placed on victim responsibility first, rather than on the skills of the driver. This has resulted in accusations of "victim blaming."

The RDIM designates the Roads Police Senior Investigation Officer (RP-SIO) as the lead investigator for all fatal collisions, though it clarifies that the role is not rank specific. Unlike a murder investigation, which has to be led by the rank of detective inspector or above, the RP-SIO in a road death may be of the lowest rank of constable. This was the case with Eilidh Cairns, Toni Rolls, and Jake Thompson, three road deaths victims whose stories are outlined in this chapter.[7]

Another useful guidance mentioned in the RDIM concerns the use of hypotheses. These hypotheses or assumptions are made by the RP-SIO "to indicate where further material may be gathered and to identify which investigative strategies are required to progress a fatal collision investigation," adding that "when developing hypotheses, it is important to remain objective." It also clarifies that RP-SIOs "should be aware of the dangers of making assumptions . . . or believing that assumptions made by others are fact" because "the hypothesis should be either modified or rejected as appropriate."[8] Further, "alternative interpretations of what might have taken place must be continually reviewed."[9] The RP-SIOs may be asked to account for decisions at the coroner's inquest or other proceedings and are required to create and present a disclosure file with witness statements and the forensic collision investigator's report to the coroner. This policy file, which contains background paperwork on how the police arrived at their decision, may be requested by the coroner on rare occasions but is never disclosed to the family. Aside from providing information on how hypotheses are derived, the police file includes all documentation on the lines of inquiry covered by the investigation, including (though the RDIM does not elaborate) covert policing techniques.

Under the Coroner's and Justice Act 2009, which came into effect in July 2013, the disclosure of all relevant material that will be presented at the inquest is available to the families of the deceased who constitute "interested parties," but information may be withheld without the families' knowledge.

The RDIM is clear that investigations should be conducted with objectivity and reviewed by senior staff members. This consists of a thorough examination of the various causes of collision, including bad driving, distraction of the driver, health and eyesight issues, and pedestrian movements, where applicable. Aside from the senior investigation officer, other roles are also defined in the RDIM. These include that of FLOs (whose role in a road death remains ambiguous, as seen in chapter 2). In a homicide, a FLO acts as a detective performing an investigative role. Their task amounts to carrying out covert operations and gaining access to information on the deceased, including diaries, mobile phones, family tree, bank details, relationship to other family members, and so on. This information is gathered as a high percentage of homicides are carried out by persons known to the victim. In a road death, however, there is no need to gather such information as the perpetrator—and relation to the victim—is already known. Strictly speaking, therefore, FLOs have no role other than giving sympathy and assistance to the families of victims. Yet according to the RDIM, they are still required to devise a family liaison strategy, "gathering evidence and information from the family in a manner which contributes to the investigation and preserves its integrity."[10] However, if the family were not present at the death and are known not to be responsible (as is the case in 99 percent of collisions), what can they contribute? If they were in the vehicle, the investigating force would have already recorded the evidence. This leaves bereaved families often being treated like suspects.

Although the RDIM seeks to clarify that "the FLO is an overt investigator" who should not "be used for any covert operation involving the family," the very nature of the FLO's job is to collect information covertly without informing the family that this is what they are doing. Most people, even murder suspects within families, are unaware of the real job of the FLO or even why they came into existence. Traditionally, FLOs were simply police officers appointed to deal with the family's questions. As such, they usually appeared in uniform, and families were well aware they were part of the police's investigative team. The scandal involved in family liaison by the police's involvement into the death of the black teenager Stephen Lawrence and the subsequent deployment of FLOs to "spy" on the family's campaign for justice, brought to the fore a major problem with FLOs in UK policing.[11] However, this is not explained in the RDIM, which demands that FLOs be as transparent as possible. There are contradictions, however, which the RDIM fails to clarify. In carrying out risk assessments on the family without their knowledge, as well as keeping the family liaison log detailing information passed to the investigative team by the FLO, the role remains controversial particularly because information is gained covertly. Though families often praise the officers assigned to them, most have no idea that everything they have said in the presence of the FLO (including in many cases, the emotions they express) has been documented for the investigative team. This is an invasion of privacy and in a clear-cut case of a road death, where there is no suspicion of homicide, unnecessary. The RDIM emphasizes that clear strategies need to take place regarding FLO deployment, including the ending of their relationship with the family (which ought to take place after the inquest, at a roundtable meeting with the SIO). In practice, this rarely occurs.

The role of the coroner is also well-documented in the RDIM. While described as "an independent judicial office holder," the coroner does not act as a mere cipher to the police investigation but is an integral part of it, employed to arrive at the facts of death after the police have completed their investigation. While coroners are said to conduct their own investigations, in effect coroners' investigations are tied to the investigations of the police, who liaise with the coroner regarding the evidence presented for the inquest. As already stated, however, the full policing report is rarely provided to interested parties. At the request of the family, the report may be disclosed to interested parties, but families are often charged extortionate fees running into thousands of pounds to cover the price of photocopying. Others are denied access altogether.

The latest guidance on road death investigations from The College of Policing, published in 2013 (*Road Policing: Investigation of fatal and serious injury road collisions*), is ten pages in length. The RDIM, on the other hand, is 144 pages. Thus the College of Policing's updated document has little to add to the RDIM.[12] However, the College of Policing's document is keen to point to the "National Decision Model" (figure 4.2) and its "Code of Ethics," which the College introduced, on its foundation in 2013, which includes Policing Principles (figure 4.3).

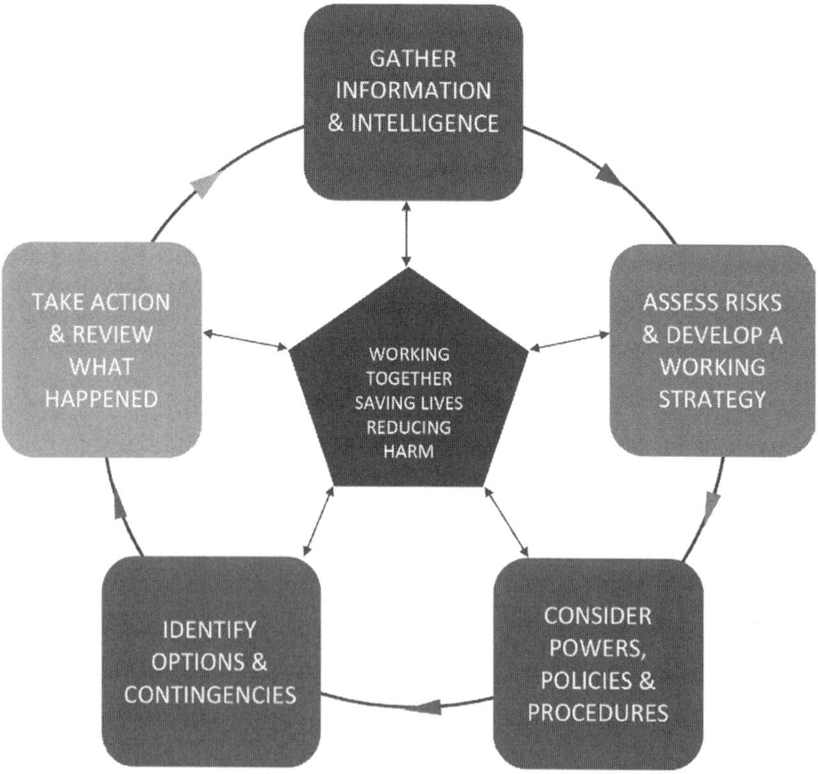

Figure 4.2. National Decision Model.

Accountability
You are answerable for your decisions, actions, and omissions.

Fairness
You treat people fairly.

Honesty
You are truthful and trustworthy.

Integrity
You always do the right thing.

Leadership
You lead by good example.

Objectivity
You make choices on evidence and your best professional judgement.

Openness
You are open and transparent in your actions and decisions.

Respect
You treat everyone with respect.

Selflessness
You act in the public interest.

Figure 4.3. Policing Principles.

In addition to official guidance, which until recently was produced in hard copy, police forces produce their own documentation based on the above (or rather, based on the RDIM).[13] Otherwise, the only other "official" publication available to police officers on road death investigations is *Blackstone's Police Manual on Road Policing*, intended as a revision text for officers seeking promotion to the role of inspector.[14] This covers basic laws and procedures, namely, The Police and Criminal Evidence Act, 1984 (PACE); and it is not without merit, helping, for instance, to avoid confirmation bias—e.g., "police officers have a duty to gather and present any relevant evidence whether it tends to prove or disprove a person's guilt."[15]

In recounting the stories of several road death victims' families, it is hoped that this will pave the way for clearer recommendations in the future, where "guidelines" are used as the benchmark for good practice and open to legal challenge if and where recommendations fall short of the mark.

TESTAMENTS OF VICTIMS

Eilidh Cairns was thirty years old when she was killed as the direct result of a road traffic collision. An experienced cyclist, she was on her way to work on February 5, 2009, cycling down a two-lane one-way road in Notting Hill Gate, London, when she was struck from behind by a tipper truck lorry and dragged under its wheels. Two hours later, she was pronounced dead. As police arrived on the scene, they directed members of the public, who had witnessed the crash, to leave the scene without taking contact details. This included a woman, who, on witnessing the incident, had immediately run to the aid of Eilidh, who, trapped under the wheels of the lorry, repeatedly called out, "please help me." On the arrival of the police, the woman was asked if she was next-of-kin. When she said she was just a passing stranger who had witnessed the incident, the police officer told her she had no business being present and ordered her to immediately leave the scene, though Eilidh was heard pleading "don't leave me."[16]

The driver informed the police that he had simply not seen Eilidh, and no action was taken against him. The police forensic collisions investigator (who, unbeknown to the family at that time, was under investigation for fraud) concluded that Eilidh must have been cycling alongside the lorry—a dangerous position for cyclists—and got trapped in his blind spot. However, police failed to interview any witnesses on the scene or to put up white boards asking for witnesses to come forward, which is a standard procedure when a fatal collision has occurred. The family complained and was told that the delay was down to the boards needing to be "constructed." Two weeks later, boards appeared but no details were provided of the time of the incident or that it had involved the death of a cyclist. The police were unable to find any witnesses. The family then decided to conduct their own investigation. Through producing leaflets and talking to people in the street, several witnesses then came forward. One witness said she had been in the back of a taxi behind the lorry that had killed Eilidh. Informing the police of this information, a search was then done by the police to find the taxi driver, who appeared as a key witness at the inquest. Two other people also telephoned the family to say they had seen the collision. This included Melissa Ross, the woman who had held Eilidh's hand before she became unconscious. Informing the police they had found a key witness, the family were told they were "interfering in the investigation" and forbidden to contact Ross again until the investigation was closed, more than a year later. The family then discovered that it had taken the police over two months to interview Ross, by which time police officers said she was so traumatized she couldn't be interviewed (an impression not shared by the family). Another witness who had contacted the family was dismissed by the police as being "flaky," "foreign," and "could not speak good English." They refused to find an interpreter for her even though she had informed the family, via a friend that she had "seen the lorry under her" but that the police kept shouting "are you *absolutely* sure of that?" The woman stated that she subsequently felt so intimidated by the police's behavior that she refused to speak to anyone again or appear as a witness. However, the witnesses who did eventually testify at the inquest, unanimously agreed that Eilidh had been in front of the lorry when she had died and that it had driven straight over her.

Dissatisfied at what she regarded as a pointless investigation, Kate Cairns, Eilidh's sister, a qualified civil engineer, questioned the police investigation. She wanted to know why CCTV cameras were not checked nor the lorry settings nor the experience and competence of her sister, an experienced cyclist who took the same journey of ten miles each morning.

Eilidh's family attended a meeting with the RP-SIO and demanded that the eyesight of the driver be tested. It took police six weeks after this request to carry out eyesight tests on the driver. When performed, it showed the driver's vision was so poor he was unable to pass the roadside eyesight test required to drive a car. This meant he should not have been permitted a license to drive a lorry. He was charged with uncorrected defective vision and fined £250. He was not charged with careless or dangerous driving as the case against him was brought three months after the crash. His lawyer argued that his eyes had deteriorated since the collision, which meant no concrete connection could be made between his vision and Eilidh's death. He was permitted to carry on driving.

The Cairns family criticized the family collision investigator whose diagrams were so poor "that when used at the inquest the witnesses could not understand it . . . nothing was clear and laid out." Having established that Eilidh Cairns had been in front of the lorry when she was hit (as stated by key witnesses) and had not come up beside him, the collisions investigator wrote in his report:

> It is uncertain how or why this collision occurred. Motorcycles and pedal cycles regularly filter down between slow moving traffic. This is generally considered safe to do so if there is sufficient room. However, it should have been obvious to an experienced cyclist that to cycle down such a small gap in lanes of traffic and put oneself in such close proximity to such a large vehicle would be hazardous.

As Kate Cairns comments:

> On re-reading Ewan's [the collision investigator's] summary statement above I see that we have jumped to the conclusion that he is implying it was Eilidh's fault. . . . The question is to what extent in the rest of the report is Eilidh's experience detailed and does it unequivocally show that she was experienced, and therefore would not have filtered?

Elsewhere the collisions investigator wrote: "The mirrors afforded the driver good views down both sides to the rear of the lorry, and there would appear to be no reason why the driver should fail to see someone cycling down his offside close to the side of his lorry if he was looking in this mirror at that time." Yet there was no suggestion, by any witness that Eilidh *had* been cycling down the side of the lorry. As Kate commented to the investigator:

> if as you suggest, she was cycling down the offside, and as you suggest he did look in his mirrors, he would have seen her. As you and he state he did not see her we can conclude that either a) she did cycle down the offside and he did not look in his mirrors as he stated he did, and should have done or b) she did not cycle down the offside at all. And yet you go on to state "*it is more than likely the cyclist has come down the offside of the vehicle.*" This is completely unsubstantiated. On what basis are you making this claim? Why are you ignoring your own reasoning? Why are you ignoring Eilidh as an individual experienced cyclist, her familiarity with the route, and the witness statements?[17]

Sixteen months later, the same driver killed Nora Gutmann, ninety-seven, on a pedestrian crossing. He was given a four-year sentence for dangerous driving (he was not wearing his prescription glasses) and an extra year for tampering with his tachograph (a device that records speed, distance, and hours driving) to evade laws on driving hours. He was banned from driving for six years. Although the Cairns family asked for the investigation into Eilidh's death to be reopened, no charge was brought against the driver for that death. However, it was revealed in court that after killing Eilidh, the driver had been in numerous accidents, which included: driving into the rear of another vehicle causing £3,000 worth of damage, colliding with a parked motor vehicle for which he failed to stop, and a week before he killed Nora Gutmann, being in a collision with a minicab.[18] Both the families of Eilidh Cairns and Nora Gutmann stated they would have preferred that the driver be banned from driving for life than have gone to prison. They remained highly critical of the police investigation teams.[19] As Kate Cairns states:

> Eilidh's case epitomizes the unacceptable failings of the justice system at every stage of the process in dealing with a cyclist death; the investigation, the prosecution, and the inquest. . . . It reveals a justice system unfit for purpose and stacked against the victim.[20]

Jake Thompson was twenty-seven when he was killed after being hit on a pedestrian crossing on the A27 in Bristol in May 2011. The police primarily decided that his death did not warrant investigating and a senior officer informed the coroner that there would be no prosecution, even before any witnesses had been found. As his father, John Thompson, wrote in correspondence: "This implied that, as far as the police are concerned, Jake's life was insignificant, no investigation was warranted and the driver was free to continue to drive with their blessing." The driver was only interviewed four months later at the insistence of the family wherein the police found him blameless and refused to investigate further. At the inquest into Jake's death, held in September 2012, it was reported that the lorry's tachograph recorded that the driver had been speeding immediately prior to Jake's death and had driven through a red light.[21] As a result, the family started a campaign for the driver to be brought to trial.

Without any hope of due process, the family decided, like the Cairns family, to carry out their own investigation, which included an attempt to find witnesses. However, it took more than two years before the police decided to conduct a formal investigation into Jake's death. This revealed that the lorry had been traveling at thirty-eight miles per hour in a thirty-mile-per-hour zone when Jake was killed and that the traffic lights were red or had just changed to red at the time of his death. The police investigation accepted that the driver had "fallen below the expected standard," but their report to the Crown Prosecution Service (CPS) stated there were insufficient grounds to prosecute. As Jake's father states:

> We got the call from our solicitor, David Robinson, to say that due to a clerical error, he had been sent a copy of the Specialist Collisions Report—a "red tagged" document normally meant for police and CPS eyes only. In it, the CPS stated that the police investigation into Jake's death had not yielded sufficient evidence and failed to make the case that being 8mph over the speed limit was "sufficient cause for a charge of causing death by careless driving." . . . People receive fines of £80 if they get caught speeding by a Gatso camera, and yet here, with our son dead, the driver walked away without charge or penalty. . . . To add to our distress the CPS stated that they considered there would be "minimal" public interest in prosecuting the driver.

The family then decided to bring a private prosecution against the driver based on their own investigations. After three years, with the support of their solicitor, David Robinson, they won a civil claim for compensation against the driver, after which the police agreed to reopen their case. Three years after Jake had died, the driver was charged with careless driving and appeared in court in September 2014. The family was informed by the CPS that the trial would take between five and six days. However, after less than one and a half days, the judge told the jury he would decide on the verdict. As John Thompson reported,

> the Judge decided the jury should not hear all the evidence or the reasons for the delay in getting the case to court. The expert witnesses were asked to submit a written report, they did not give evidence under oath and did not answer any questions. In his summing up he agreed the driver had been driving carelessly but he could not see the connection between this and Jake's death. He was unable to recognise that had the driver been driving carefully he would not have crashed into Jake. His comments are also in contradiction to CPS Guidelines. According to the judge, the driver is free to continue driving carelessly.

On November 20, 2013, Toni Rolls alighted from a bus and minutes later was killed on a pedestrian walkway in East Sussex. Six hours later, her daughter, who lives in London, was informed by local police that her mother had died. Unable to provide further information during their visit, one of the Metropolitan Police officers telephoned the police sergeant in Sussex who had been first on the scene. The sergeant was then put on the phone to Toni's daughter but for some reason refused to directly confirm that Toni was dead, instead repeatedly saying, "she is in the hands of the coroner." Her daughter, not understanding the meaning of "coroner," thought this meant her mother was still alive and being cared for by a consultant. It was not until the next morning that she learned via Sussex Police's website that her mother had been killed by a thirty-six-year-old driver on the A259 near Seaford. This information had not been passed to her prior to the press report being released, in contravention of media guidelines provided in the RDIM. The next day she received a telephone call from a FLO, who described himself as an intermediary between the police investigation team and the family. She had no idea until they met that he was a serving police officer with the investigative team. Having been told that her mother required an autopsy and that the police investigation could not begin until the daughter identified the body (although it had already been identified), on November 22, she attended the mortuary with a close friend.

The FLO stated she should expect to see some facial swelling and two black eyes, but that otherwise her mother would appear as if she were sleeping. What she saw bore no relation to this statement. As she said:

> There were deep gashes in parallel lines cut into the left side of my mother's skull, a long drip of blood that had poured from an ear and stopped before reaching the neck in suspended animation and what appeared to be half a brain missing at the back as the head was concaved and sloped sideways. The rest of the body that was on view (from the neck to the upper torso) was dressed in an antiquated white-laced garb to [presumably] hide the scars from the recently completed autopsy. I was horrified and almost immediately ran out of the room. I pleaded to James, to look. . . . He retuned seconds later, his face ashen. He looked at me, stating angrily but calmly "this is *not* what was described." Overwrought with grief, I sat down and sobbed uncontrollably. As I did, I became aware of three people watching me, two police officers and the coroner's officer, who I learnt, much later, was also a police officer. I remained completely unaware that I was under surveillance and that my reactions would form part of a police file.[22]

During the identification, another (female) police officer had arrived and there were thus three police officers (including the coroner's officer) in the tiny antechamber next to the mortuary. They engaged in chatter and were laughing. When Toni's daughter asked for her mother's possessions she was informed by the coroner's officer that all her mother's clothes had been destroyed because they were stained and damaged. Not only was this later disclosed to be untrue, but it was against police guidance to destroy the clothes as these were vital evidence and the property of the next-of-kin who has the right to their return. She was then asked if she wanted her mother's handbag. When she said yes, the coroner's officer placed the bag on her lap, without informing her that it was covered in human tissue, including brain matter.

Three days later she wrote a lengthy letter to the FLO asking for an explanation of what had occurred. He replied saying that he could no longer act as her FLO. She was not provided with any further details of her mother's death. A few days later, a key witness made a comment in a local newspaper. He said he had been the driver of the bus Toni had been on just before she died and that he had witnessed her being killed. Communicating with the daughter on social media, and later privately, the driver said she had been standing on the white line that separates the bus stop from the road when the car had hit her. He also claimed, though the police verified but later turned out not to be true, that he had been the first person on the scene at her death.

A road policing inspector who was also in charge of FLOs visited Toni's daughter six days later. He informed her she was interfering with the police investigation, that she was not allowed to talk to the bus driver, and that her social media accounts were being monitored. Following this visit, which lasted six hours, she made a formal complaint to the police. She believes this complaint stopped the police from conducting the investigation into her mother's death and was a major reason why a junior police constable was appointed as RP-SIO while her boss, a police sergeant, acted as deputy SIO. Information received more than a year later showed that the police investigative team went into overdrive in targeting the daughter rather than investigating Toni's death. This included carrying out intelligence checks with other police forces to determine if she had a history of mental illness or "anti-police" feeling and creating a covert dossier collating emails to whoever she contacted in the police or related organizations (e.g., the coroner). As to the investigation into Toni Rolls's death, the coroner's file revealed several unsigned witness statements, two of which belonged to witnesses who had seen nothing. The next-of-kin then decided to conduct her own investigation. She met up with the bus driver who had been told by the police that he had to "stick to his story of not seeing anything" or he'd lose his job. However, the police still maintained that the bus driver had been the first person on the scene and that her mother had bled to death for fifteen minutes on the road.

A year after the inquest documents revealed by East Sussex ambulance service showed that Toni Rolls had not only died on impact but that the first people on the scene had been an army medic and a female doctor who had confirmed in their emergency call she had died instantly. It is not clear if the army medic or the doctor were ever contacted by the police, but no information about them was conveyed in any documentation to the coroner though Sussex ambulance service had the mobile number of the medic on file.

The ACPO lead for road death investigations informed Toni's daughter in writing that she was entitled to view any reports, pictures, photographs, videos, drawings, or other material that may have been taken by the police as part of their investigation. Though she managed to see the police body-worn video at her local police station, and photographs of the scene, after several months of persistent requests and only if a lawyer was present, the only information she ever received from the police was the initial assessment made from the first officer at the collision scene, the same sergeant she had spoken to the night of her mother's death. The sergeant had written that there were four hypotheses which could explain why Toni had died (the details in brackets were provided by the family):

1. She had been running across the road [even though she was eighty-three and walked with a limp];
2. She had been drunk because alcohol was smelt at the scene [toxicology reports showed no alcohol in her system but a bottle of whiskey that she had just bought from a nearby supermarket had smashed when the car hit her];
3. She had underestimated the speed the car was traveling and therefore thought she could "just make it" [which suggests number 1]; and
4. The driver of the vehicle who killed Toni did not stand a chance because she had been wearing dark clothing—[photographs reveal she had been wearing a bright purple Norwegian anorak with reflectors on the back and cuffs and light grey trousers]

The RDIM states that creating hypotheses is the first step in conducting an investigation. But where it makes clear that hypotheses need to be based on *evidence*, no evidence was considered when the on-scene officer wrote her preliminary report into the death of Toni Rolls. Prior to evidence being gathered any opinion is simply bias, as has already been indicated and which research has shown overwhelmingly targets the victims of cycle and pedestrian deaths, never the driver.[23] The facts that the driver admitted to "often bumping into the back of people's cars" (as heard on body-worn video) and an officer stated "the driver broke to avoid a man crossing the road but then accelerated and hit the woman" were never submitted in evidence. Furthermore, when her daughter examined the scene and sent copies of the pathology and police forensic collisions report to independent experts they verified that Toni's injuries could not have come from her crossing the road but that she must have been facing the oncoming car or walking in the other direction (which could not have been the case) at the time of her death. This evidence was not welcomed by the police (or the CPS).

The forensic collisions expert stated in his report that Toni Rolls's eyesight was failing because "she needed reading glasses." When questioned at the inquest what needing reading glasses had to do with failing to see an oncoming car, the collisions investigator said it was to prove she had "eyesight!" At no time was the driver's eyesight tested, though the collision report said he wore contacts. The driver admitted at the inquest to having been looking in the direction of the central reservation at the time of Toni's death and thus not looking ahead of him. He described her figure in his witness statement as being just a "shadow."

Johnny Smith was sixteen when he was killed on a pedestrian crossing outside his college in a small town somewhere north of Leeds. Speaking at a reception for road death victims in 2014, his parents expressed dismay with the police's investigation into his death, particularly the way that officers had invented hypotheses as to what might have occurred. "The police said he was wearing dark clothing," Johnny's mother remarked, "and that the driver couldn't see him." His father added:

> That's exactly what we were told—that Johnny was wearing dark clothing, that he just stepped out and ran across the road, that he'd probably been drinking. He was sixteen for Christ's sake, he didn't drink, he was responsible, he was on a pedestrian crossing. I mean *on it*, it wasn't his fault.

Johnny's parents and Toni's daughter are far from alone in expressing dismay at hypotheses created by police officers as part of their investigations, particularly ones that contradict perceived facts.

After reports on the death of Toni Rolls were published on social media, Michael Doherty, a justice campaigner, contacted Helga Akitt whose brother, James Sutton, forty-seven, had been killed by a police car on Hasting's seafront four months after the death of Toni Rolls, also on the A259. Helga pointed out the similarities between her experience and that of Toni's daughter, remarking, "Not only does this express exactly what I have gone through, they are the *same* family liaison officers." Helga asked about CCTV cameras because there were several close to the scene where her brother had died, but officers told her that there had only been one in operation along the road that night more than half a mile away.

Contacted shortly afterward, Helga stated that what struck her the most about the police was the unprofessionalism and insensitivity of their behavior. This included a female FLO who turned up at James's wake, "barging into the house and declaring 'wow, doughnuts, I love these,'" upon which the family asked her to leave. The inspector in charge, who informed Toni's daughter that her Twitter account was being monitored, informed Helga that her Facebook pages were also being scrutinized. She was also similarly warned not to have contact with witnesses though Helga had no intention of doing so.

Helga believed that a thorough investigation would be carried out into her brother's death, but the family soon felt that the police were merely covering their tracks. First they were told the police had been following a speeding vehicle, but it was later revealed that it was traveling around twenty miles per hour. There was also the question of the police car's incident data recorder (IDR). Each police vehicle is fitted with an IDR (similar to the black box fitted in airplanes). This records whether the vehicle's siren and lights are on and the exact speed the vehicle is traveling. The police informed Helga that the IDR in the car that killed James had malfunctioned around 4 p.m. that afternoon and there had been no time to get it fixed. The family commented:

> We wanted to know *why* that car was in operation? It all seemed too convenient that the black box broke down and was only noted *after* my brother was killed. To this day we don't know if the sirens were going or the lights were flashing.

To confuse matters, Helga had at first been told that her brother had been killed by a speeding police car in the middle of the road and had thus "failed to acknowledge the sirens," but this was later changed to saying that James had "stepped out into the road," so even if the police had not had their sirens on they could not possibly have seen him. Even though the IPCC found the police not guilty of misconduct, the family felt that the real facts of the case were never established. As Helga states,

> It's difficult because it was the police that killed my brother, so it was always going to be a difficult situation; I believe they protect themselves and each other as a force, you know they wanted to deal with this very quickly; I thought it was wrong that the officer who killed my brother wasn't questioned for twelve days.

Helga was also puzzled to learn that the police car had been attending to a Grade 1 incident. A Grade 1 incident is one noted as an emergency requiring immediate police attendance. This occurs where (i) there is a risk of danger to life, (ii) immediate threat of violence, or (iii) serious injury to a person, damage, or property. In the case of James Sutton, who the police state they hit while pursuing a Grade 1 emergency call, it later emerged that they had been following a suspected disqualified driver, which is not categorized as a Grade 1 emergency. Nor did it make sense to the family that the police should have been traveling "in excess of 55 mph" when the suspect was driving at twenty miles per hour. After James was killed, the control room ordered all other police vehicles to stand down in the pursuit of the vehicle, which was stopped two hours later in a different county.

An IPCC report published in 2009 casts doubt on the legitimacy of police pursuits given that approximately forty people die each year in UK collisions involving the police with between one and eleven police pursuits out of one hundred leading to a death. And yet, of those police officers arrested and taken to court, only a small percentage are ever found guilty and none charged for dangerous driving.[24]

In the case of James Sutton, the car under pursuit was *not* regarded by the control room as a Grade 1 incident (an incident which required speeding and the use of lights and sirens), a view contradicted by PC Morris, the officer who killed James, who stated at the inquest that in hindsight and in similar circumstances, "my actions and decision making would be the same."[25] Though his actions had been contrary to police guidelines and IPCC recommendations, there was no suggestion that he had made any mistake. Instead the family were told that James's "awareness of the car might have been impaired by 'alcohol or cannabinoids' as he 'entered the pathway of the vehicle.'" The pathology report indicated only that James had died of "multiple injuries," and no one suggested prior to the inquest that James's intake of alcohol had anything to do with his death.[26] It was the attempt to discredit her brother that distressed Helga the most. As she said:

> He'd been out with friends, he'd been drinking so they said it was his fault as he'd been drinking, he was like a shadow coming up with dark clothing, they couldn't see him . . . I've read a lot after my brother was killed and that kind of terminology "dark clothing" "like a shadow" is often repeated . . . if my brother hadn't been drinking I don't know what their excuse would have been. But I have no doubt they would have come up with an excuse.

In all of the cases mentioned, none of the families expressed any desire for retribution or imprisonment of drivers. Instead, concern was expressed regarding the behavior of the police and their seeming incompetence and ability at being able to conduct a road death investigation. Criticism focused on (i) why police were so careless, particularly in failing to find and interview witnesses; (ii) why forensic collisions investigators did not seem up to the task of conducting proper investigations; (iii) why RP-SIOs were uninterested in determining the facts; and (iv) the role of FLOs who were patronizing and unsupportive. Most of all, no one could understand why, when there is a reasonably good guidance for police officers to consult, the RDIM, it can be so readily ignored. Though other changes were desired (e.g., that drivers who kill be subjected to the European law of Strict Liability and those found to have driven carelessly have their licenses revoked *for life*), it was the lack of proper protocols on behalf of the police that families were unable to challenge that caused the greatest amount of distress.

POLICING ATTITUDES

In early 2017, the All Party Parliamentary Cycling Group held an Inquiry into Justice and Cycling at the House of Lords. As part of this Inquiry, police officers from two English police forces were asked to speak on the topic of enforcement and police investigations. Police constable Mark Hodson and PC Stephen Hudson from West Midlands Constabulary spoke about the Close Passing Initiative they had introduced in Birmingham as a preventative measure to avoid cycle deaths and injuries, and Detective Chief Superintendent (DCS) Paul Rickett from the MPS spoke about policing investigations in London. While the initiatives produced by West Midlands police were encouraging and praiseworthy, with no blame placed on the victim (i.e., the cyclist or pedestrian), the attitude of DCS Rickett provided an alternative account which suggested a victim-blaming attitude.[27]

Both communications are presented here to show that although negative strains toward police investigations do exist in UK roads policing, there are also officers not only willing to challenge this underlying status quo but also whose experience of dealing with road traffic collisions place the onus of harm on drivers and the need for good communications between the public and the police.

The West Midlands "Close Passing Scheme Initiative" is a recent project that has received much positive press coverage.[28] PCs Hodson and Hudson devised the scheme as a means of preventing cycle and, by association, pedestrian deaths in the city of Birmingham. The scheme is simple. An undercover police officer on a bicycle selects a handful of roads in Birmingham where killings or serious injuries of cyclists are known to take place. Working in two-hour shifts with a backup vehicle nearby (a police motorcyclist) and video cameras attached to the front and back of the bicycle, the officer films anyone committing an offense. The police cyclist also has a police radio so that assistance can be called for, if required. If drivers are seen coming too close to the police cyclist—either on the side or at the front of the vehicle or commits any other driving offense (e.g., going through a red light)—they are pulled over and asked to attend a fifteen-minute course on safe driving. This consists of information on behavior and the reasons why cyclists take the positions they do on the road. In many cases, the driver will be shown the video of themselves engaging in poor practice. If drivers are receptive to the course, which always takes place at the scene, they will be given some literature and informed that if they are caught driving in the same way again, they will be faced with prosecution. If they refuse to attend the course, the video of their poor driving is sent to the crown prosecution service, who will decide whether charges should be brought against them. In all but one documented case, drivers have been willing to attend the fifteen-minute talk.

As a matter of course, and particularly when drivers claim they did not see the cyclist, the officers will test the driver's eyesight. One person failed the road side test for vision and was apprehended and prevented from driving;

other offenses included drivers with no insurance and those driving while using a mobile phone. PC Hodson explained that as traffic officers in the motorcycling unit, they were often asked to attend cycling events and to deal with cyclists engaged in poor decision-making such as cycling on the pavement (which violates the Highway Code). When asking cyclists why they did so, the officer was repeatedly told by cyclists that they found it too dangerous to cycle on the road because drivers would come too close, giving them little consideration. PCs Hodson and Hudson devised the Close Passing Initiative after realizing that only when drivers faced the threat of prosecution would this change their behavior and make cycling safer. As PC Hodson states,

> What you quickly realize, when you're a road traffic officer is that the only thing that seems to stop people offending on the road, large scale, is the threat of prosecution which is why average speed cameras work so well; people always adhere to the speed limit in areas of average speed cameras; it's an unfortunate fact but it's true; so we needed a scheme whereby first of all drivers had their attention focused on cyclists and became more aware of them because when we analysed the figures we found that 75% of road side collisions involving cyclists occurred at junction locations. Now we can't stand a police officer at every junction in the West Midlands waiting for someone to pull out in front of a cyclist because in 98% of those collisions, the collision was the driver's fault, they had pulled in front of the cyclist at the junction and there were no incidents of cyclists not having lights on, there were no other environmental factors that were contributing to the collisions so it was purely the fact that the drivers were failing to see the cyclist even though the cyclist was doing everything right according to the law. So we had to concentrate driver behaviour and the way to do that was basically make the cyclist a threat to their licence, if they were to interact with the cyclist the wrong way, that they would be punished for it and be expected to be punished for it.

The Close Passing Initiative involves a matter of waiting and then cycling. Since the officers use different types of bicycles and clothing (one day they may use a folded Brompton and be dressed in jeans, another day a racer dressed in Lycra), drivers have no means of identifying who is a genuine cyclist and who is a covert police officer. As PC Hudson states, "as a result, they've always got in their head, 'Is that a police officer? Did I pass too closely? Could I be prosecuted?' It changes their behaviour immediately. Whether they agree with what we do or whether they don't agree with what we do."

The two police officers also decided to take on third-party prosecutions by accepting and documenting cyclists' own video evidence. The officers recognized that some of the video recordings were so good and identified such bad driving practices that it was easy to present to a court to prosecute the drivers as a result. Since the initiative started (at the end of 2016) more than two hundred offenses have been dealt with between just two officers. Since they are part of a police investigation team with limited resources, it has not been possible to extend the scheme, though West Midlands Police have reported a 52 percent decrease in videos being sent to them by cyclists since the scheme started. Positive feedback has also been received from other police forces, with more than half of police forces in England and Wales intending to replicate the scheme. What the West Midlands police officers also discovered was that the drivers they were stopping were not their usual suspects (young males between the ages of eighteen and twenty-five) but those who had been driving in excess of ten to fifteen years and who had not had any further driver training since they passed their test. This shows that placing police officers on the actual road where harm occurs also prevents confirmation bias.

The initiative has now been extended to pedestrians, particularly to the way drivers behave at pedestrian crossings. As PC Hudson states:

> One highlight of the analysis was the finding that over a third of pedestrian KSI's [killings or serious injuries] occurred on or at pedestrian crossings . . . which again begs the question what are drivers paying attention to at such vulnerable locations? . . . These new operations primarily designed to protect pedestrians will of course naturally protect all other vulnerable road users as they significantly concentrate driver's attention in the most vulnerable of areas.[29]

The initiatives and presentations by West Midlands Police contrast quite radically with the views presented by DCS Rickett, Head of the Metropolitan Police's Road and Transport Command, whose role is partly funded by Transport for London, a local government body.

The officers of West Midlands Police accepted that 98 percent of cycle casualties were caused by careless or dangerous driving. In contrast, DCS Rickett suggested that cycle injuries stem overwhelmingly from the behavior of cyclists rather than drivers. On the Cycle Superhighways alone, a newly developed scheme by Transport of London to ensure cycle safety, DCS Rickett commented:

> There's been massive investment in London with Cycle Superhighways. Yet everyday, indeed travelling here today you see the Cycle Superhighway empty and the roads filled with cyclists . . . one of the things we lobbied for as part of the cycle superhighway journey through Transport for London was to say, if a Cycle Superhighway is built and it is there we should be able to enforce its non-use. But we can't.

DCS Rickett offered no explanation why these superhighways were not being used nor did he mention the number of serious incidents that have occurred since they were introduced. He also ignored the criticisms against the superhighways from the cycling lobby and others, including a London coroner.[30] Research produced for a local lobbying group discovered that the superhighway link in central London has caused more casualties than before it was built.[31] Additionally, since 2011, six cyclists have been killed by drivers on cycle superhighway 2 (CS2), which runs from Aldgate to Stratford in East London, including a thirty-two-year-old woman who became trapped under the wheels of a coach on February 6, 2017, just two weeks before DCS Rickett appeared before the House of Lords Select Committee.[32] The superhighway in south London has also come under criticism for being so slippery that cyclists have received serious injuries.[33] DCS Rickett failed to mention these incidents, though he is the head of road policing in London. Instead he complained that cyclists "are choosing to use the roads and ride alongside the empty highway."

In addition to placing the onus on cyclists to use superhighways DCS Rickett also suggested that cyclists should be equipped with proximity warning systems to protect themselves from close-passing cars. Such devices, which work when a signal is picked up by a passing vehicle that has the technology installed (at present HGVs), are indeed a good idea because they relay to the driver that a cyclist is in close proximity. However, DSC Rickett's suggestion for their use was to help cyclists avoid collisions and not for drivers to avoid getting too close to bicycles. He failed to acknowledge that cycle deaths and injuries mainly occur at road junctions and are caused by bad *car* drivers (as the West Midlands police officers identified) and not HGVs, which are more likely to pick up the signals of cycle warning systems. Such systems are also not much use to pedestrians killed mainly on crossings by drivers who are speeding or not looking.

Asked how he thought investigations into road deaths could be improved, no mention was made of enforcing existing guidelines such as the RDIM or the College of Policing's own inadequate *Road Policing* guidance. Instead he referred to an initiative set out by the College of Policing to start an undergraduate policing degree of which collision investigation would form a part. This is problematic because "collision investigation" as part of a mainstream degree would still not provide the detailed forensic expertise held by those who have studied forensic science; nor would it ensure that protocols were maintained and carried out. There is, at present, no dispute that road policing officers receive no formal training; what is problematic is that there are no obligatory standards for conducting investigations and, therefore, no means of holding any officer accountable for failing to adhere to standards. A university degree would not change this scenario.

Asked about referring cases to the CPS (which occurs in all criminal cases), DCS Rickett stated that the police are bound "by the Attorney General's Guidelines and it is absolutely the case, whether it is a road traffic collision investigation or a crime investigation [that] the threshold test has to be applied and it has to be met before we would refer it to the CPS." There are, however, no Attorney General's guidelines for police officers; the "guidelines" are presented in the CPS Code. The "threshold test," except in all but the most minor cases, is not a matter for police officers to decide but for crown prosecutors. As the CPS clarify on their website:

> Crown Prosecutors are responsible for determining the charge in all but minor cases, advising the police during the early stages of an investigation, reviewing cases submitted by the police for prosecution, preparing cases for court and presenting those cases at court. In each case reviewed, the prosecutor will consider whether there is sufficient evidence and, if so, whether the public interest requires a prosecution. Although Crown Prosecutors work closely with the police, they are . . . an independent governmental organisation.[34]

If the police decide there is insufficient evidence, the CPS are unlikely to disagree. Where there is insufficient evidence, the CPS simply hand the investigative report back to the police and request further evidence. In cases of homicide, detectives always inform the CPS of a suspicious death even before sufficient evidence has been collated, so that an appropriate barrister can be found and the death is recorded. Though many police forces do send all their collated evidence into road death investigations to the CPS for advisory purposes, this is not a common practice. Indeed it is derided by the CPS who expect the police to make their own decisions. As DCS Rickett states,

> the police still retain the absolute authority to say whether or not the case moves the threshold test for referral to the CPS in the first place. And personally, as a relatively senior police officer of twenty nine and a half years service I would defend that position very strongly. If we follow your train of thought [that we should refer all cases to the CPS like we would a pub fight] the threshold has been removed and we're basically giving the whole decision-making process over to the CPS which is not what the attorney general's guidelines are directing us to do and it's not, as my understanding is, it's not the position that the CPS want to be in.

When asked if anything needed to be changed to the Highway Code, a code which provides details for all vehicles (including cyclists and pedestrians) and which is both a legal code (in parts) and otherwise offers guidance in others, DCS Rickett was entirely focused on the cyclist.

> There's a lot of evidence out there to suggest that actually lives could be saved if the wearing of helmets was mandated, for example. So I think there might be elements of the Highway Code in relation to cyclists say that could be more robust than they currently are in terms of guidance or mandation.

In the United Kingdom, the wearing of cycle helmets is not compulsory, but there is no evidence that wearing a cycle helmet would make any difference to the incidents of road deaths or the prevention of serious injuries.[35] The only difference they do seem to make is to prevent confirmation bias from occurring where police officers might otherwise not investigate a serious incident of road death as a result of the victim not having worn a helmet. This does not, however, help the plight of pedestrians nor explain where DCS Rickett's opinion that cyclists need to take responsibility over drivers derives.

In the early 1980s, the Police Foundation published a small book on road users and the police. Although it did not look too deeply at police attitudes, it did offer at least a partial explanation why drivers seemed to be favored when they broke the law. Perceiving motorists as generally innocent of any crime, the authors argue that targeting motorists risks alienating a group of people from engaging in "honest activity" and risks spoiling the police's own effectiveness with the community.[36] That motorists might be excused for "accidentally" breaching a law and killing a person was put in perspective at a seminar on Road Death Victims. As Terence Morris states:

> If 4000 people—a number roughly equivalent to the number of those who die on the roads in this country—died as the result of physical assaults involving deadly weapons such as a baseball bat, knives or firearms, it would be regarded as something sufficient to classify our society as one of the most violent in the world.[37]

Sadly, more than twenty-five years later, the United Kingdom remains one of the few countries in the world to remain complacent toward drivers who kill.

CONCLUSION

Since there are no statutory guidelines for policing investigations in the United Kingdom, individual police forces are permitted to be run as independent authorities. In the case of the Metropolitan police, this means decisions are being made without seeking advice or recommendations from the CPS. The problem with a nonenforced investigation process is that it increases the discretion of the police to ignore guidelines.

Should guidelines be made mandatory then the situation for many victims would be transformed as would the police's relations with the public. The culture of defensiveness when complaints against the police are made would also be better managed by examining whether certain protocols (e.g., not destroying vital evidence or securing the scene *as if* a crime had been committed) had followed procedures. The only time ambiguity would arise is where no guidelines existed or where the guidelines themselves proved ambiguous—which could be challenged and raised in Parliament if necessary. Universities and major companies usually deal with complaints against a backdrop of guidelines and ethical codes. In this regard, the police service is in a state of chaos, largely because its own *Code of Ethics* (devised by the College of Policing in 2013) is so general as to be meaningless. At present, both road death victims and their families will continue to be failed by ill qualified forensic collision inspectors and road policing officers acting on an ad hoc basis.

One major change of law could, however, help transform both negative policing attitudes and the behavior of drivers. The Law of Strict Liability, enforced across Europe except for five European counties (Britain, Cyprus, Ireland, Malta, and Romania),[38] is a law of tort (i.e., a civil law) that offers a ground for lawsuits to compensate parties for damages or injuries offered. It places liability on the drivers should they maim or kill a pedestrian, cyclist. or fellow car driver. It is reasoned that such a law makes drivers more aware of pedestrians and cyclists for similar reasons to those given by the constables of West Midlands Constabulary—that the onus is then placed on the drivers to show they were not responsible and should not pay compensation toward the victim. If the attitudes of PCs Hudson and Hodson are correct and the only means to change motorists' behavior is by threat of losing their licenses, this would seem to be the best way forward. It would also prevent police officers from taking the stance that the responsibility lies with victims' behavior.

5

Police Support Networks

This chapter focuses on nonpolicing bodies that contribute to poor policing practices. Its intent is to reveal the flaws that are either built into the institutions concerned or have developed over time owing to structural flaws. Though any number of police support institutions could be discussed, from border control to social services to trading standards to medical experts—the latter of which, in one notorious case led to a woman being wrongfully convicted for child murder[1]—this chapter focuses on just three: coroners, pathologists (medical examiners), and crown prosecutors.

While it is difficult to separate out the motivations of different institutions, it seems more than likely that the persons concerned forget, or are indifferent toward those on the receiving end because of an adversarial legal system in which the roles of the prosecutor or coroner are merely required to tie up loose ends for the police investigation. This may also be seen as morally unproblematic since for the coroner, the real victim is already dead and the prosecutor's job is to find the accused guilty as charged.

For a prosecution to be successful, however, the evidence supplied must be watertight. Thus, not only do prosecutors need to trust the police investigation, they need to trust that they are both working for the same end. Trust implies you do not betray those you rely upon, so to expect that either the police or the Crown Prosecution Service (CPS) should hold the other accountable is somewhat whimsical. Nevertheless, it is common for the CPS to blame the police when a case fails and vice versa because they are independent bodies whose reliance on each other is simply part of the legal framework. In the United Kingdom, which advocates an adversarial system of justice, its purpose is not to find the "truth" but for lawyers to battle out arguments for or against the guilt or innocence of the accused. One miscarriage of justice may be one too many for most people's conscience, but prosecutors are more concerned with getting a conviction than the actual innocence or guilt of the person standing trial. In 2017–2018, a survey revealed that 97 percent of defense lawyers working in criminal practice in England and Wales complained that either the CPS or the police failed to disclose evidence, while one-third thought that the failure to disclose had resulted in miscarriages of justice. In response, the CPS said the survey provided a "skewed view,"[2] and commenters on the story in the online police magazine *Police Oracle* blamed defense lawyers for hiding material from prosecutors.[3] In turn, the British police have recently introduced a national consent form asking victims of rape (qua complainants) to hand over personal data for examination, particularly that held on mobile phones. In a Catch-22 scenario, victims have been told that while providing electronic evidence is "voluntary," if victims refuse to provide police with access to their phone records and other data, the police have stated they may not charge a suspect and "the CPS will have to take a view about whether or not the case can proceed."[4]

Where there is no criminal trial but a person dies in suspicious circumstances or the cause of death is unknown, it is necessary for the police to do an investigation and an inquest takes place. The inquest is led by a coroner, a lawyer, who, acting with an assistant (usually but not always, a serving police officer), concludes the police investigation, thus providing the impression of having overseen the police's work. Because "the law" represents the state and there is no higher authority in a democracy, the coroner's word—as a member of the judiciary—is seen as having an authority over that of the police. Though it is said that "unquestioned power leads to hypocrisy" and "to avoid moral corruption, power should be questioned,"[5] the Coroners Rules for England and Wales clearly state that "no person may address the coroner as to the facts."[6] The inquest is therefore a peculiar type of court where argument between parties is not permitted and where "a coroner must disallow any question put to the witness which the coroner considers irrelevant"[7] (i.e., one which may incriminate a witness) and where, if a jury is appointed, a coroner may direct the verdict. Though focusing on practices in England and Wales, a comparison with the United States involving a medical examiner (coroner/pathologist) and the District Attorney's Office (equivalent to the CPS) reveals that there is nothing unique in the way cases are handled within the United Kingdom.

CORONERS, INQUESTS, AND PATHOLOGISTS

Since its inception in the late thirteenth century, the establishment of the office of coroner has been to inquire into the manner of the death of those who have died from violent or unknown causes by holding an inquest. In the US system, the coroner (medical examiner) is also the pathologist who performs the autopsy and then decides the cause of death according to his or her own examination of the body. In contrast, coroners in England and Wales are typically solicitors in local practice, employed by the local council to conduct inquests into the deaths of those who have typically not seen their doctor or another medical professional in the two weeks before they died. This gives the United Kingdom the unenvious title of having the highest rate of inquests in the world. Working closely with the police, coroners heavily rely on the pathologist's postmortem report, often heavily influenced by the police with which the coroner has a close relationship. This is unsurprising because in England and Wales the local council also fund the local police.[8] Unlike their colleagues in the High Court, coroners have no specialist training, and there is often doubt about the consistency with which they handle medical evidence and legal argument.

The purpose of the inquest is not to assign culpability but to answer the question *how* the person died. When a person dies in circumstances that involve the police but the death is deemed not suspicious, the coroner (rather than the courts) is said to conduct an investigation independent of the police. But except for requesting an autopsy, which in cases of suspicion would be carried out at the request of the police by a forensic pathologist, the coroner's investigation relies entirely on the police file. Prior to the coroner's involvement, evidence has been gathered by the local police. This evidence is passed on to the hospital pathologist (who performs the autopsy) by the coroner's officer. Inquests may therefore often be little more than a recital of this evidence. It is true that the coroner takes requests from "interested parties" (usually the family of the bereaved) as to whom to call as witnesses. But the decision to comply with such requests is usually decided on by the coroner and the police.

A further obstacle for justice is the rule against self-incrimination. This rule is intended to prevent a person from being compelled to say anything which might incriminate them at a criminal trial as an inquest does not exist to incite blame or find anyone guilty. Though this rule is not unique to an inquest, it is enforced in stronger terms than it would be in criminal proceedings. In the criminal court such a privilege means that "a suspect cannot be required to provide the authorities with information that might be used against him," which "places obvious restrictions on criminal investigations."[9] It also means that suspects will not be held accountable or in contempt of court if they fail to provide such information when asked. To be forced to do so would be in contravention of Article 6 of the European Convention on Human Rights (i.e., the right to a fair trial) though why this should be the case is unclear, "even after legal and moral perspectives are taken into consideration."[10] If self-incrimination is problematic in criminal cases, it is undoubtedly more so at an inquest, where no questions may be put to witnesses that may incriminate them as being responsible for the death of a victim. Furthermore, there is no prosecutor or defense counsel, no arguments permitted to be placed in front of a jury, no room for maneuver to challenge witnesses to be clearer, and "difficult" questions, which may lead a witness admitting culpability, are met with a heavy bang of the coroner's hammer (metaphorically speaking) with witnesses told (at the coroner's discretion) that they do not have to answer. While the inquest is supposed to get to the facts of the matter, to decide *who* has died, *where* the death took place, and *how* the death occurred, as inquests are not permitted to attribute blame or find fault with a particular individual this makes them rather a show court. This may be unproblematic in cases where a person with a long-term illness has suddenly died, but in deaths which involve a third party (e.g., a lorry driver) or when the matter involves a death in police custody, the legitimacy of the inquest is questionable because the main protagonist can simply decline to answer, cannot be cross-examined, and key witnesses may or may not be called, depending on the coroner's discretion. This is the reason why many families come away dissatisfied with inquests.

That inquests should be anything but straightforward is indisputable. Nor is there much dispute that the so-called "independent" office lacks any real independence since it relies almost entirely on the police file. If the police investigation turns out to have been poor or nonexistent or if the death took place in police custody, this will be reflected at the inquest in terms which seldom reveal more than was known before the inquest took place. This also holds true of the pathologist's report—as will be discussed.

The closeness with which the police and the coroner work is demonstrated in the various case histories outlined in this book, together with documentation supplied by participants via transcripts and subject access requests. In the case of Toni Rolls, the family requested that the senior investigating officer (SIO) be called as a witness at the inquest. The coroner refused to do so, stating:

> I did not know they were appointing one officer to correlate all communications . . . but I have never contributed to or received input from that officer. My only dealings with Police in the run-up to this inquest have been a meeting with the SIO to go through the evidence and decide on the witness list. My impartiality is entirely intact.[11]

Communications that arrived in a subject access request several months after the inquest took place revealed that after writing the above reply to the next-of-kin, the coroner immediately wrote to the SIO in question, stating: "I've dictated my reply—and you'll get a copy when it's typed. Don't t5hink [*sic*] I need any more at the moment thanks."[12]

Unbeknown to the family, a meeting had already taken place between police officers, FLOs, and the coroner's officer, revealing the heavy codependence of the coroner's office with the police. A transcript of this meeting (held January 20, 2014) revealed that as part of a strategy to discredit the family for raising questions regarding the police investigation, the coroner's officer volunteered to write to the next-of-kin's GP to state "she has a mental health issue" due "to her complaints to the police." It was also the coroner's officer (not the SIO who was also present) that was tasked with creating the police file submitted to the coroner as the basis of the inquest proceedings.[13] The lack of independence between the coroner's office and the police was, in this case, undeniable, with the CEO of the Local Police Commissioners Office (which is also supposed to be independent of the police and the coroner) stating that they had set up a specialist task force to include the coroners.[14] As to the inquest itself, key witnesses were never called and, had the family not conducted their own investigation, would never have been known. They included the last person to speak to Toni Rolls alive and the first two people at the scene after she was killed. One, an army medic, had telephoned the emergency services to declare that she had died immediately on impact, and the other, a female doctor, confirmed this was the case. The family were never informed, either by the police or the coroner at the inquest, of the existence of these two people. Instead the family of Toni Rolls had been informed by the FLO that she had bled to death on the road, for around fifteen minutes before she died, after which paramedics tried to resuscitate her. Other evidence was also withheld. This included footage of a police officer's body-worn video (BWV) taken at the scene, which could have indicted the driver but was never disclosed. At the inquest, the officer who took the video admitted to not having seen the recording and noting that it had gone into storage. When the driver admitted to having been distracted at the time he killed Toni Rolls (admitting he had been looking to his right at a man on the central reservation and, therefore, had not noticed the woman in front of him when he accelerated), the comment was dismissed by the coroner as irrelevant.

While it is true that "the coroner decides what constitutes relevant and admissible evidence, and has considerable discretion at all stages of the investigation,"[15] the information presented to the court is decided on in conjunction with the police, whether directly (as in the case of Toni Rolls, killed by a distracted driver [see chapter 4] when the coroner met with the SIO to decide which evidence to use and which witnesses to call) or indirectly, via the police file. Where a jury is called, as it must be in inquests that involve deaths in police custody or cases of possible corporate manslaughter, "the coroner may recommend, implicitly or explicitly, a particular verdict, or advise that a choice between two or three particular verdicts exists."[16] This occurred in the case of James Sutton, who (as discussed in chapter 4) was also a road death victim.

The law is quite clear on who selects a jury for an inquest: "When the coroner needs a jury for his court, a crown court official will select at random a group of people from the jury list."[17] This random group of people will be called to sit for jury service for a maximum of two weeks unless they are assigned to a case which extends beyond this limit. After that case is dismissed, however, so is the jury. Nothing is stated in the rules permitting the *same* individuals to be called up—as a group—to take part in jury service again as the *same* jury after their original service has come to an end.[18] Even though the appointment of juries has changed over the years, very little has been done to ensure that juries should not be chosen to suit the coroner (and therefore the police) as they were prior to 1983. As Anthony Morris, the coroner for York, wrote in 1980:

> The coroner issues a warrant to summon a jury specifying the number of jurors to be called to the coroner's officer. The coroner's officer then selects the jurors and issues a summons to each person so selected. The coroner should not interfere with this selection and the summoning of juries as this may be grounds for quashing the inquest. . . . The coroner's officer is invariably a police officer. For practical purposes therefore, the coroner's jury can be seen to be selected by the police.[19]

The appointment of juries by the police (namely the coroner's officer) was challenged in 1983 when Lord McIntosh of Haringey argued that:

> The coroner's warrant is directed to the coroner's officer who, in turn, issues summonses to a number of adults sufficient to make up a jury. There is advice from the Home Office about how to use the electoral roll and summon jurors on a random basis, as is the case with other juries, but it is still the case that in some areas coroners' officers do as they think fit. It was suggested in another place that they might go out and take people going to or from meetings of the National Front or the Communist Party. . . . there is evidence that in some parts of the country the coroners' officers, who tend to be police officers, look for retired people who are less likely to seek to be excused, and less likely to make expensive claims for loss of earnings. Of course, the discretion in the hands of the coroner's officer is itself a matter of concern, because unfortunately, there are deaths in police custody and the idea that a police officer, being a coroner's officer, should have any real discretion about the selection of a jury when the case concerns a death in police custody is worrying, to say the least.[20]

The subsequent bill made clear that the "selection of jurors will therefore no longer rest with the coroner's officer, as at present." And yet, the Coroners and Justice Act 2009 (which came into force on July 25, 2013) rescinded this rule, permitting coroners (and thus coroner's officers) to summon people from the electoral register to attend jury service (see Section 155).[21] Though no rule stated that individual jury members could be recalled to sit again at another case in the future, this seems to be precisely what happened in the James Sutton case, where the rules were ignored. Instead of asking a Crown court official to select a group of random people, the coroner (or his officer) asked members of a jury who had been dismissed seven weeks previously to sit again on James Sutton's case. The coroner made this clear to those present before the jury were sworn in. He informed the court that the *same* jury had sat less than two months previously, denying this caused any conflict of interest as the previous case had involved a cleaner, Roger Lower, age forty-seven, who was killed on the railway.

Roger had been electrocuted while carrying out his duties as a rail side cleaner, but the jury ruled that his death had been an accident.[22] Two years later, however, the rail and cleaning companies were fined £3.6 million for breach of health and safety regulations—putting into perspective the meaning of "accident."[23] Surprisingly the coroner's decision to recall the same jury to sit at the inquest into James Sutton's death, killed by a speeding police car, was not questioned at the time, even though the coroner's officer (a police officer) had strong ties with the local roads policing department, and it had been one of their officers who had killed James. It is difficult to see how exactly the same set of people that comprised one jury could have been asked to sit at another inquest once their jury service had finished. Juries are supposed to comprise individuals chosen at random. Once a jury is dismissed, it is therefore legally ambiguous how the same set of individuals could be recalled to comprise a new jury. Yet this is precisely what occurred in the case of James Sutton. The unprecedented recall of the same jury members raises questions about the motives of the coroner and breaches of official regulations.

James Sutton's inquest was held eleven months after the death of Toni Rolls. Both cases were similar in that the victims were pedestrians killed by a car while (supposedly) crossing the same road albeit several miles (and four months) apart. However, James was killed by a police car, and significant evidence either failed to be disclosed or was glossed over at his inquest. The first anomaly concerned the police driver's claim that he had been answering an emergency call at the time of James's death and had thus put on the car's lights and sirens ("the blues and twos") even though it was clear he had not been responding to an emergency situation but looking for an unlicensed driver who was eventually found in another county driving twenty-five miles per hour. The second anomaly concerned the police cars Incident Data Recorder (IDR) (which would normally have filmed the incident), which police stated had failed around 4 p.m. that day—coincidentally at the same time the officers went on duty, thus begging the question why they had not driven another car. With both lawyers—that for the family and that for the police—agreeing on the verdict of road traffic collision, the coroner requested the jury to conclude that James had died as the result of a "road traffic collision" reminding them that the toxicology report showed that James had been drinking alcohol before he died.

With the coroner directing the jury as to the verdict, the jury had little to do but agree, thus removing the purpose of appointing a jury in the first place. While the jury could have chosen "unlawful death" or even "narrative verdict" (leaving the conclusion open) they were "guided" to accept a ruling without further debate or inquiry. In accepting the phrase "road traffic *collision,*" the coroner was contradicting a claim he had made a year previously. Though "collision" had replaced "accident" in coroner's rules more than two years earlier, the same coroner had ruled at the inquest of Toni Rolls that she had died as the result of a road traffic *accident*. When asked by Cynthia Barlow, Chair of the charity Road Peace, if the coroner would use the term "collision" as a summing up of Toni Rolls's death as stated in the chief coroner's guidelines, the coroner gave a resounding "No," stating that he disliked the word "collision" and *preferred* the term "accident" so would continue to use it. At the inquest of James Sutton, however, the same coroner stated that he had been using the term "collision" as preferable to "accident" for the past six or seven years. The inconsistency was not lost on either family.

While it is true that "the coroner's court is not concerned with personal liability, that is, with deciding who is responsible for a death," nevertheless, "coroners' interventions, through their use of inquest procedure and their summing-up, can shape a jury's verdict and prepare the ground for future court actions over a personal liability."[24] By the same token, however, where a jury is absent, as is typical of most road deaths, the coroner may also show bias in favor of the police investigator's report. This seems to have been the case at the inquest into the death of Eilidh Cairns who was killed in February 2009.

To recap: In February 2009 a tipper truck lorry killed Eilidh Cairns while she was cycling to work. When the police initially failed to investigate her death, the family conducted their own investigation, finding eyewitnesses who would be prepared to testify. The police then took over the investigation and excluded the family from any further involvement. The family requested that the driver's eyesight be tested. The police ignored the request for more than three months. It was then discovered the driver had poor vision. He was subsequently found guilty of driving with uncorrected defective vision and fined £200. He was permitted to carry on driving and sixteen months later killed Nora Guttmann on a pedestrian crossing while driving without his glasses. He was then found guilty of dangerous driving, received a four-year prison sentence, and banned from driving for six years. The case of Eilidh Cairns was never taken into consideration.

When the family was notified that the inquest into Eilidh's death would take place on January 22, 2010, they asked the coroner for an adjournment. While a coroner must adjourn an inquest where a person is charged for murder or manslaughter, coroners have complete discretion as to whether to grant an adjournment in any other case. The Cairns family sought an adjournment for several reasons: (i) the prosecution of the driver had yet to take place; (ii) additional disclosure evidence was required; (iii) the family wanted additional witnesses to be considered; (iv) the police forensic investigator would not be able to appear as he was on trial for fraud; (v) the counsel of their choice was not available on that date; and (vi) Kate Cairns was expecting a baby in March and would have to travel several hundred miles to attend the inquest. The coroner refused to adjourn the inquest on all counts because it did not suit the police, who, she argued, had waited long enough for the inquest hearing.

Though key witnesses had positioned Eilidh cycling *in front of the lorry*, the replacement police collisions investigator—who had not attended the scene—said it was unlikely that Eilidh had been cycling in front of the lorry but had probably been to its side when it pulled out. Asked by the family solicitor to show evidence of the fact by providing images of the scene, the collisions investigator stated he could not because he had not seen any. When later on in proceedings photographs of the scene were found (by the coroner), they showed Eilidh's bicycle propped up against railings several hours after the collision had occurred.

As the transcripts of the inquest show, the coroner continually interrupted witnesses, refused an interpreter for a key witness whose English was so poor she could not fully understand the questions put to her, and dismissed an eyewitness who saw the cyclist *in front of the lorry*, insisting instead that the cyclist must have been *alongside the lorry* (the narrative provided by the police collisions investigator). When the solicitor for the family asked the driver to confirm his position in relation to the bicycle, the coroner informed the solicitor that the question was unfair and told the driver not to answer because he might incriminate himself. Even though he had already been charged with incorrect vision and was soon to be put on trial for this offense, the coroner ruled that Eilidh's death was an accident.

The family won the right to take the case to Judicial Review. This was held on October 18, 2011, on the grounds that the coroner failed to adjourn the inquest or to consider sitting with a jury under S.8 (3)d of the Coroner's Act 1988 or to conduct an inquiry that satisfied rule 26 of the Coroner's Rules. The coroner, Dr. Shirley Radcliffe, defended her decision, stating:

> it has been suggested that I acted unreasonably in that my office did not disclose police statements and investigation reports to the Cairns family until they made a request for that material four days before the hearing. I did not give such disclosure for several reasons. The inquest concerned a tragic road accident which was not unduly complicated . . . I can say that [disclosure] would be a very costly and onerous obligation for coroners and police forces to satisfy, given the large number of simple road accident cases which have to be heard . . . the family of the deceased will often not be legally represented and may have no desire to be provided with statements and reports.[25]

The High Court agreed. The judge, Justice Silber, stated, "I do not think there is any justifiable complaint that can be made against the coroner for the way she handled the inquest." However, since the Coroner's and Justice Act 2009 became law in July 2013 coroners must provide full disclosure to families. As to "simple road accident cases," chapter 4 has shown that the idea of a road death being "simple" or referred to as an "accident" is doubtful.

One could be forgiven for thinking that in light of the publicity surrounding the second Hillsborough inquest in 2016, held into those who had died at the Hillsborough football stadium in 1989 which resulted in a verdict of unlawfully killing, that inquests are generally fair and insightful. However, the second inquest was the result of years of campaigning by both academics and bereaved families. The original inquest, held in November 1990, had resulted in a verdict of accident. It took two public inquiries and an independent panel, led by the criminologist Phil Scraton, who researched extensively on the case, investigating police files and interviewing officers and family members, to establish the truth. By the time the second jury reached its conclusion, with a specially appointed coroner, some twenty-six years after the tragedy and two years since its commencement, making it "the longest jury case in British legal history,"[26] the general public already knew that police officers had provided false statements in 1990 by claiming that fans had been drunk and ticketless. In addition, the former chief superintendent, David Duckenfield, who had been in charge of policing at Hillsborough on that day, now freely and openly admitted responsibility. For those who believe that "justice" was finally served for the Hillsborough victims, then the verdict of unlawful killing gave them justice. Unfortunately this did not extend to the way that the victims and their families had been discredited. They remain discredited by the police, who continue to slander fans and families who to this day have never received so much as an apology.

Nevertheless, in many cases, even for those who may remain unsatisfied with a coronial verdict, an inquest is not without benefits. An inquest may provide the only opportunity for families, friends, and civil rights workers to account for events regarding a person's death while providing perhaps "the only opportunity for the interests of families and friends of the deceased to be represented and for key witnesses to be cross-examined."[27] This was certainly the case at the inquest into the death of Toni Rolls, where the driver revealed he had been looking in another direction and had failed to see her standing directly in front of him. Though the power to try a person for a crime remains outside coroners' jurisdiction,[28] the inquest "cannot be regarded as something entirely separate from the criminal justice system" because "evidence obtained under oath at the inquest can be used in subsequent proceedings in other courts, and many coroners would accept that the inquest may serve as a 'dummy run' for a later trial."[29] For example, in the case of Christopher Alder who died in police custody, the CPS refused to prosecute even though "the violence and gross negligence of the police was caught on a 12-minute video." After the inquest ruled that he had been unlawfully killed, the Director of Public Prosecutions decided to review the decision.[30] For most inquests, however, coroners will generally censure any questions which could possibly lead to a witness incriminating himself. Consequently, the inquest remains at best a half-hearted process. Phil Scraton and Katherine Chadwick point out in their seminal text:

> personal liability has no place in the coroner's court. If personal liability emerges directly during an inquest then in some circumstances the inquest must be adjourned either for the person involved to be present and/or represented, or for the DPP [Director of Public Prosecutions, that is, CPS] to investigate and/or institute proceedings in the criminal courts. As liability is not an issue, there is no prosecution and no accused. Thus the coroner's court sits uneasily alongside the other courts.[31]

In the culture and proceedings which surround inquests, there is a structural bias against families of the bereaved, which, in failing them, exonerates those who might or should be held accountable. This is especially true of those who die in police custody given that there is "something of a special relationship" that develops "between the coroner and the local police."[32]

Even though the Coroners and Justice Act 2009 created the appointment of a Chief Coroner, his role is purely perfunctory because he refuses to get involved in individual cases and will only set issues on guidance for coroners. Though the governance for coroners lies with the Ministry of Justice, it plays no role toward ensuring the fairness of procedures because the general public may only contact the Ministry if the coroner has committed a crime (e.g., discriminated on grounds of race). Unlike the CPS, coroners are not subject to Freedom of Information Requests and may act with complete discretion over proceedings, without the rise of any judicial eyebrow. Nor are coroners anymore obliged, as they were under the old law (rules 39 and

57(1), Coroners Rules 1984), to take, keep, and disclose their own notes of evidence at an inquest which in previous years formed part of the record of the coroner's court and which could then be consulted. Though coroners may appear to act in a similar role to crown prosecutors, the purpose of the inquest is somewhat misleading because it exists to discover how someone has died without the court being able to rule that anyone is to blame. Even the reliance on the pathology report as some objective measure with which to determine cause of death may be a misnomer because the nonforensic pathologist relies on information presented to them by the coroner's officer to determine cause of death. Where the coroner's officer is a police or an ex-police officer, now working as a civilian and employed by the local police force, this can lead to confirmation bias.[33]

For example, the autopsy report on Toni Rolls contains comments provided by the coroner's officer days before the police investigation even began. Though the pathologist had not been present at the scene (which would be extremely uncommon even for forensic pathologists), his report read:

> This 83 year old lady, who alighted from a double-deck bus and walked to the rear of the bus while crossing the road, failed to see an oncoming car. The vehicle struck the lady despite applying the brakes. She died on the scene.

The General Medical Council (GMC) investigated a complaint by the family as to the impartiality of the pathologist's report because the family were concerned with the claim that their mother *failed to see an oncoming car*, which had not been (and never could be) established. In his defense, the pathologist wrote to the GMC that he did not understand why he was being criticized by the family but wanted them to note that the family had been rude to both the coroner and the coroner's officer [*sic*]. Since the family had never met the pathologist and bar making a complaint to the GMC would never have heard of this "rudeness," this was a further example of the coroner's office seeking to discredit the complainant and to justify the outcome of the inquest. In response to the comments given on the autopsy report, the GMC replied as follows:

> The [pathologist] is not expected to work to the forensic standards of the Home Office and ACPO guidelines. In instructing him or his colleagues to undertake the case, HM Coroner is implicitly commissioning the lesser degree of detail in the post-mortem report. If the police disagreed with this approach, they would have requested HM Coroner to have a Home Office Pathologist . . . the pathologist's post mortem report is a report combining hearsay evidence, factual observation and professional opinion.[34]

As for the comment on whether Toni Rolls *did* see the oncoming car, the GMC state, "[the pathologist] is simply repeating the information . . . from the police and Coroner's officer." As previously stated, histopathologists in England and Wales employed by the coroner are not on any official register, are not trained in forensics (so cannot and do not look for vital signs and in many cases do not perform the autopsy themselves), and (as is now known) are given the explanation of cause of death by reports provided by the coroner's officer. This is problematic particularly when the result of the inquest is "unlawful killing." If the death of a person who has died was thought to be "unlawful" on discovery of the body, the police investigation would have been entirely different at the start. Rather than the coroner paying £96.80 for a hospital pathologist to carry out a postmortem, a Home Office forensic pathologist would have been instructed by the police to carry out careful and detailed examination of the body (at a cost of £2,860—with £260 paid for by the coroner), and SOCOs or CSIs would have made detailed examinations of the scene. Thus, as Dean Jones has argued, the decision made at the scene where a body is discovered has huge consequences. If an inquest does rule that the deceased was unlawfully killed or is halted midway for the CPS to bring charges (e.g., new evidence has been found), it is too late to carry out a forensic autopsy because the body will most likely have been cremated and other vital forensic clues will have been lost. Thus, not only can the result of the system lead to homicides not being recognized (as Jones argues),[35] but since 2009 the term "verdict" has been replaced by "conclusion," suggesting that an inquest is simply a matter of logical reasoning.

There may be a serious issue in England and Wales regarding the divorce between forensic pathologists and what are known as histopathologists, who perform autopsies on a self-employed, unregistered basis. However, in the United States, the pathologist and coroner form one role, that of medical examiner. This can have serious implications of its own because any independent autopsy is thus carried out by a member of the judiciary. An example is the case of Joseph Osborne, who was charged with killing his five-year-old stepson, Charlie, in 2002.[36] Though the postmortem did not reveal anything suspicious regarding Charlie's death and his three-year-old brother, Sam, who shared the same room as Charlie, told police at the time that his brother was restless, Steven Hayne, the medical examiner, determined that Charlie had died of suffocation. No suspect was found. Five months later, police decided to interview three-year-old Sam a second time. This time Sam seemed to remember, in great detail, events that had occurred that night, including Osborne coming into the room, spanking Charlie, and Charlie taking his last breath. However, aside from the testament of the three-year-old, there was no other corroborating evidence. The medical examiner (qua coroner), Hayne then ordered Charlie's body to be exhumed and a plaster cast made of his decomposed face. The examiner then compared the notes of the "death mask" to those he had taken at his autopsy and claimed that he could now determine the size of the hand that had suffocated Charlie. The death mask was the main evidence produced by the prosecution at Osborne's trial.

> Hayne testified that Charlie was suffocated, and that his injuries were consistent with an adult person having covered the child's nose and mouth with a hand. More specifically, he testified that the death mask marks "would be consistent with a person placing their hand over the child's face. . . ." He added that in his opinion a "large hand," which he said would "favor a male's hand," caused the child's injuries.[37]

Obsorne was found guilty of murder and sentenced to life imprisonment even though the testament of a "death mask" was regarded as absurd by the president of the National Association of Medical Examiners (NAME), as was the claim that wounds on a face could tell the size or gender of a hand.

Writing for the *Washington Post* on Stephen Hayne's activities, the journalist Radley Bilko revealed over several years how he had conducted more than 1,700 autopsies a year (as well as working two full-time jobs) as opposed to the recommended limit of 250 given by NAME, and that his testament had helped to convict two men of rape and a thirteen-year-old boy of murder, all of whom were later exonerated or had their convictions overturned. Though Hayne was fired from performing autopsies in 2007, an appeal to exonerate Osborne, brought by the Mississippi Innocence Project in 2016, was denied. As Balko states,

> The courts don't seem to have much interest in overturning Hayne-tainted convictions, at least not without DNA. . . . It's understandable (if not justifiable) why those judges would be reluctant to issue rulings that could affect thousands of murder convictions. . . . The federal courts are a different matter . . . in order for a defendant to get a new trial in federal court, he must show that he has new evidence; that the evidence he has could not have been discovered at the time to trial . . . and . . . the defendant must file his claim based on the new evidence within one year of the time that evidence could reasonably have been discovered. . . . When we're talking about bad science and bad forensics, the one-year rule puts defendants in an impossible bind.[38]

Though Hayne is barred from performing autopsies for the district attorney (chief prosecutor), in a final twist to the tail, it was discovered in 2012 that he never actually qualified as a medical examiner because he'd walked out of the examination for the Certificate in Forensic Pathology. He is, however, still acting as an expert witness.

THE CROWN PROSECUTION SERVICE

Before the CPS was established in England and Wales in the late 1980s, the police prosecuted most of their own cases in the magistrate's court while instructing their own lawyers to act on their behalf in the crown court. "If the police insisted on prosecuting a weak case to further their crime control goals, or bring more serious charges than were warranted by the evidence ('overcharging'), there was little or nothing the prosecutor could do about it."[39] It was out of such dissatisfaction and bias (whether actual or potential) that the CPS was established.

The Criminal Justice Act 2003 transferred the police's power to prosecute to the CPS in all but minor cases, allowing the police to maintain discretion to offer warnings and cautions (e.g., for harassment). At least that's how the CPS was set up to work *in theory* as an independent body, separate from both police and government.[40] In practice, while the police role seemingly ends at the point of investigation, the CPS will usually only prosecute on the recommendation of the police. This was made clear by Chief Superintendent Paul Rickett, Head of Road Policing for the Metropolitan police, when he spoke to a House of Lords select committee in February 2017:

> The CPS in my experience have always taken the firm line that if you don't think you've got the evidence don't give it to us, we're not here to make that assessment for you because that would be a constitutional shift. . . . There's a threshold by which we would make that referral, the threshold by which the CPS would make their decisions.[41]

In a real sense, therefore, the establishment of the CPS did not radically change policing powers because the police's lawyers simply became the prosecutors appointed to act under the umbrella of the CPS.[42] While prosecutors may question policing decisions, which they necessarily must do when evidence is lacking or where there appears to be no case to answer, prosecutors rarely contradict the police. Furthermore, "prosecution is discretionary, like stop-search and arrest. When the police do not seek to prosecute they may: delay the decision . . . release the suspect . . . or take no further action."[43] The CPS are not the decision-makers and do not thus decide prosecution cases. This is similar to the system in the United States where the Attorney General's guidelines for prosecution "requires a prediction of what will happen in court."[44] It is against this "prediction" that we can see why certain actions come about because once predicted, embarrassment may easily be caused if matters do not go to plan.

The CPS is not therefore so much a "decision-taker" as a "decision-confirmer or reverser," yet as "it is even more difficult to reverse a decision to prosecute a case . . . discontinuance rates are low even though acquittals remain high."[45] Where a case has been brought to court, there is naturally an unwillingness to admit mistakes. Therefore, confirmation bias remains high and may be the sole reason why a court case is dismissed by a judge.

Strictly speaking, the police investigate and charge an offender, while the CPS prosecute—where "prosecution" is the direct action of taking someone to court. However, the public often mistakenly assume that the *decision* to prosecute rests *with* the CPS. When police officers present their file to the CPS, the decision as to whether to charge someone with a crime, and, therefore, to prosecute them for an offense, has, however, already been made. And yet it often remains the case that the CPS (rather than the police or their actual local prosecutor) is held responsible when no subsequent trial takes place. The following offers an illustration. It is a notification published online from a demonstration that took place on July 3, 2009 for the failure of the CPS to prosecute drivers in the case of two cycle deaths, Anthony Maynard and Eilidh Cairns.[46]

London Cycling Campaign—Demonstration Statement—3rd July 2009

We are cyclists of London, gathered here this afternoon, in a quiet protest and short vigil in memory of all our fellow cyclists killed by the drivers of vehicles; several more during this year already.

In particular we think of Eilidh Cairns, 30, who was killed at Notting Hill Gate by a tipper lorry driver on February 5th this year, and of Anthony Maynard, 25, who was killed north of Henley by a van driver exactly a year ago.

We make our protest here at the London Crown Prosecution Service (CPS), to remind Ms Dru Sharpling, Chief Crown Prosecutor, of the decision of her colleagues at Reading CPS, when last year they inappropriately, remissly, and to our minds unforgivably, ordered that the van driver who struck Anthony (and his companion) from behind would not face charges. We do not hold Anthony's life so cheap.

You, the CPS at London, will shortly be reviewing the case of Eilidh Cairns who was also hit from behind on a one-way straight road.

Our protest is on behalf of all cyclists. Across Europe, motorists are presumed to be at fault in motorist-cyclist collisions. In the UK, even faced with prime evidence of a dead body, a driver does not have to prove his innocence. Instead the CPS decides whether charges can successfully be brought against the motorist, and can then choose to drop a case entirely. In Anthony's case (and as is claimed in Eilidh's case, and in the cases of many others) the van driver's defence that he simply didn't see the cyclists was accepted by the CPS as an adequate accounting for the death of a highly-principled and well-loved citizen in the prime of his life.

In a time when the nation as a whole is encouraged to exercise, and use forms of transport other than the car, and when climate change is seen as a real threat, cyclists need to feel that they have the full and equal protection of the law when on public roads, and not a law apparently interpreted (or simply set aside) to the maximum advantage of the driver, no matter how culpably careless. The CPS was in dereliction of its duty last year. We fervently hope that it will adopt a different perspective, starting with the forthcoming case of Eilidh. Allowing drivers to kill with complete impunity just will not do, and does not meet the nation's needs and priorities.

We append a quotation from Christopher G. Thompson, 'District Crown Prosecutor, Oxford Rural', in a letter sent by him to one of the Reading Cycling Club committee who had written deploring this failure to prosecute (dated 16 March 2009):

"the fact that no prosecution has followed in this case does not in any way mean or suggest that drivers may drive carelessly around cyclists or that cyclists will not be afforded the protection of the law where appropriate."

In what must have been a considered letter, the phrase affording cyclists the protection of the law "where appropriate" is chilling: NO! We demand the protection of the law. Full stop.

The statement "*the CPS decides whether charges can successfully be brought against the motorist,*" is neither true nor accurate. The decision to bring charges rests solely with the police, with the CPS decision being one which considers whether the charges brought would lead to a successful prosecution. In certain cases, the CPS may ask the police to find more evidence, but if it were the case that the CPS looked at the police files presented to them as some form of overview body—similar to the custodians mentioned in chapter 2—then the CPS would make their decisions independently of the police. This only occurs in extremely rare cases (usually owing to public pressure). The decision to charge or, in this case, not to charge will have been decided by the police investigative team. The CPS (or rather the individual prosecutor assigned to the case) is unlikely to find some reason to prosecute if the police investigation states that the CPS threshold test for prosecution has not been met. The failure to prosecute thus rests squarely with the police investigating team, which is not to say that the police are always at fault when no prosecution is brought; after all, there simply may be insufficient evidence. On the other hand, things can easily go wrong, particularly in cases of disclosure.

The police are duty bound to list all material that has been collected as part of an investigation even if it "may undermine their case or strengthen the defence case."[47] All such information is sent to the CPS, with material not to be used as evidence filed by the CPS, under one or more "schedules of unused material." It is within these schedules where evidence helpful to the defense is often found and which often remains unlisted and poorly filed. As Hannah Quirk clarifies:

> scheduling involves more than just bureaucratic cataloguing: it requires judgments about the legal significance of material, the consideration of multiple possible defences and potentially complex legal argument. Police officers are neither qualified nor trained for such a role; more than 20% of decisions to discontinue cases by the CPS are due to the police having failed to establish an essential legal element of the offence charged.[48]

The material that Quirk uncovered in examining police schedules included:

1. A box of unread material including original statements;
2. Details of identification parades that were illegal or where the defendant had not been picked;
3. An interview with a main prosecution witness who had been arrested initially as a suspect;
4. Details of someone wearing an identical shirt to the defendant, who had been arrested but not charged;
5. The police command and control log [which] contained an eyewitness's report consistent with the defendant's, otherwise uncorroborated, account.[49]

Though up to prosecutors to check and challenge all the material presented to them, "others prefer not to create work for themselves . . . as to do so would make their workloads unmanageable."[50] Yet the CPS have a duty to do so as the Criminal Procedures and Investigations Act 1996 (CPIA) makes clear that all material that has come into the prosecutor's possession must be disclosed to the defense, even that "which might reasonably be considered capable of undermining the case for the prosecution." If there is no such material the CPS should "give to the accused a written statement that there is no [such] material."[51]

On February 27, 2018, the BBC Radio Four program, *File on 4*, examined failures affecting justice in the magistrate's court as a result of nondisclosure of information to defense lawyers.[52] The program focused on complaints from solicitors for the defense who were not provided with full information from either the police or the CPS. If they had been, this would either have led to an immediate dismissal of certain cases or the suspect being found not guilty sooner. One of the cases concerned William, a teacher who was charged with sexual assault by one of his students while shopping for lunch in a local store. Accused of inappropriately touching a girl (with her friend acting as an eyewitness), William was arrested. At the police station, he asked to see CCTV footage but was told the camera in the store had been too far away to record the incident and the images were unclear. Police also said there were no facilities at the police station to view the CCTV footage. William was released on bail and suspended from his job. Abu Kibla, his solicitor, asked to see the CCTV footage but was denied. After six requests to the CPS the footage was disclosed, nineteen days before William was due to stand trial. The footage showed William passing the two girls with a sandwich in one hand and a drink in the other, making it impossible for him to have placed either one of his hands anywhere near either of the girls as he had been accused of doing. Having told the CPS about the footage, the defense expected the case to be dropped, but William was still brought to trial where magistrates dismissed the case, citing the CCTV images as the reason. If the CCTV evidence had not been disclosed, it is likely William would have been found guilty, lost his job, and been placed on the sex offenders register. When questioned, Thames Valley Constabulary claimed that they carried out a "thorough investigation," including "the sharing of information among partner agencies" (i.e., the CPS). The director of legal services for the CPS, Greg McGill, stated that prosecutors were right to bring the case to court based on that fact that there had been a complaint "and CCTV evidence that put the people together" in the same store—an argument, which, as seen in chapter 2, is a classic illustration of confirmation bias leading to miscarriages of justice.

It seems clear that the police and the CPS were only interested in securing a conviction because neither Thames Valley Police who had charged William nor the CPS admitted to having done anything wrong. Instead a statement from the CPS claimed: "The prosecution put their case, the defence make their arguments and the court makes their decision. That's the criminal justice system in action."[53] But as William said, "had I been found guilty, I would be permanently on a paedophile register. It's a life-changing allegation." As it stands, William is most likely to now have a file on the PND as a suspect in a sexual assault case, a file he will never discover (unless he makes a subject access request to the police force concerned) and which, as was shown in chapter 3, he can never erase. Though not guilty of any crime, this information may be used at any time in the future to arrest him for any sexual crime.

A further example of nondisclosure concerned Matt, an estate agent who in 2015 became embroiled in a professional disagreement with a rival firm. Having driven to his rival's office, an argument between himself and the manager escalated when the manager physically assaulted Matt who was then dragged into the street by other staff members. As he curled up on the ground, he was repeatedly punched and kicked by five employees and he required hospital treatment. He reported the battering to the police but in a play of Kafkaesque proportions was the one charged with assault. Reviewing a schedule of unused material, his lawyer noted that the complainant and his work colleagues had originally been interviewed as suspects, but their statements had been marked as nondisclosable. After several failed requests for the interviews to be produced, Matt's solicitor finally obtained them through the magistrate's courts. These revealed that three community gardeners had seen Matt being attacked. Had Matt's solicitor not fought to see this undisclosed material, he would never have known about the three witnesses who were not mentioned in the police file or any other documents presented to the CPS. When the CPS were informed that key witnesses had been found and agreed to give evidence, the CPS dropped the case, a day before the trial. By that time Matt had been on bail for eighteen months. The CPS refused to admit that mistakes had been made even when confronted with vital evidence.

Since the police and the CPS work closely together it is not possible to say *who* is responsible when material, such as this, goes astray. Once material has been handed over to the CPS, it is their responsibility to make it available to the defense, but it is up to police disclosure officers to make the CPS aware of all material to be used in evidence. In Matt's case, the CPS knew about the eyewitness statements because they would not have dropped the case otherwise. In William's case, as CCTV footage was vital to William's defense, the police and the CPS deliberately withheld the information to secure a conviction. That the CPS did not disclose the footage to the defense should therefore cause alarm given the CPS's rationale "to be independent from both the police and government because it was agreed that suspects and defendants needed an extra layer of protection. It was to be accountable, not to defendants, but to the law in a neutral fashion." Yet, the natural affinity of CPS thinking with police thinking makes this aspiration "unrealistic" not only because "the CPS is more tied into the police than it ever has been" but as "the police now have more influence over prosecutions than at any time since 1986."[54]

In 2011 Christopher Killick was sentenced to three years imprisonment for the sexual assault of two severely disabled men. Though charged by the police in 2010, the CPS originally decided not to prosecute, but one of the victims took the case to the Court of Appeal which ruled in the victim's favor, arguing that victims have the right to challenge CPS decisions without resorting to judicial review—at the time, the only means of challenging the CPS. Two years later, the British government introduced the Victims Right to Review (VRR), at that time, welcomed by Keir Starmer, the Director of Public Prosecution. The decision to introduce the VRR has not, however, been a resounding success.[55]

In one of the only successful cases to be reviewed—that of Lord Janner (accused of historic child abuse)—the lawyer responsible for conducting the review was appointed independently of the CPS (most likely due to the high profile and media attention surrounding the case), so the VRR was anything but usual. Further confusion arises with the use of the term "victim"—defined by the CPS as "a person who has suffered harm, including physical, mental or emotional harm or economic loss which was *directly* caused by criminal conduct."[56] Given that those who raise concerns may not be direct victims but bereaved families, the definition is far from clear as is the notion of "criminal conduct," which is far from straightforward. This is because, in many cases, criminal conduct has yet to be established, which is why, for example, families of road deaths face a disadvantage. If criminality is yet to be determined, but the CPS has decided not to prosecute, there is little that a VRR will achieve. This is further complicated by the fact that, unknown to family members, the decision has been made by the police. Therefore, where the police have decided that no criminal charges are to be brought, a right to review has no practical application except in *seeming* to offer some appeasement to victims where none exists in practice. This is why the Janner case remains the solitary example of a successful right to review, though every victim who is told that the CPS will not prosecute is also told they have a right for this decision to be reviewed.

For example, the police decide they do not wish to prosecute a driver for an offense or argue there is no case to answer. The file goes to the CPS with the police's recommendation not to prosecute. The CPS automatically rejects the case, stating it is not in the public's interest to prosecute. The "victim," or bereaved family member, is given the right to question this decision, under the VRR, but if no crime is seen to have taken place, the case is not deemed worthy of review. Thus families complain that the CPS has not taken them seriously and simply dismissed subsequent evidence presented to them. In the case of Toni Rolls, the police file to the CPS stated that "this elderly woman of 83 ran across the road." When her daughter informed the CPS that her eighty-three-year-old mother not only walked with a limp but was also last seen, by a key witness, standing on the white line of the bus lane, the response, by the CPS was that "that makes no difference, the fact was, she was in the road and hit by a car."

After Joao Lopes killed Nora Gutmann, a ninety-seven-year-old Holocaust survivor, on a pedestrian crossing in central London, sixteen months after he had killed the cyclist, Eilidh Cairns, Kate Cairns wrote to the prosecutor also requesting a review of the decision not to have prosecuted Lopes for dangerous driving. Aside from serious typographical errors (including misspelling the name Eilidh throughout), the CPS prosecutor disputes the evidence of key witnesses presented at the inquest and bases his response on a police investigation report that was incomplete as the police collisions investigator was, at the time, under arrest for fraud. Witnesses clearly placed Eilidh in front of the lorry at the time of her death, but the prosecutor states that it was only "presumed that she was in front of the lorry before the collision" and that there was no "evidence to conclusively prove how she was riding her bike," which, in any case had never been an issue. The rest of the letter is scattered with standard responses sent out to victims who seek a review including: "there is too much open to speculation," "it is not in the public interest," and the final instruction: "If you wish to have a meeting please contact your [police] family liaison officer."

CASE STUDY: A FALSE CHARGE OF RAPE

The story of George is an example of how the CPS seek to support policing decisions even when there is no case to answer. It will resonate with many who have faced wrongful arrest or a miscarriage of justice. The case has been widely publicized online and in newsprint; however, the names have been changed to protect the identity of the family for George, who has learning difficulties, to be able to lead an independent life without further accusations or harassment.[57] It should be noted he had been under supervision from social services since he was a toddler and had been receiving specialist help with his education at the time of his arrest. His mother, Jennifer, thus spoke on his behalf. Prior to his arrest, the family had no complaints with the police; their only contact having been as victims of robbery several years before during which they thought the police had been "very thorough."

In 2012, when George was age eighteen, his half-sister, Gina, fifteen, who lived with his father in another part of town, accused George of having repeatedly raped her when she was between the ages of ten and twelve and George between the ages of thirteen and fifteen. Although George stayed for weekends at his father's house, the two families—Jennifer's ex-husband, his wife, and their daughter Gina, and Jennifer, her husband Mark, and their daughter Ella had only minimal contact. This was because, prior to Gina's accusations against George, she had made previous accusations against the family on Facebook. These included claims of rape against George's stepfather, Mark. Jennifer had not reported the abuse to the police because of Gina's age and because she was convinced that her conduct had been prompted by her former husband's wife, who, consumed by jealousy, had harassed and cajoled the family for years. Thus, despite the horrendous nature of the accusations against her son, Jennifer had never doubted his innocence. The accusations, after all, were nothing new. She was surprised if not shocked that when the inspector first visited the family he showed no interest in any of Gina's previous accusations or in looking at the Facebook pages, which Jennifer had kept for the record.

> I tried desperately to explain the allegations that had happened previously and everything that I was saying was being dismissed; what I obviously know now is this person came to visit me with a very closed mind, obviously had his own agenda and didn't really have the ability to investigate impartially and look at two sides of the story.

George was arrested and then interviewed without an appropriate adult being present. By this time medical checks had been carried out on Gina with the medical examination clearly stating, "'hymen intact'—she's not had sex." The family were shocked that the case was not immediately dropped, and instead, George was granted bail for three months, providing he did not remain at the family home, where it was said, he might pose a risk to his younger sister, Ella. At just eighteen and with mental health issues, he could not look after himself but without finding somewhere for him to live, he would have to go to prison. At first Jennifer asked her brother if George could stay with him on the understanding that an agreement could be made with social services with the view of George returning home. Her brother agreed to help for the three months that George was on bail. At the end of the three months, however, the family were told that bail would be extended for two further months while the CPS decided what they were going to do with the case. With her brother no longer able to look after George, he went to live in a flat that the family usually rented out unfurnished. The family lost several thousand pounds in rental income, which helped pay their mortgage. Suddenly they were faced with additional utility bills and council tax. The flat also had to be furnished. According to Jennifer, this was nothing compared to the mental and physical strain the family were suffering, not least because George's name appeared in the national press. As Jennifer said, "I was so frightened that somebody would know he was living there because by the time he was charged he became almost fair game because his name and address was posted in the newspaper." George's mental state also meant that Jennifer had to split her time between caring for George and spending time with the family.

The case shows how police work closely with other agencies aside from the CPS. Through making a subject access request, Jennifer later discovered that the officer in charge of the investigation had informed social services that Jennifer had taken the decision to remove George from the family home when in fact bail conditions had demanded that George reside elsewhere. Jennifer also read that social services had been informed that the inspector had given her and her husband safeguarding advice designed to keep George away from his youngest sister with closely supervised contact being required at all times. Jennifer, who had recorded every conversation that took place when officers visited her, was adamant that no instructions had been given. That conversation never occurred. Instead the family had been told that George was forbidden to see his younger sister Ella, which placed a further strain on the family.

Nearly eighteen months after George was first arrested and the information had come to light that the accused had lied, the CPS took him to court. The prosecution opened proceedings by stating that the Crown offered no evidence against George, citing that the complainant had not been telling the truth. The case was dismissed. As Jennifer says:

> I understand and I fully respect when somebody makes an allegation it needs to be investigated; what I took umbrage with, is the way that [George's] case was handled and from my own point of view, there was already substantial evidence to prove malice; we had a medical examination to say that the little girl had not had sex and that was [eighteen months before]. . . . At that time it should have been done and dusted; it shouldn't have gone any further which would have meant that my family would have suffered for only a very, very short period of time which would have enabled us to have a better coping mechanism and we would have been able to get on with our lives much quicker; unfortunately it went on [for eighteen months] by that time I was so distraught, I had to resign from my job and my son was removed from his family home for a prolonged period of time resulting in . . . post traumatic stress.

Though the CPS dropped the case for lack of evidence, a question remains as to why they failed to do so eighteen months before when it was clear that Gina's evidence was untrue. Section 3.6 of the Code for Crown Prosecutions clearly states that:

> Prosecutors review every case they receive from the police or other investigators. Review is a continuing process and prosecutors must take account of any change in circumstances that occurs as the case develops, including what becomes known of the defence case. Wherever possible, they should talk to the investigator when thinking about changing the charges or stopping the case. Prosecutors and investigators work closely together, but the final responsibility for the decision whether or not a case should go ahead rests with the CPS.[58]

Dismissing cases at the last minute is neither new nor unique, as Maeve McClenaghan in the *Bureau for Investigative Journalism* states:

> In 2012 there were 45 homicide trials that failed because the CPS provided insufficient or no evidence after a not guilty plea. This was equivalent to one in twenty homicide cases and a rise of 50% from 2010. Such trial failures are recorded as due to "no evidence," and the defendants are acquitted. The term also encompasses cases when the prosecution decides to pass on chasing for one particular charge, instead opting to add the charge to another, more serious crime.[59]

The same report notes that "one senior judge described the CPS's performance as a 'disgrace,'" another as "a lamentable state of affairs," and a third told the CPS that the court would "not put up with this kind of disdain." That this is the fault of the police is speculative because "in some cases CPS barristers are arriving at court without sufficient evidence, having not read case files and without key witnesses. Such failings can lead to a case being thrown out." Furthermore, the costs involved can be extortionate. "In 2014–15, the CPS spent £21.5 million on preparing cases that were not heard in court." Of this sum, £5.5 million related to cases that collapsed attributable to "prosecution reasons," including nonattendance of prosecution witnesses and incomplete case files.[60] A 2015 inspection found that just "18.2% of police charging decisions were incorrect. Incorrect charging decisions should be picked up by the CPS before court, but 38.4% of cases were not reviewed before reaching court."[61]

CONCLUSION

Conspiracy theorists often accuse police of having close relationships with judges and other members of the judiciary through association as Freemasons.[62] However, this chapter has shown that there is no need for such theories as links between the police and other state organizations are already intrinsic and only need to be brought to light. A spate of miscarriages of justice in different countries and continents and police jurisdictions has shown that poor police investigations lead to poor jury outcomes. These practices continue. Whether they continue out of laziness, maliciousness, or poor practice is a moot point, but what seems clear is that no one has a vested interest in *losing* and can rarely, if ever, admit to having made a mistake.

Not adjourning an inquest when the main police collisions investigator is on trial for fraud made the inquest into Eilidh Cairns seem something of a farce. Had this been a criminal court, the prosecutor or defense counsel would have had the right to suspend proceedings until all evidence had been collated, but not at an inquest where rules are entirely down to the discretion of the coroner. To the police, an inquest may simply herald the end of an investigation but to the families concerned, who, in many if not most cases, will be unaware of the process and the reason for the coroner's court, they can be forgiven for believing that its objective is to provide families with answers. To the family of Eilidh Cairns, however, it seems unreasonable to suggest that her death was an "accident" when it could have been avoided if only the driver had been wearing corrective lenses—or if the driver in the case of Toni Rolls had only been looking in front of him at the person about to cross the road instead of looking to his right and accelerating. Or in the case of James Sutton, when a police car claimed to be responding to an emergency with sirens blazing (implying that James was somehow stupid not to have seen or heard the car) when the main objective evidence—the car's black box recorder—had purportedly broken down at the beginning of the shift. In the latter case, someone should have taken responsibility for the car's machinery not being in operational order. Why should an inquest be simply a place where facts maybe discovered but no action taken and where "lessons learned" are ignored?

How can the CPS be permitted to withhold information from the defense or bring cases to court without sufficient evidence or wait until the last minute to drop a case, even while an innocent person suffers as a result? The CPS rely on the police to supply evidence of criminal behavior. Where they fail to do so the public is not protected by the Victims' Right to Review (VRR), which is little more than a public relations exercise. Commenters may hold the CPS responsible as prosecuting authorities, but the decision to charge is a policing matter.[63] Though the CPS may ask the police for more information, when the police do decide a prosecution is warranted but have supplied insufficient evidence, it is unlikely the police file will even be read, for why waste time on reading a document that the police have said is not "charge-worthy?" Since the police are the investigators, they have failed to investigate, do not wish to charge, or have investigated and reached a decision but have insufficient evidence, the CPS can do very little. After all, the CPS is only a legal body, acting on information provided to them by the police. Yet, as seen in the case of the cycling lobby, the public remain largely ignorant of this process. By this lack of transparency the police remain beyond criticism, the local prosecutor remains unknown, and the onus of responsibility is placed in the hands of an anonymous institution—the CPS.

6

Accountability

A Gray Area

The methods used to discredit victims and complainants as revealed in this book do not fall under the criteria of police corruption or misconduct as defined by policing agencies and criminologists.[1] These latter practices include soliciting or accepting bribes, using excessive force, tampering with evidence, blackmailing witnesses or having illicit affairs with victims, and the whole range of criminal behaviors that apply equally to members of the public. Dealt with in England and Wales through public misconduct hearings, many remain skeptical in the ability of police agencies to deal with corruption because "traditional police departments are noted for their tendency to close ranks and protect corrupt colleagues behind a 'blue wall' or 'blue curtain' of silence."[2] The "tendency to close ranks" may be especially true of the sorts of behaviors depicted in this book which fit no specified category. The general public might be forgiven for thinking of these practices as unethical, but none of the illustrations given are found in the College of Policing's *Code of Ethics*, which sets standards of professional behavior in England and Wales.

That codes of professional ethics fail, or fail for being too general, may be down to "ethical behaviour [being] tempered by an officer's personal set of values and beliefs, overlaid by a lesser or greater extent by those relating to police occupational culture."[3] It is against the background of such a culture, where the matter of accountability comes to rest. Given that covert techniques, disbelieving victims, and slandering complainants are well known in policing circles (even perhaps encouraged by some PSDs) the question remains why such practices continue, even after the establishment of an independent police complaints commission.

To understand the failure of police institutions to deal with this matter, the police complaints system, as it currently exists in England and Wales, is examined. Since the actual complaints system seems at odds with the way the police service is commonly regarded, both by policing agencies and the mainstream media, a discussion on public relations in policing will lead toward a better recognition of how policing culture has become estranged from the guiding principles established in the nineteenth century.

In a world saturated by academic texts, the treatment of police complainants remains a neglected area of research. As seen in chapter 1, police officers may discredit victims and complainants in several ways: by disbelieving a crime took place, by stigmatizing a person for a previous conviction that has nothing to do with present circumstances, by alleging the victim is under the influence of drink or drugs, through threats or actual arrest, or by diagnosing victims, occasionally with the support of psychiatrists, as mentally ill. These methods, identified more than forty years ago by Steven Box and Ken Russell, remain prevalent today. Research has shown that certain victims are more likely to be discredited in some ways rather than others. For example, victims of rape and sexual assault are overwhelmingly neutralized (disbelieved or ignored), as are those who report crimes of antisocial behavior, whereas malicious arrest is a tactic commonly used against whistleblowers, including police officers. Victims of road deaths, particularly cyclists and pedestrians, are commonly derided as having been responsible for their own death, without any guilt being considered on the part of the driver (except in cases of drunk driving, determined by a breathalyzer or blood test without the requirement for further police investigation). Mental illness was seen as a way to silence a whole range of disparate individuals, showing that stigma remains commonplace. Through using the word "delusional," police officers wrongly equate anyone branded mentally ill or disabled as being incapable of truth telling or objectivity.

More recent means of discrediting victims and complainants include the use of surveillance, harassment on social media, data sharing of information on the victim or complainant with third parties (revealing a gray area in the Data Protection Act 2018), and illegitimately interfering in a person's private life, contrary to Section 8 of the Human Rights Act. Yet, while these practices exist, there remains little that a person can do about them given that such behaviors do not fall within the remit of police misconduct.[4] The situation is no better for police officers themselves. Those who were interviewed as part of this research were astounded at their treatment by colleagues when they witnessed police malpractice and sought to report it. Although the public have no recourse to make complaints to an independent body (contrary to expectations, as discussed herein), police officers are not permitted to complain about their treatment to the Independent Office for Police Conduct (IOPC) either but are expected to bring matters to the attention of their Police Federation representative. In all cases, it is usually the same police force that handles complaints and, within a policing division, often the police officer's line manager.

THE POLICE COMPLAINTS SYSTEM

The majority of those interviewed for this book made formal complaints about their treatment via the form provided on the website of the Independent Police Complaints Commission (since January 2018 the IOPC), expecting their concerns would be independently investigated. Unbeknown to them, however, the IOPC only investigates complaints against the police where a police officer may have been involved in a death. Otherwise the same local force against which the complaint has been made investigates the complaint. This is a common practice in other countries[5] and leaves the courts the only reliable form of redress, which is beyond the financial remit of most people. Even where police are sued and complainants win compensation, the police themselves often face no criticism. One such case is that of Leroy McDowell and Wayne Taylor, two black men in their thirties who complained of police harassment after they were stopped and searched for being in a supposed "drugs-related area." Though no drugs were found on either of them, they were maliciously arrested for threatening a police officer. Both men suffer from sickle cell anemia and asked for medical help but this was denied. After the prosecution case against them failed, they decided to take the police to court for wrongful arrest, malicious prosecution, and negligence. The matter was settled out of court with each awarded £19,000 in damages. The police officers concerned were admonished, no liability was accepted, and the duty officer, who had failed to provide them with the necessary medical attention, was merely "given advice."[6]

The police complaints system in the United Kingdom is seriously flawed. If one complains via the form on the IOPCs website or directly to the local police force concerned, the effect is the same. The force's professional standards department (PSD) initially reviews all complaints and makes the decision whether there is a case to answer. If there is, they decide if a complaint could be resolved by Local or Informal Resolution (which requires the agreement of the complainant) or formally investigated by the same force. Local resolution (LR) is a way of handling complaints by dealing directly with complainants, but if complainants decline a meeting with the police, they are likely to be derided as being obstructive. In any case, LR is extremely limiting in scope.

The Police Reform and Social Responsibility Act (PRSRA) came into force in 2011. It decided that LR would be the best means of dealing with a complaint but only if the complaint was about conduct that would "not justify criminal or disciplinary proceedings against the person being complained about," and would be unlikely to lead to a disciplinary hearing.[7] In other words, even if proved, there would never be a satisfactory outcome for the complainant and the person being complained about would at most receive a ticking off. Aside from this, the use of the term "local resolution" is misused by several policing agencies. Several respondents were told their complaint was being dealt with by LR but not one was asked to attend a meeting; in one case, when a complainant repeatedly suggested meeting with the police team as a means to resolve her concerns, this was denied. In all cases, complainants received a response stamped by the force's PSD, even when the person dealing with the complaint was a colleague or line manager. In no case was the person conducting the complaint from another department or another police force.

Where a complaint is to be investigated, the complainant receives a holding letter giving the time frame by which the investigation will be completed. Usually given as two months, in several cases such "investigations" took more than six months and sometimes even years. More often than not, the final letter will admit some responsibility without upholding the complaint in which case the complainant will be informed if they have the right to appeal and if so, to whom, the IOPC or the PSD. Although the IOPC never examines initial complaints, they do accept appeals at the discretion of the local police force.

Complainants have no choice but to follow this decision-making process. If they attempt to appeal to the IOPC where the police have not granted permission, the IOPC will not hear the appeal. Even when appeals are permitted to be brought to the IOPC, the IOPC may either inform complainants that they should contact the local police force for resolution, or the IOPC may simply uphold the findings of the police force concerned, casting doubt on their own value as an independent body. Since a third of the IOPCs investigators are former police officers, this is perhaps unsurprising. In any case, the IOPC lack the power to require serving officers to provide direct evidence to them and have been criticized for their lack of thoroughness, with families resorting to coroner's courts and even the European Court of Human Rights.[8] Though rumors suggest this may change in the future, at present the IOPC remains a rebranding of the former IPCC.

The initial setting up of an independent police complaints commission in 2004 was devised as a result of a report published in 1996 which criticized the then Police Complaints Authority because "people did not trust the police to investigate themselves."[9] Created to increase public trust, the establishment of the IPCC, however, made no difference to the way police investigated complaints, with 95 percent "handled exactly as they were under the old system—the police investigate themselves."[10] Thus, it is not surprising that the IPCC was highly criticized. Aside from showing favoritism toward the police, criticisms have included:

- A failure to provide effective oversight for the work of the police investigators who handle complaints;
- Complaints being rejected despite evidence in their support;
- Cases of indifference and rudeness toward members of the public;
- Casework managers with no legal qualifications, relevant experience, or even minimal training;
- Decisions being reversed by the threat of court action.[11]

The process by which PSDs handle complaints has also been criticized since the recognition of wrongdoing "involves no admission of guilt and is not noted on the officers' records."[12] At best, most officers receive "operational advice" from managers, but most complainants do not realize that the complaint system is "not oriented toward punishment or blame."[13] Nor do most people recognize that the complaints system is geared toward accepting the status quo, with complainants who question the outcome being branded as "vexatious." As a police detective explained:

> Vexatious—that's a new word. I don't know if I've said it on Twitter or on Facebook, it's a word that's been bastardized from the Freedom of Information Act and the Data Protection Act and basically, it's a get out clause for the police, so you give them a request or you ask information of them that they cannot, they are refusing to give you, so people will ask again, then they suggest you are being vexatious. My issue with being "vexatious" is that, if you vex somebody, you cause them to worry, you're annoying them. If you're going to accuse somebody of being vexatious, then somebody has a reason to be vexed . . . [but] if you've nothing to be vexed about, there's no need to worry.

PSDs informed many of the victims and complainants interviewed for this book that they were being vexatious or would be regarded as such if they did not accept the decision of the PSD. In all cases, the use of "vexatious" did not refer to its legal definition, as a "vexatious litigant." This phrase is applied to "individuals who persistently take legal action against others in cases without any merit, who are forbidden from starting civil cases in courts without permission."[14] As clarified in *Information Commissioner v Devon County Council & Dransfield* [2012] UKUT 440 (AAC), (January 28, 2013), "the ordinary dictionary definition of the word 'vexatious' is only of limited use, because the question of whether a request is vexatious ultimately depends upon the circumstances surrounding that request."[15]

None of this is made clear to complainants. Instead, PSDs use the term "vexatious" *as if* it refers to the legal definition, when in fact it is only being used in a dictionary sense. The IOPC also misuse the term stating: "A complaint is vexatious if it is possible to demonstrate it is without basis . . . and . . . it would tend to, or is being made with an intention to cause worry, upset, annoyance or embarrassment."[16] Confusion between "vexatious" and "vexatious litigant" would thus appear to be a means of preventing a complainant from seeking legal redress. Use of the term "vexatious" is a simple means of stating that there is no basis to a complaint and, therefore, nothing to investigate.

The problem of accountability is compounded by other members of the criminal justice system (e.g., coroners, prosecutors, and judges) being even *less* accountable than the police themselves. Those caught up in the system thus have nowhere to turn. For instance, when a family member of a road death victim made a subject access request to the coroner via the local council, she discovered that the inspector of roads policing had set up a covert dossier on her as the next-of-kin in which those requested to participate included the coroner, the crime commissioner, officers from the College of Policing, the National Crime Agency, her local police force, and an officer from another police force who was working on secondment from the College of Policing. Correspondence revealed that those invited to contribute to the dossier submitted information infringing data protection legislation. When an additional complaint was subsequently made regarding this "dossier," the inspector argued that it was set up "to support [her as] the next-of-kin." How a dossier could possibly be a support mechanism was not explained. Complaints to the Information Commissioner's Office (ICO), which had written repeatedly to the coroner and the police to reveal information (a subject access request which should take forty days to process took in one case more than a year to receive), also failed. Having sent hundreds of documents by special delivery to the ICO, the complainant was ignored. The ICO then confirmed it had lost all the papers and would no longer be reviewing the case. When the complainant informed the ICO that all relevant documents were available to download online, the ICO stated that its policy excludes them examining online documentation. It was later discovered that policing requests at the ICO were being handled by a member of the College of Policing.

In other cases, participants remained completely dumbfounded at the purpose of the IPCC. Helga Akitt, whose brother, James Sutton, was killed by a police car in East Sussex, stated:

> I wasn't happy with the investigation so I contacted the IPCC who then in turn told me I needed to make a complaint to Sussex Police which is ironic because Sussex police are the people who killed my brother. So that was kind of a no

> go—to me that was kind of ridiculous and I expected the IPCC to be on my side and to help me and I felt that they failed me.

As to reforming the police complaints system in England and Wales as a whole, Kevin Donoghue of Donoghue solicitors suggested a five-stage plan to cut police complaints.[17] In responding to Donoghue's comments (which, in theory, are perfectly reasonable) the actual experiences of those complainants are taken into consideration.

1. Scrap the Police Reform and Social Responsibility Act (2011).

This act, which came into effect on November 22, 2012, states that if the complainant is dissatisfied with the outcome of the initial investigation, a "Chief Officer" in the same force should deal with the appeal unless the complaint justifies criminal and/or misconduct proceedings. Donoghue states: "taking Chief Officers out of the equation will help to put genuine independence back into the complaints process." However, this would only work if the IOPC was itself an independent and efficient body, which, as seen, is highly questionable.

2. Replace Professional Standards Departments with independent IOPC units.

Allowing a police force's PSD or internal investigations unit to investigate their own officers is a clear conflict of interest. By taking the complaints investigation process away from them and putting it in the hands of independent investigators:

- the public will gain confidence in the system;
- complaints and appeals will be properly investigated;
- senior officers will take the complaints process more seriously; and
- serial offenders in the police will know that they cannot get away with repeated police misconduct.

However, as seen, the IOPC already *claims* to be independent, so it remains to be seen if independent investigators (given many are and would continue to be ex-police officers) would change the way complaints are handled.

3. Incentivize police forces through financial rewards and penalties.

Donoghue suggests that linking police funding to an independently vetted complaints system would entail chief constables prioritizing police complaints and improve the conduct of their officers, which would not only lead to fewer complaints but also to fewer instances of police misconduct. He also suggests that linking this system to police staff (who work behind the scenes) would ensure an improvement in standards as a whole and a more positive attitude from staff. However, the danger lies that even more complainants would fail to be recorded and more complainants discredited to conceal police malpractice.

4. Annual continual professional development courses on the law, conduct, and complaints to be made compulsory for all police staff and officers. As Donoghue states:

> "Police neglect or failure of duty" is the most common cause for complaint. . . . by ensuring that all officers attend regularly updated training courses on the law, conduct, *and* complaints they would be better able to serve the public. Training should include "soft skills" like civility and politeness. This would help cut complaints about the police's high-handed and arbitrary behaviour.

Donoghue does not provide examples or mention the types of unethical practices that complainants regularly encounter or the fact that people are discredited precisely for challenging the way officers behave. It is, in many cases, not the initial action that causes a serious breakdown in trust; it is what happens next.

5. Cultural change to be led and instigated by senior police officers.

Donoghue argues that the police do not take complainants seriously because most concerns do not interest lawyers. However, Donoghue accepts that recourse to law is not the main priority for complainants to the police in the first place. "Often, the police's apology, which is free and could have been given before getting solicitors involved, is more valuable to my clients than the money." While this is undoubtedly true, as chapter 4 has shown, when it comes to policing attitudes, it is often the most senior officer, not the rank-and-file constable, who is at fault. This has certainly been the experience of the complainants mentioned in this book. Of those interviewed for this book, not a single complaint was upheld.[18] When asked about their desired outcome, the response from complainants was unanimous: Each wanted an apology and an acceptance of wrongdoing with the idea of litigation being far removed from a complainant's intention. Instead, as shown in numerous case studies, making a complaint to the authorities is precarious and carries the risk of being discredited in ways that may damage reputations and careers.

Box and Russell concluded that the main reason for the failure of police organizations to deal with complaints is the perceived threat to professional and bureaucratic interests. Complaints are dismissed and victims blamed to prevent morale from deteriorating. This allows the police institution to see the victim qua complainant as the problem, while the organization "closes ranks to protect its own and its reputation."[19] Therefore, it is difficult to see, even if each of Donoghue's grounds were accepted, how the cultural attitude which discredits victims and complainants and gets away with bias in investigations, is likely to change.

RESPONDENTS

Whether the public are right to trust the police given their ability to discredit both victims and complainants (let alone that group of people that have not formed part of this study, suspects and convicted criminals) remains a moot point. The evidence, according to Timothy Brain, speaks for itself, with Home Office statistics reporting that 62 percent of people believe the police do a decent or excellent job.[20] No reasons are given why nearly 40 percent of those polled think the opposite, and no differentiation is made between people who have not had any dealings with the police at all or been involved with the police with investigations or in other ways. Nor do the figures reveal if any of the 62 percent found themselves as suspects in policing investigations—or perhaps, that figure falls to the other 38 percent. Information is scarce and the reasons for public mistrust ignored by the Home Office and many other policing agencies. Victim satisfaction surveys, for instance, do not apply to "all" victims, or even a majority but carefully decide that "victims" are those who have been violently assaulted (but not harassed or raped) or have been the victim of burglary or car theft (but not road traffic collisions or deaths). For "victims" who do not fit the given criteria, their satisfaction or discontent is clearly irrelevant. Other polls choose people "at random" such as the Crime Survey in England and Wales. But a quarter of those asked to complete the survey refused to participate. With one in five crimes not being recorded by the police and when families of victims are also ignored, it would come as no surprise if trust in the police wanes as soon as a person becomes involved in a complaint or investigative procedure. Indeed a news report on undercover officers revealed that when they tried to tackle an armed man in East London, and were injured in the process, crowds of onlookers cheered for the man to get away, while failing to help the two officers whose injuries included a broken wrist.[21] Mistrust in the police has far-reaching consequences for officers as well as the general public.

Given that victims who have sought a right to review are largely ignored by the Crown Prosecution Service (CPS), it is not merely "the police" as an institution that is failing the public but prosecutors, pathologists, coroners, and even judges. However, it is policing complaints and the treatment of victims that remains the most problematic area because "policing by consent" depends on public trust.

Stella summed up her experience with the police as follows: "I can't believe that I've ever trusted them as much as I have." A qualified barrister and law lecturer, Stella came into contact with the police after her mentally ill son went missing and she read on his Facebook page that he intended to kill himself. Relieved when half an hour later she received a call to say that he had been found, she arrived at his location at the same time as a police sergeant. Her son, Simon, had cut his arm from a piece of glass he had found in the road, but it was not a serious injury and the blood had already dried. Stella stood back on the officer's advice, as he spoke kindly to Simon, telling him to put the glass down and that everything would be okay. Simon still held the glass in his hand but had calmed down and was engaged in conversation with the sergeant when six police cars and a van pulled up, blocking the road at each end. Out jumped a dozen officers; two ran at Simon, dosed him with pepper spray, and then tasered him. Stella, accompanied by her elder son, could only watch. She screamed, "Stop Taser" repeatedly—as police officers had not given any warning before the deployment of the Taser guns.[22] Police officers went to taser Simon a second time, but the sergeant who had been speaking to Simon stood in front to protect him and was himself tasered.

Most people are aware that a Taser is an electroshock weapon that when used with a cartridge fires two small dartlike probes into the body to deliver an electric current which causes the muscles in the body to seize and the person to experience a momentary loss of consciousness.[23] In some cases, it has been known to kill.[24] Referred to as conductive energy devices (CEDs) by the College of Policing, it is less well-known that officers may legally choose to remove the cartridge placing the Taser in "drive-stun mode."[25] In drive-stun mode, the Taser is applied directly to a person's body. This causes extreme pain without rendering the victim unconscious. On the third and fourth time Simon was tasered, the gun was applied direct to his hip and lower back to cause excruciating pain. The United Nations (UN) has called the use of Tasers a form of torture, with Amnesty International pointing out that this is particularly true when used in drive-stun mode.[26] In addition the UN has also severely criticized the UK government for allowing police officers to use Tasers on children.[27]

The police led Simon away, throwing him into the cage of a police van meant for violent offenders. He was left with burn marks to his body, violent shaking that lasted forty-eight hours, and posttraumatic stress disorder. No explanation or apology for the police's behavior was offered. Stella made a formal complaint to the police but heard nothing. She is convinced the actions that followed were the direct result of her making this complaint.

Several weeks after her complaint was recorded, Simon and his brother were arrested by police officers after leaving a club in the town center for allegedly causing an affray. They were held all night in a police cell before being released without charge. Stella asked to see her sons. She was especially concerned about Simon given his mental health issues. The police officer on duty refused her request. On discovering that the inspector in charge of arresting both her sons that night was the same police officer who had ordered Simon to be tasered, she made a second complaint.

Having received no response to her complaints, Stella raised concerns about her son's treatment and the use of Taser on social media. She had every right to do so because the police had breached protocols presented in the College of Policing's own guidelines.[28] She was then hounded on Twitter by unknown police officers who engaged in taunting her and retweeting their taunts, a form of harassment that had gained some notoriety when the Metropolitan police's helicopter division targeted an innocent woman on the social media platform.[29] After Stella closed her Twitter account, local police officers contacted her employers demanding they take disciplinary action against her for lying about her son's experience. Fortunately, working in a law department has some advantages when it comes to dealing with the authorities. Until this day, however, not one officer has been held accountable, either for the actions taken against Simon or the ways in which officers have behaved toward her.

Stella is far from alone in having lost all trust in the police. After Sharon intervened to protect her mentally ill daughter who was being held down by a police officer for screaming in the street, the officer hit Sharon, leaving her with a broken nose and a fractured skull. To cover his tracks, the officer claimed he had been acting in self-defense. Sharon was maliciously arrested, subsequently charged, and prosecuted by the CPS. Witnesses, whose names she had given to her barrister, never turned up to court. They later informed her that they had been told by police officers to stay away. She took her case to the Court of Appeal. Held a year later, she was fully exonerated, and the judge advised Sharon to take civil action against the police for the injuries she had incurred.

Aside from these injuries, officers also took the decision to write to her employer. Unlike Stella, however, Sharon lost her job, though she had worked in the social service department of her local council for nearly twenty years. Her employers refused to accept unfair dismissal, even when she was exonerated, unless the police force concerned put the record straight. They refused to do so. As Sharon states of the police:

> I trusted the police before. I had no reason to distrust them. Now I don't trust them at all. I acknowledge that there has to be some good police but they are all tarred with the same brush, because of the corruption that is involved, and when you are enlightened to that corruption you know that you can't trust them because they have a police code of silence—it does exist.

Asked how she thought the police could get away with such behavior, Sharon said:

> They know that they're not going to be held accountable. They know that the public funding is an endless money pit that they are going to be protected, to have the best lawyers available to them all paid for by the public funds, they know that even if they're found guilty, they're not going to be sacked, they'll get a slap on the wrist and a "don't be naughty again" and that's it. They do it because, in a nutshell, they can. They've actually said that to me. Now the thing is, if the officers who were guilty of the corrupt act, if they didn't have every penny paid for them, if the money awarded to the victims had to come out of their pensionable pay or their salaries per month so clawed back into the public purse, I think they'd think again about being corrupt as well.

Kay, whose story is told in chapter 1, echoes Sharon's sentiments. A physically disabled woman who had reported antisocial behavior to the police for several years only to find herself maliciously arrested and placed on a mental health database, she was asked how her views of the police had changed.

> I will never report anything to the police ever again. I will not have anything to do with them ever again. . . . I'll never help the police, nothing to do with me, or be a witness. I will never help them ever again; they disgust me. . . . It just gets you down.

Malik agrees. An international student from Bangladesh who came to the United Kingdom to study for an MBA, he was burgled and beaten up by known robbers who had been wearing electronic tags at the time. When the case came to court, the police did not inform him, and thus, he made a complaint. He believed his concerns would be taken seriously. Instead, he was told he needed psychiatric help. As he said:

> I don't trust them anymore, what they say, what they are doing, I mean, I cannot depend on them if I am in a critical situation, if I am in trouble, I don't think. I haven't taken any action, actually, at the moment I can't do it, I am an international student but I have learnt. Police don't take proper action. Like this

> incident. I call them. First they do the routine things but people got away. . . . It's like they are scrutinising me like I am the one who has done the crime—they need to really focus on the incident of the matter, what happened, ok and then figure out quickly.

Interviews with twenty-six complainants and media reports from the families of Hillsborough and the Undercover Policing Inquiry reveal that denigration of innocent members of the public who "annoy" the police continues as a little known fact. As Theodore, whose story was told in chapter 3, states:

> I don't think either of the originating officers had the integrity to admit their mistakes. Had they done so I would have dropped the complaint there and then, with the confirmation that "Ok, they cocked up in a big way and I hate it but there you go, that's life."—I can deal with that but to continue the torment as they have—and it was torment—I think that's absolutely outrageous and I think they're prepared to do that to anybody. Had they done that to somebody that I love or care about I think my reaction would have been not to play by their game, their rules, I think I would have done something stupid, I'm sure of it.

There are, as seen, rarely repercussions when things go wrong, showing that codes of ethics—with their emphasis on being accountable and transparent—are ineffectual. Equally worrying is the failure of the Home Office, the ministry responsible for policing in Great Britain, to accept responsibility for *its* errors. When a report announced that "10% of Home Office data provided to banks was inaccurate resulting in people being wrongly declared a 'disqualified person'" and "8% of driving license applications were wrongly refused or revoked," a respondent from the Home Office stated, "none of this was in any way a fault or lack in Home Office staff,"[30] which begs the question, whose fault was it? When the so-called pediatric expert Roy Meadows provided fabricated statistics on child deaths against Sally Clark who was subsequently wrongly imprisoned for the murder of her two children, Meadows was rightfully struck off the General Medical Register. Unfortunately there is no oversight for either Home Office officials or the police, which is no doubt why police departments spend millions each year on public relations exercises and actively relish taking part in procedural dramas.

PUBLIC RELATIONS

It should come as no surprise that police forces around the world rely heavily on communication strategies, with the British police alone spending more than £36 million each year on public relations (PR). Given an age of austerity in which police forces constantly complain of budget cuts, police communications departments have seen a steady increase in funding.

In the United Kingdom, PR currently include press releases and Twitter accounts but exclude television programs, which are commissioned and paid for by television companies, though this was not always the case. When the Central Office of Information was established in London in April 1946 it produced thousands of films, including several hundred on the police and criminal justice system. Some of its most popular features included *British Policeman* (1959), *Unit Beat Policing* (1968), and *Snatch of the Day* (1975).[31] Though overtaken in the 1970s by fictional police dramas, *Z-Cars*, *the Sweeney*, and the ever lovable *Dixon of Dock Green* (1955–1976) and US TV shows, *Hawaii Five-O*, *Kojak*, and the *Rockford Files* to name a few, a more recent development in the televising of police programming has been the increase of police procedural dramas. Termed "factional" TV programming, these reality documentaries, constantly broadcast on mainstream media, combine real investigations with slick camerawork and incidental music. So popular have such programs become they are now made across the world, in Australia, Brazil, Mexico, Germany, the Netherlands, France, and above all, the United States where "the most successful example of the genre is . . . the US syndicated programme *COPS*, which has run for over 23 seasons. *COPS* attests to the now long-lasting popularity of the genre with viewers."[32] Series in the United Kingdom include *The Met: Policing* (BBC, 2015–present), *Secrets of a Police Marksman* (Channel 4, 2016), *Traffic Cops* (BBC, 2003–present), and *24 Hours in Police Custody* (Channel 4, 2014–present). These reality television shows either follow officers making routine calls, on hot pursuit of miscreants, or at the station engaged in "police-speak" trying to solve a crime. They openly curse—this is reality TV after all—and then, as if suddenly remembering the presence of an entire television crew, look at the camera, hand over mouth, and apologize. For those who have never encountered the police in their day-to-day lives or been involved in an investigation, such airtime does the trick of convincing viewers that the police organization operates as it does on TV. Such programs are not afraid of revealing corrupt officers either, so long as the message is put across that these form a rogue minority who will be penalized. To give one example:

In episode one of the sixth series of *24 Hours in Police Custody*, shown on Channel 4 in 2018, a member of Bedfordshire's police surveillance team is discovered trying to extort £1,000 from a married man for visiting a prostitute. After he is sentenced to eighteen months imprisonment for misconduct, his boss, Chief Inspector Jerry Waite, takes the opportunity to address the camera:

> There's no place for corrupt police officers . . . they need to be driven out. Policing's hard enough in today's society. I'm just grateful for the fact that somebody who shouldn't be a police officer has been brought to justice.[33]

This is followed by Bedfordshire's Chief Constable, Jon Boutcher, also addressing the camera. He informs viewers that the police were not happy with the leniency of Suffling's sentence so complained to the judge. As a result the court increased Suffling's sentence to three years. Proud of his power to interfere in the sentences handed out by the judiciary, Boutcher states:

> I have nothing against DC Suffling but we have a higher standard to display. There is no brushing under the carpet of what happened, there is no protection of police officers who commit crime; we cannot police our communities without the consent and support of those communities. And that's why transparency . . . is so important to policing, not only in Bedfordshire but also across the country.

If the aim of the program was to create greater assurance in the police or to boost confidence among officers, then it certainly paid off. Bedfordshire police received "multiple messages of praise" for the way they handled the program, thus fulfilling a PR objective—of reinforcing the brand, with the Chief Constable proclaiming that "the programme marks . . . a defining moment in British policing."[34] Outside the nuances of public entertainment, however, as this book has shown, there is little to suggest that either policing attitudes or the attempt to challenge unethical practices has changed in any real respect.

There is no doubt that policing programs do not merely exist to credit the police for the work they do but to provide an image of a chaotic society against some established order. Whether to instill fear or amusement in the public (both of which may be entertained), the only real moral persons are the police themselves with "other" members of the public—whether victim or suspect—reinforcing those stereotypes and myths revealed in the previous chapters, particularly when it comes to sex or race.[35] This is also true of the mentally ill who are nearly always presented as worst off, culpable, and encountered in TV cops series far more often than police officers encounter nonmentally ill suspects (whether real or imaginary). Suspects, victims, or perpetrators are denounced as nonpersons, with officers "defiling them for their very status as disordered, homeless, poor or 'other.' In this context, officers may unwittingly participate in a process that fosters the subject's felt, though often unspoken, victimisation,"[36] as seen in the 2011 riots. Thus, far from being positive, "reality programs about the police present a skewed view of law enforcement work where order maintenance and crime control are continuously emphasized and where the notion of a highly authoritarian officer is routinely depicted."[37] In these cases, "viewers are likely to believe that crime is rampant, are likely to report higher levels of victimization and are likely to push for tougher crime policy legislation."[38] Others have suggested that such programs reinforce the police as a separate professional body, protectors of the public that deal with the conflict between good and evil.[39] As Jessica Fishman argues,

> Positioned as an urban savior, the cop-hero emphasizes the public's power to authority figures, who, invested with the power of the state, are deemed responsible for maintaining law and order. In fact, not only is the public dependent upon the police to solve crime, but also to fix other problems. . . . Always available [the police] are uniquely qualified to serve justice and administer general aid to humanity.[40]

Such observations are not new. In his book *Police State* published in 1970, Brian Chapman made the observation that "what finally links the policeman to the priest, the soldier and the artist is the instinctive horror all have of chaos, and the professional lives of each are concerned with attempts to fashion some pattern and coherence from the tangled strands of human existence."[41] Who better, therefore, to remind the public of their place in the collective than the police who do not deal with individuals but "types?"

In 2015 when the BBC aired a new reality TV series showing London's Metropolitan police at work, the stereotyping of the public was done with great effect. In the fourth episode, viewers follow patrol officers as they are called out to a possible death in north London. The scene begins with the police control room receiving a call. The man on the line says: "I've just been to visit an old friend of mine and I think he's dead." Two police patrol officers are then shown in a police car heading to the scene. While staff in the control center continue speaking to the caller, officers enter a flat with the postcode on screen, locating the premises in Camden Town. As a constable rifles though the man's belongings, a voice-over states "this might be a crime scene." (In reality, if there was any suspicion of an actual crime having taken place, the officer has just contaminated every bit of DNA and failed to follow protocol by calling a senior officer).[42] Another constable picks up a photograph and says "that appears to be him and his wife in happier times" and then turns to an urn and states: "that's the ashes of his wife, 27 July 2011." The section ends with the first officer stating:

> It is quite sad to know when you're gone no one's going to miss you. I think you can be in such a busy and bustling city and feel very alone [cut to image of homeless people] the community feel is gone.

As this is a police procedural drama, it would be easy to accept, having seen the state of the dead man's flat, where his body is visible among sheets and debris, and where pornographic posters line a wall above his bed that he had indeed been unloved and uncared for, if not exactly homeless. Except, the story is a fiction. First, the dead man had not been "alone"—as the emergency call by his friend revealed, a friend who regularly met with the man to go fishing. Though the man had died through alcohol poisoning (as revealed at his inquest), it was not stated that his drinking problems had started after the death of his mother, with whom he had been close—his mother who appeared in the photograph identified by officers as his wife and whose ashes were contained in the urn.[43]

Knowing the man had no next-of-kin (information which the officers at such short notice could only have learned from questioning the man's "friend") and there being no one around to enter the property or challenge the narrative (the man in question died over the Christmas period, so few of his neighbors were around), officers presented a picture of the "loner," who, to the TV viewer, could not even be identified. In showing an image of a homeless person, the program's producers clearly wanted to present an inner city with housing projects, homelessness, and extreme poverty, all of which were emphasized by providing the wrong postcode. In reality the area portrayed was far removed from the one where the man actually lived, in Bloomsbury, central London, near the British Museum.

POLICING CULTURE

When the police were created in the early part of the nineteenth century, they set about imposing standards on the populace.[44] This included breaking up congregations of men assembling in the streets, which was seen as a "perceived attack upon a traditionally sanctioned freedom."[45] Heralded as moral overlords, the Chief Constable of Leeds led a campaign to restrict pub opening hours, leading, in the latter part of the nineteenth century, to a huge resource of police hours being put into "public-house surveillance" as "Leeds chief constables saw themselves as natural allies of the temperance movement."[46] Given special powers and seen as "a group apart from society" that took "delight in being the possessors of secret powers and secret knowledge," it was somewhat inevitable that these "blue locusts"—as they were commonly called—would regard themselves as separate and superior to the general populace.[47] Though Sir Robert Peel had heralded the police as being members of the public, it was somewhat inevitable that this was never going to work. Though no different than anyone else, police constables were given inexorable power over their fellow citizens, which even today requires continual justification, particularly in times when police officers are found to be corrupt. In many ways, therefore, the institutional powers of police officers remain unchanged today, notwithstanding PR exercises and television procedural programs, which provide new means to substantiate the moral superiority of a relatively small group of people.[48]

In 1998, Satnam Choongh carried out a series of interviews in England and Wales with individuals who had been maliciously arrested by the police but not charged with any crime. Unlike the case studies mentioned in this book, where malicious arrest occurred after individuals raised concerns with the police, the case studies Choongh identified derived from the police arresting people in the street. Those targeted included people of color (black and Asian people in equal proportion), other ethnic groups (e.g., travelers, gypsies), and the homeless.[49] Choongh distinguished the treatment meted out to individuals in these groups as *police* cases as distinct from *criminal* cases. In criminal cases, a person is arrested and charged on suspicion of committing a crime. In contrast, *police* cases target individuals to "achieve police goals" these being "to subordinate sections of society viewed as anti-police and innately criminal."[50]

The idea that some people are innately criminal and in need of control is the underlying ethos of policing, regardless of where one lives in the world. Police officers stand on the thin blue line between order and disorder, thus supporting the group-speak of "delinquents," "yobs," "evil doers," or "culprits," which fit the political and sociological patterns of policing taught on college policing courses.[51] However, the general belief that human nature is *defective* has a much longer history with its roots in the Judeo–Christian tradition, finalized as a *political* philosophy in the seventeenth century. The beliefs of Thomas Hobbes detailed in his book *Leviathan* (first published in 1651) form the bedrock of classical criminology and still underpin policing and criminological courses. Human nature is regarded as intrinsically flawed, with each person engaged in a war of all against all (the state of nature). Without the rule of law human life is "nasty brutish and short," so an authoritarian sovereign is required to create and maintain order.[52]

That a philosophical theory more than three hundred years old should justify a policing culture that sees itself as both "modern" and "of the people" may seem incongruous. Yet Hobbes's philosophy is as prevalent today as when *Leviathan* was written during the English civil war. Individuals agree to give up their *natural right*—their right to do whatever they like—in exchange for the protection of the state. This agreement is called the "social contract" and, in modern times, can be understood as a tacit consent to obey the law. Through recognizing the necessity of a sovereign to keep the deviant characteristics of human nature at bay (notwithstanding these characteristics being part of one's own nature), those who refuse to adhere to the rules are punished, enabling everyone else to live in peace—or so the theory goes. On a deeper level, it is not difficult to see how this general view of humanity pervades much of the Western worldview, with the need for both laws and an imposed morality that justifies the authoritarian nature of the state.[53] Reattributed to modern-day policing, the autocrat is replaced by parliamentary democracy, while tacit consent (the social contract) applies to obeying the law and *policing by consent*.[54]

The belief that human beings live in peace due entirely to the rule of law and the social contract has come to underpin many contemporary theories in policing, from social control to broken windows theory. However, it is the social disciplinary model of policing, first established in the courts of New York, that has seen *policing by consent* put to the test.

In 1995 Mike McConville and Chester Mirsky revealed how social discipline was being applied to defendants in New York. In exchange for a lighter sentence, those charged with a crime were told to plead guilty whether they were guilty or innocent. Avoiding the expense of court and thus due process (the need to call witnesses), defendants were given just fifteen seconds to accept the sentences offered. They were told that if they refused to do so the outcome would be far worse.[55] This method of "plea bargaining" was gradually exported to other countries around the world, namely England and Wales. While in 2015 it was estimated that "44% of documented miscarriages of justice in the United States involved cases where the defendant had pleaded guilty," the situation in England and Wales was recorded in 2014 as standing at 70 percent.[56] As McConville has recently said:

> Increasingly, England and Wales is dependent upon pressurizing defendants into pleading Guilty and avoiding trial and does so with various institutionalized threats and sweeteners.[57]

When carrying out his research into *police* cases in England and Wales, Choongh discovered that the social discipline model, as meted out to defendants in plea bargaining cases in the United States, had been adopted by police agencies in the United Kingdom in other ways. This was expressed not in terms of sentencing but in "the police objectives of reproducing social control . . . by extracting deference and inflicting summary punishment."[58] The similarity with the "plea bargaining" cases was the assurance that such behavior is "not subjected to scrutiny by a court," thereby targeting the most vulnerable in society.[59] As Choongh states:

> Having identified the "criminal classes," the police are then justified in subjecting them to surveillance and subjugation, regardless of whether the individuals selected for this treatment are violating the criminal law at any given moment.[60]

Though the case studies in this book reveal that discrediting individuals does not discriminate among the sexes, race, or class, there is no doubt that an authoritarian attitude lies at the heart of policing culture—a pervading ethos which has not changed since its inception. Choongh acknowledges that, "despite the lack of any law which requires citizens to show respect to the police, officers clearly expect respect to be forthcoming and will not condone any challenge to their authority," which leads to "resentment on the part of the citizen and encourages the very type of challenge which so annoys the police."[61] Making certain people appear *special* necessarily lowers the status of those others not in the superior social group. While police officers may pick on the most vulnerable—namely the poor and the unemployed—the police institution, by its very nature, holds the public in contempt. When "policing strategies appear to revolve around efforts to neutralise the anti-authority elements in society by forcing them to accept, as one officer put it, 'the authority of the cloth,' how could this be otherwise?"[62] Disregarding guidelines and the law, the police then behave in a manner which "knows best." As Choongh illustrates: In one case a black youth was detained for five hours at the police station contrary to PACE regulations, simply because he wanted officers to return his watch. "Although he quickly realized that he was not going to get very far and announced he would leave the station, his temerity in challenging police control in the station was not allowed to go unpunished. He was arrested."[63]

Choongh noted that regular detainees recognize that police bullying can be avoided if they say nothing, whereupon officers label them "good as gold," while anyone who challenges police authority—by swearing, criticizing, complaining, demanding, or making any type of request—is labeled "obnoxious."

Because those who are arrested without charge and are likely to engage in plea bargaining are mainly poor or powerless to know their rights, and while, as seen in chapter 2, the PEACE method of investigative interviewing is supposed to ensure fairness in police questioning, police officers were reported to behave in exactly the same way in England and Wales as their US counterparts, using "the opportunity of interrogation to ask detainees *any* question they want, and in any *manner* they want, regardless of whether it relates to the original suspicion . . . they have no rights."[64] Both inside and outside the police station such behaviors send a signal to those the police have targeted (usually from the same backgrounds as themselves) that they are the authorities who cannot and should not be challenged.

That "police see themselves as the embodiment of authority" and deliberately target those who disagree or question this authority still prevails. As one witness told the author, regarding an event witnessed in London in 2015:

> I saw two police officers harassing a group of Muslim men . . . One man was handcuffed and being forcefully restrained on the ground and he was clearly in pain . . . A man went up to the police and shouted "what the fuck are you doing, can't you see you're hurting him?" upon which he was arrested and shoved into the back of a police car for "using foul language." I said to the police, "I bet you use far worse language when you're in the pub with your mates." The police officer told me to mind my own business, stating, "anyway I'm a Christian, I uphold moral values." . . . I've seen police officers do this several times, just harass ethnic minorities who are doing nothing . . . they do it because they can.

This treatment can only operate within a system which believes that the use of aggression or force is right even if it targets innocent individuals. This utilitarian philosophy dispenses with the rights of a minority on the presumption that it maintains public harmony. It is underpinned by the anthropocentric view that places human beings as separate and superior to the nonhuman world and, thus, posits *certain* humans as superior to others.[65] An anthropocentric worldview operates on a deeply engrained dichotomy: For some people to hold power, there must necessarily exist those who are power*less*. Because *in reality* no person is worth less than or more than any other, this position creates perpetual antagonism or distrust of those in power and vice versa since neither can survive without the other. Appeal to "democratic values" is overridden by the utilitarian principle that what matters is the "greater good." This permits individuals to be sacrificed—discredited or actually harmed—as if the greater good is *more than* the sum of those individuals who comprise the public. As security is awarded only to those who fulfill certain credentials imposed by the state, whatever these might be (e.g., white, married, middle-class, employed, etc.), it risks members of the public outside this criteria being more likely to be targeted by the police whenever some *perceived* criteria are not met. Given that these criteria remain hidden (in routine activity theory, for instance, a person is regarded as more likely to be a criminal if they are single than married), the methods by which members of the public are judged is not only kept hidden but remain spurious because, of course, no theory can be applied to officers themselves. To compensate for any perceived insecurities this may cause, police officers are promoted not as superior *moral* beings but as heroes willing to put their lives on the line for the public they serve—a fiction which not only sets the police further apart from the general public but masks police malpractice, including child sexual abuse.[66] As Samuel Jones states:

> Cultural allegiance to the "hero cop" narrative has contributed to the construction and preservation of a schema that enables and protects sexually deviant police officers. The circumstance enables exceptionally dangerous officers to shroud themselves under the cloak of law enforcement's reputation for trustworthiness to commit unspeakable offenses against our nation's most vulnerable group: our children.[67]

As seen in the literature and case studies, however, this applies not only to children, but to anyone who questions police authority, including fellow police officers whose "'Blue Wall of Silence' correlates with a plethora of counterproductive and hazardous results."[68]

To be clear, there need be no actual heroics involved for the police-as-hero rhetoric to be espoused. The term "hero" is the ultimate prize reserved for that group which is seen as *essential* to the collective's survival, even though few members of the public have contact with police officers on a daily basis. Even where policing may be regarded as high risk, not every police officer who may protect a member of the public will be regarded as a hero. Officers who run to the scene of a suspected terrorist attack are, of course, always regarded as heroes even if no actual heroism is involved,[69] while the sergeant who stood in front of Simon to protect him from being tasered by his colleagues is not and will never be a hero. Caring and heroism do not mix.

This raises a further problem with the use of the term "'discretion'—the bedrock of policing."[70] Though usually understood as referring to policing decisions whether to charge a person for a minor crime, it does not explain the activities of individual officers who, when questioned regarding their decision-making, might claim they were using their power of discretion. When the police officer told Melissa Ross that she was forbidden to attend to Eilidh Cairns as she lay dying in the road (see chapter 4) it can hardly be said that police discretion guided his decision-making. Yet nowhere do police guidelines state that a stranger is not permitted to help a dying cyclist or that only family members are allowed to offer sympathy or support. And when, in the case of Simon, the police sergeant was tasered in the course of protecting this vulnerable young man, it would seem equally obtuse to suggest that he too was acting out of discretion, rather than saying he was being human. But if one officer is *humane* and another acts in deference to his own policing powers (ignoring the cries from a dying woman), one needs to ask what *values* lie behind these particular motivations?

Anna Kopec-Massey's work on the role of empathy in social enterprise can help answer this question. Empathy, Kopec-Massey argues, is an ability "to understand what the other person is feeling," as well as "the emotional instinct to help and feel something of that person's suffering." Empathy performs "an important function in society as it contributes to our understanding of right and wrong and individual gain versus collective gain."[71] Serving both an emotional and cognitive function, empathy contributes to organizational behavior and to the way social organizations treat members of the public. As an instinctual phenomenon, "empathy may lead a person to act (e.g., in witnessing a person in pain) for in feeling the suffering of another . . . we connect in a shared reality exposing the human need for mutual dependency."[72] As an emotion, a cognitive process and an activity (which has been identified in infants as early as eight months old), it must thus be asked what has gone wrong when a person (such as the police officer arriving on the scene of Eilidh Cairns' death) fails to identify with "the other" and act appropriately—out of empathy for another human being? This lack occurs when instead of identifying oneself as part of the whole—be it the species *human being* or, in a wider scope, as part of nature—one aligns oneself almost exclusively with a specific group—be it a particular culture, ethnicity, religious affiliation, nation state, political party, or more narrowly, a specific organization. Though it is rare for individuals to take just one identity rather than several, where a particular group takes primary place among one's concerns, respect for others becomes problematic. In the sphere of social enterprise, Kopec-Massey argues, this is illustrated by "family run businesses [which] may exhibit a high level of empathy due to the relationship ties, obligations and ethics of care . . . but . . . may become directed to self or family-interest rather than to the greater social or collective good."[73]

Police officers refer to the policing institution as a family. The "police family" relates not only to colleagues but also to policing agencies across the world. Left out of this "family" are the general public who the police are supposed to represent. Within a public facing office, placing the family first should be seen as extremely problematic, for the very notion of a "police family" disbands the reason why the police service was established. The police *may be* the public, in the same way that every person is part of the human race, but allegiances and interests are served to this group *ahead of* or *despite* the general public who are not even related. Those closest to the police family—their "cousins" so to speak, tolerate policing behavior as they exist to support it—lawyers, coroners, politicians, all of whom have the same vested interest within *their* institutions as the police have in theirs—to uphold a superior social position—as law enforcers. There is a difference, however, as the "families" of the judicial system are less intact than those of the police, though no less incestuous. If the public are not part of the family, it should come as no surprise if a police officer's natural empathy is conditioned to limit itself to the policing institution contrary to Sir Peel's original recommendations. Often compared with the military, the comparison, is, in this sense, inequitable. The military *necessarily* stick together to fight a warring party, whereas the police are supposed to act, foremost, if not entirely, for the public good.

An absence of empathy "defines some of the worst things in society" and "has been shown as a key characteristic that psychopaths do not possess; in terms of feeling remorse or guilt."[74] Could it be this which permits an officer to shoo away a person aiding a dying woman lying under the wheels of a tipper truck lorry? Could it be a lack of empathy which fails to recognize the vulnerability of a disabled woman being tormented by her neighbors, as illustrated in chapter 1? Or an absence of empathy that is responsible for maliciously arresting a woman who complains of abuse at her son's school? If poor policing is the result of a lack of empathy, then the whole meaning of police discretion is questionable. The following statement by a police volunteer is illustrative of this point:

> A mentally ill man was causing trouble on a train, shouting and kicking passengers. He had been stopped by two Metropolitan police officers in one corner of a carriage who were travelling off duty. A BTP [British Transport Police] officer was called to the train. He spoke to the man who soon calmed down and started to trust him. When we arrived at the mainline station . . . the officer took the man off the train by gently holding his arm. He told the man to sit down on a seat on the platform as he took out his handcuffs. The man pleaded with the officer not to cuff him so he called for back up. Minutes later, five officers arrived on the scene and proceeded to handcuff the man who had, until then been sitting patiently, doing nothing. As the officers arrived he flew into a panic. Screaming and cowering, I watched as officers pushed him onto the ground and placed his arm behind his back. They literally dragged him along the concourse to the police station. I have no doubt that had the [original] officer not had the intent to cuff him the man would have willingly permitted himself to be led to the station un-cuffed.

If a lack of empathy is a pathology, this may explain why police officers are often indifferent or lacking in what most of us would regard as natural concern. The hierarchies of the police institution, with its need to call managers "Ma'am" and "Sir" and its deference to itself as a family already sets the police service apart from any other occupation (except the military); deconstructing these cultural structures would therefore be a first step in breaking down the boundaries between the organization and the public. Given that empathy is a requirement "to act fast in times of danger or crisis," which is "a pivotal motivation for promoting the survival of others,"[75] it should be at the forefront of policing, taking precedence over the "hero-cop."

In England, the mass demonstrations that took place in 2009 and 2010 illustrate how far the negative view of human nature is entrenched within UK policing. Writing in 2009, Her Majesty's Inspectorate of Constabulary

(HMIC) identified significant shortcomings in the police being able to manage peaceful protests caused by the attitude of viewing crowds as defensive and potentially violent, rather than peaceful.[76] The mass riots that took place in 2011 across Britain should therefore not have come as a shock. As discussed in chapter 2, these occurred following the shooting of Mark Duggan by Metropolitan police in Tottenham, north London, on August 4, 2011. Many reasons have been cited for the riots but most believe that the deciding factor was Duggan's death and the way police officers dealt with the immediate aftermath of the shooting. Officers failed to inform the family of his death and confronted peaceful demonstrators, who had congregated outside Tottenham town hall seeking answers, in full riot gear. The claim that the police were the likely cause of the riots was ignored by policing agencies and in the mainstream media. Two academics even wrote of the event: "how reliant we are on the bravery and public service ethos of the thick blue line of officers standing between chaos and order,"[77] thus repeating the Hobbesian mantra that without authoritarian rule chaos would ensue.[78] It is somewhat ironic therefore that "the thick blue line" had failed to prevent the riots from occurring in the first place.

Interviews with those who took part in the riots revealed the cause to be more complex, with police behavior having a much larger effect than realized. As Raeka Prasad reported for *The Guardian*:

> One 17-year-old Muslim, who was in full-time work in Tottenham, north London, and took part in the riots, told researchers of an episode when he was stopped by police on his way to school when he was 13: "One of them said to the other one: 'Mate, why don't you ask him where Saddam [Hussein] is. He might be able to help out.' They're supposed to be law enforcement. I hate the police. I don't hate the policing system, I hate the police on the street. I hate them from the bottom of my heart." Another rioter, aged 34 and also from north London, described an incident when he was aged 12, claiming he was thrown into a police van, handcuffed, beaten, kicked, spat on and called "nigger" and "black bastard." In later life he said he had never "gotten over [his anger] with the police," compounded, he claimed, by three instances in which attempts were made to fabricate charges against him, including one involving a knife.[79]

These comments—a reverse of the Hobbesian position—show that people act on the basis on how they see reality, determined not merely by opinion but individual experience.[80] As another interviewee claimed:

> [The police] just generally class you as someone that's bad like that . . . it really irritates me because I'm not like that kinda bad person, it's just that I get frustrated at police people thinking they can just talk to you like you're some, any other hoodlum, and know you're stupid . . . and talk to you like you're a

> five-year-old and you don't know what you're doing, but I'm the police, so you have to listen to me.[81]

The fact that the College of Policing needs to remind senior management that people in the United Kingdom have the right to peaceful protest unhindered by the authorities is worrying.[82] It suggests that the "us" versus "them" mentality remains prevalent, regardless of legislation or guidance.[83] Perhaps it is time to rethink public protection and crime fighting given that the police—as a separate body, with its unique powers—has, since its inception, been too open to abuse, with officers who raise concerns trapped behind "the blue wall of silence."[84] For a new organization to emerge, however, requires turning police culture and its concepts on their head and to recognize that the real heroes (if indeed there need be heroes) are those who act from their common humanity and not for the opportunity to gain commendation or for any other public recognition. After all, while the police are supposed *to be* the public, as Sir Peel said, the public *are* the police.

CONCLUSION

The view of an "us" and "them" society where police officers operate from a different set of values than the general populace may not be as apparent as it appeared some 250 years ago, but it still exists, at the edges, encountered by victims and complainants, in poor policing investigations, the use of surveillance, and a "we know best" attitude which denies many the opportunity of justice. If the state is supposed to act as role model to the populace in terms of integrity and ethics, then it has a long way to go given the failure of policing agencies to address a flagging complaints system where complainants can be discredited with impunity. Undoubtedly this leaves state authorities with a problem—not the traditional one of why anyone should obey the state given cases of injustice, but why consent should freely be given to a state authority whose power can be so readily and harshly overreached? Given that democratic governments can ignore criticism even when evidence is presented against their own policies, it should come as no surprise if the police are not held accountable when things go wrong.[85] If politicians can openly ignore facts—and we are, to an extent, living in a postfact world—then, depressingly, the institutions that represent the state—the courts, police officers, coroners, pathologists—are unlikely to change because the incentive to do so does not yet exist.

Police investigations depend entirely on the public coming forward, not only to report crimes but also to act as witnesses. Without public support, policing services cannot work. In this sense policing by consent is no mere catch phrase. Knowing that officers may behave as they like, often with the full support of members of the judiciary—and even the government—may not be a sentiment that those in power wish revealed, as it heralds a flagging system hanging on by the skin of its teeth. Nevertheless, the revelations and case studies revealed in this book should act as a wake-up call to those who want to see integrity and human rights at the heart of the legal system, rather than on the periphery.

The purpose of law is to mitigate harm. Yet access to legal services remains unaffordable to most people, especially (though no doubt not exclusively) in the United Kingdom. This must be seen as part of the problem in challenging malpractice within the policing system because the only way most people can ever hope to hold the police accountable (as well as protect themselves) is via the courts. In a true democracy, each individual should have access to free legal advice, particularly given the fact that those they come up against have lawyers to support them at every stage (particularly senior officers within the police service) and given that the CPS can act to entice people to plead guilty, against their better interests. As McConville and Marsh state:

> The very "rights" once said to be the "British tradition" . . . have either not existed in fact or have been dismantled by judges, aided and abetted by official inquiries . . . and by politicians engaged in populist "law and order" campaigns. At root, while espousing fidelity to individual rights and upholding them occasionally, there has been almost unconditional support for police practices in the face of known police illegality.[86]

Though not ideal, a National Legal Service, run through taxation, similar to the NHS could help redress this balance or at least permit ordinary members of the public, who are discredited or harmed by police officers, to have the same recourse to legal action as the rich. Just as there will always be people who are willing to pay for private health care, this would undoubtedly not change with the introduction of a legal service (since most NHS consultants work both for the general public and in private practice). Assuring that legal advice is available at the point of need would create a healthier, more equal society, and help challenge the efficacy of those policing practices and behaviors that remain largely hidden from public view.

Cultures transform when efforts are made to put policies into practice that are transparent and aim to meet expectations; they do not change on their own. Treating people well should not be a matter of "belief" or "disbelief" but one of accepting a concern and carrying out an investigation. In many cases, poor treatment by police officers of the public is so blindingly obvious, as the cases in this book reveal, it remains shocking that they still occur without any redress and without any acknowledgment of failure on the part of the police service or their cohorts.

The extent of this failure goes beyond the valid but often unfair criticism that police are failing to solve crimes or catch those terrorizing local neighborhoods.[87] It also goes beyond the criticism that individual officers are to blame for their colleague's behavior or that alternative models are unavailable. As the Close Passing Initiative elucidated in chapter 4 shows, policing initiatives may have profound benefits for the public and break the mold of the patriarchal "us" and "them" culture, which for too long has been permitted to prevail. It also shows that in every profession, including the police service, there are those who wish to genuinely benefit society.

Conclusion

This book has shown that the police's self-referential attitude—its "inner uniform"—may lead to bias in policing investigations, a breakdown in social order, and a lack of public trust. This is exacerbated by police officers using their power of discretion to subdue a right to criticism. As many members of the judiciary support the police in their endeavors even when things go wrong, the police remain unaccountable. This leaves members of the public with no means of redress.

Chapter 1 began with a brief discussion on the nature of police discretion and the distinction between "victim" and "complainant." With officers habitually disbelieving certain victims and where the justice system demands criminal convictions for the "status" of victimhood to be conferred in some cases but not others, the chapter revealed how the ambiguity between these terms has led to both victims *and* complainants being discredited by officers. Though discrediting complainants was shown to be nothing new (as Steven Box and Ken Russell revealed in 1975), research reveals that the same tactics are still being used today. These include defamation of character, malicious arrest, and regarding the complainant as mentally ill. New means of discrediting complainants were also revealed. These include writing to complainants' employers demanding they be sacked and using the (new) tools of social media, particularly Twitter. Several examples were provided of women who had gone to the police with claims of abuse and harassment, only to be accused of wasting police time. They were subsequently murdered. Aside from these cases, several incidents of people hit by police vehicles showed how officers may seek to discredit those they harm to conceal any fault on their part.

The chapter then focused on the Hillsborough stadium disaster that occurred on April 25. 1989, leading to the deaths of ninety-six football fans.

It was discovered that the same tactics of abuse identified by Box and Russell had been meted out to those suffering from bereavement, with officers openly mocking the victims of the tragedy. The Independent Panel (2012) into the events of Hillsborough revealed how officers' accounts had been doctored to suit a particular media image of the police, exonerating senior officers while blaming victims. Though the second inquest held in 2016 concluded that fans had been unlawfully killed, no means of redress has ever been available to survivors' families.

The chapter ended with the story of Kay, one of several participants interviewed for the book. Kay, a middle-aged disabled woman who complained to the police of repeated antisocial behavior from her neighbors, including violence, was discredited by officers in various ways. Police failed to inform her that CCTV footage installed to catch criminal activity was being overridden without her knowledge; she was maliciously arrested and forced to move homes; and when found innocent of all charges was placed on a covert police database as being mentally ill.

The chapter showed that other victims, including police whistleblowers, may be subjected to similar or different policing practices but with the same aim—to silence their concerns to protect the institution from any unwelcome criticism. The experiences of Chief Inspector Clara Williams and Detective Superintendent Pete Jackson were given as two examples and case studies were provided by two other participants, both police officers, maliciously arrested for raising concerns about colleagues.

Chapter 2 examined bias in police investigations. Implicit bias was shown to have several meanings, from being equated with personal preferences (particular likes or dislikes) or held to be synonymous with unconscious biases—which, being unaware, means individuals cannot be held responsible. Popularized by Harvard University with its Implicit Association Test (IAT) and sold to corporations around the world, implicit bias was thrown into question when applied to police agencies and to police practices as distinct from theory. With onus placed on individual responsibility, implicit bias was seen as an excuse for institutional forms of bias such as racism.

Discussion then turned to confirmation bias—an umbrella term with various branches including hypothesis bias, premature case closure, and tunnel vision. Confirmation bias was seen as appropriated by police when officers believe they are in the right even when evidence points to the contrary or has not been adequately gathered. Convinced of a belief without exploring alternative views is a major cause of miscarriages of justice, wrongful arrest, and disbelief in victims' narratives and may account for dozens of homicides being dismissed as suicides or deaths by natural causes. The case of Ricky Reel provided an example. When Reel's body was found in the river Thames a week after he went missing, officers immediately ruled that he had committed suicide even though a racist attack prior to his disappearance points to the likelihood that he had been killed.

In the United States, the method of interrogation known as the Reid technique was shown to be a further tool in creating bias. The Reid technique permits officers to openly mislead suspects to gain a confession. Several notorious cases were presented on how the technique had contributed to several miscarriages of justice, including that of Marvin Anderson, who served twenty years for rape, even though the real culprit had confessed to the crime over twelve years previously.

Miscarriages of justice associated with various forms of confirmation bias were revealed to have occurred in Sweden, the Netherlands, and the United Kingdom. In the United Kingdom, confirmation bias was also revealed as a major component in discrediting complainants and those not found guilty of any crime.

A case study examined the treatment of Georgina Halford-Hall. Maliciously arrested after raising concerns regarding child abuse at her son's boarding school, she was subsequently arrested and tried for breaching the Data Protection Act. After full exoneration, the senior officer responsible for her arrest accepted the poorness of the police's investigation when abuse at the school came to light several years later. Bias against Halford-Hall had prevented any investigation into the school's activities from taking place. The case of Christopher Jefferies, vilified in the press for his personal appearance, was also discussed. Though he was of any crime, officers had jumped to the conclusion that Jefferies was guilty of the murder of his tenant, Joanna Yeates, and had passed this information onto the press.

The chapter explored how bias might be avoided. This included an examination of the Dutch model of contrarians who oversee police investigations in the Netherlands. It was shown that even though oversight bias remains prevalent, the complexity of what leads to bias is not fully recognized. Though the Independent Office for Police Conduct in England and Wales (IOPC) has sought to avoid bias by recommending the introduction of a system similar to that employed in the aviation industry, this offers merely an attempt to shift the blame in the police to one of learning.[1] Such an initiative is unlikely to undo the damage done to victims of police behavior because it suggests that individuals, rather than the institution, are responsible when things go wrong, thus maintaining the status quo of the police institution as a whole.

Chapter 3 focused on describing covert policing practices, the purpose of which remain ambiguous, unethical, or in breach of the Human Rights Act. The "spy-cops scandal" was presented as a known example of such ambiguity coming to light in recent years, which is the story of a secret section of the

Metropolitan police, who from 1968 to 2008 were known as the Special Demonstration Squad (since rebranded: the National Public Order Intelligence Unit) and officers were deployed to infiltrate political groups. Revealed in 2010 by two police whistleblowers, Mark Kennedy and Peter Francis, the story came to light via two *Guardian* journalists, Rob Evans and Paul Lewis. They revealed the lengths police officers will go to garner information, taking the identities of dead children, and having sexual relations and children with innocent members of the public.[2]

Much less known but more common than the activities of the SDS are the covert roles played by police and family liaison officers (PLOs and FLOs). The chapter revealed how these officers covertly monitor individuals and innocent members of the public but receive little public attention. As revealed, however, the role of PLOs is to infiltrate and befriend demonstrators to gather information, while FLOs investigate those bereaved by homicide, road deaths, or other tragedies. Since the majority of those being monitored are innocent of any crime, this has led to family members and peaceful protesters being treated as suspects simply by voicing an opinion or being related to someone involved in a police investigation.

Aside from the deployment of officers for specific investigative purposes, covert monitoring of innocent members of the public was seen in records held on several police databases. This includes the United Kingdom's Police National Database (PND), set up in 2011 as a national register for those working with vulnerable adults and children. By 2013 the database held more than 1.8 billion records on innocent civilians, with records being kept until a person reaches one hundred years of age. Noted as "police intelligence," these records may not be readily accessed even by the subject concerned, in contradiction to the Data Protection Act 2018.

The chapter discussed the implications of keeping such records and showed the effect with regard to employment. Other databases included the National Domestic Extremist Database (NDED), which counts among its files that of John Catts, a peaceful antiwar demonstrator with no criminal record. Aside from these records, it was revealed that the British police hold more than nineteen million images of members of the public which the European Court of Human Rights ruled in 2012 should be deleted for breaching Section 8 of the Human Rights Act. However, to date, neither the police nor the government has made any attempt to erase these images.

Two case studies were provided of police complainants who found themselves covertly diagnosed as mentally ill without any psychiatric assessment having been conducted. Alec, a farmer, applied for a shotgun license but was targeted by police when it became clear they had made a mistake confusing him with his father. As Alec's story revealed, two psychiatric reports were commissioned by police officers without any doctor having actually met with him, while a letter of referral from his GP (stating he had no mental health issues) was ignored. In a completely different scenario, Theodore complained to police regarding the noise of HGVs illegally using his road in the early hours of the morning. Though confirmed as problematic in a local government report, police officers chose to dispute his claims. Instead, officers informed his local mental health board that he was seeing and hearing things. Neither Alec nor Theodore felt they could ever trust the police again, with Alec having to abandon the family business and move to another part of the United Kingdom in order to gain employment.

Books on the police ignore the issue of police investigations into road deaths, which is surprising as every year in Britain around four times the number of people killed by murder die in road traffic collisions. Chapter 4 examined policing behavior toward the most vulnerable road death users: pedestrians and cyclists. It showed that while guidelines exist for road death investigations as for homicides, there is no obligation for officers to adhere to published instructions. This revealed a deep malaise within many investigations and may explain confirmation bias and the discrediting of victims not just in road death cases but across the spectrum, from missing persons to murder. Interviews with victims' families revealed the extent of the problem. They included one of the most harrowing accounts to come to light in recent years, that of the death of Eilidh Cairns, killed by a tipper truck lorry in 2009.

After police refused to properly investigate Eilidh's death, and with the police collision investigator charged with fraud, the Cairns family conducted their own investigation, finding key witnesses the police had ignored. The family also demanded that the police test the eyesight of the lorry driver. It took the police nearly three months to do so when it was discovered the driver had defective vision. Too late, according to the defense, to make a case for dangerous or careless driving (it was argued that his eyesight might have deteriorated since the death of Eilidh Cairns); the driver was fined and permitted to carry on driving. He then went on to kill Nora Gutmann, a ninety-seven-year-old Holocaust survivor on a pedestrian crossing. The preventability of Nora's death and the bizarre circumstances surrounding the investigation into Eilidh's death (including the pending court case against the forensic collisions expert) revealed a fine line between corruption and incompetence. This was exacerbated in other cases, namely that of Toni Rolls, killed by a distracted driver on a pedestrian walkway; Jake Thompson, killed by a speeding lorry on a pedestrian crossing; and James Sutton, killed by a speeding police car. In the case of James Sutton, officers claimed that the police car had a malfunctioning recording system when it was booked out that day. This meant that video evidence of the collision, which should have been available as evidence, was nonexistent. In all these cases, families were left to piece together the facts of the events surrounding the deaths of their loved ones, with officers either conducting poor investigations or taking no interest but, in each case, blaming the victims for his or her demise.

The chapter then focused on the attitudes of police officers toward road users, particularly cyclists. The head of the Metropolitan police's Units Road Policing division made clear that he thought victims were largely to blame for their own demise, refusing to accept that most drivers are at fault. A different scenario and attitude was presented from two police constables working for West Midlands Constabulary. As transcripts from a House of Lords select committee in 2017 reveal, police constables Mark Hodson and Steve Hudson recognize that 98 percent of cyclists who are killed or seriously injured on Britain's roads die near junctions owing to the behavior of drivers. In actively trying to prevent future deaths by working as undercover cyclists stopping careless drivers who disregard the safety of vulnerable road users, these officers created the Close Passing Initiative. Though it is unknown if the scheme will help to improve police investigations of drivers who seriously harm or kill cyclists, the actions of PCs Hodson and Hudson show that poor policing investigations are the result of poor supervision and training.

With institutions within the criminal justice system all too ready to support, if not actively contribute toward, poor policing practices, chapter 5 focused on other members of the criminal justice system that work closely with the police. Those discussed include coroners, pathologists, US medical examiners, and crown prosecutors (the CPS). It was shown that the anomaly in England and Wales between forensic pathologists—paid for by the police and hospital pathologists paid by the coroner—has led to serious errors within police investigations because hospital pathologists are not trained to look for nonbiological causes of death. This means that autopsy reports, written for the coroner, contain statements from the police as to the cause of death. That such reports should contain mere hearsay evidence is fully acknowledged by the GMC.

In examining the role of the coroner's court, the law against self-incrimination revealed the unlikelihood of discovering the facts of a case, even though this is the sole purpose of an inquest. Documents regarding the death of Toni Rolls showed the extent to which a coroner's office may intrude into the police investigation. In the case of James Sutton, it was revealed how breaches were made in calling the jury, while the inquest into Eilidh Cairns showed how the coroner favored bias in the police investigation.

In the United States where the medical examiner performs the dual role of pathologist and coroner, bias was seen as being no less likely to occur, as illustrated in the case of Joseph Osborne. Accused of murdering his five-year-old stepson, Osborne was found guilty when the medical examiner ordered the exhumation of the child's body several months after burial and created an imagined hand print from a death mask. Though the evidence of the handprint was scientifically disputed, Osborne was sentenced to life imprisonment where he remains to date. In the interim, the examiner was struck off from the medical register after it was revealed he had never actually qualified in forensic pathology, though he is still permitted to be called as an expert witness.

The CPS, established in the United Kingdom in the late 1980s, was then discussed in relation to police organizations. While the CPS are supposed to act independently of the police, it was seen that the opposite is the case. Crown prosecutors base their decisions whether to prosecute a suspect based entirely on the recommendations of the police. That members of the public are unaware of this process, through no fault of their own, was illustrated with a poster by the London cycling campaign.

Several examples where the police and the CPS failed to disclose evidence to defense lawyers were then provided, drawing on recent discoveries from BBCs *File on 4* journalists, which show the failure of several police agencies to properly examine evidence, leading to a host of false charges, arrests, and miscarriages of justice. The Victims Right to Review scheme, whereby a victim can challenge a failure to charge a suspect by asking for a review of the case, was also examined and shown to be lacking. The strong links between officers and prosecutors was then discussed in relation to George, a teenager falsely charged with rape. Even when police discovered that his accuser had lied, eighteen months later the CPS still decided to prosecute, though on the first day of trial the case was dropped.

In a criminal justice system where the question of responsibility when things go wrong remains abstruse, a major problem lies with accountability. Chapter 6 aimed to address this issue, starting with the failure in the United Kingdom of a coherent and workable police complaint system. As shown, most complaints about the police are investigated by the officers own professional standards department (PSD), which has no vested interest in upholding complaints against its own members. As a result, the complainant is usually informed there is no case to answer, or a process to discredit the complainant occurs to support the officer in question.

Examples were presented of how officers and other policing bodies attempt to silence complainants, including misuse of the term "vexatious" and by sharing data with other organizations, which, like the Information Commissioner's Office (ICO), have their own police representative ensuring a lack of transparency and justice. Some remedial suggestions on how the police complaints system may be improved were suggested, but it was seen that an ethos of hegemony that sees complainants as a perceived threat to the bureaucratic interests of the police halts the possibility of progress.

Two major case studies illustrated the point: Stella, a barrister whose mentally ill son was repeatedly and unnecessarily tasered by officers, was hounded by police on social media and in her workplace after she made a complaint. Another, Sharon, was victimized after protecting her daughter from a street brawl. Violently assaulted by a police officer, Sharon was maliciously arrested for assault by the same officer. Even when exonerated, with the judge advising her to take civil action against the police, Sharon had no financial means of doing so because officers had contacted her employer, resulting in the loss of her job.

Police forces in the United Kingdom spend more than £36 million per year on PR, money which does not include police procedural dramas, which follow officers in the line of duty. The purpose of making such programs was seen as presenting an image of the police as protectors of the public, without whom there would be chaos. This led to an examination of police culture and the social disciplinary model of policing, which was found to be still prevalent in cases of plea bargaining, whereby a suspect is dissuaded from legal redress.

An understanding of the nature of empathy was then discussed alongside the attitude of the police institution as a "police family," which excludes nonmembers and leads to a lack of consideration for others. The treatment of Eilidh Cairns and the attitudes of police officers to those who took part in the Tottenham riots in north London in 2011 were provided as examples, with the need for a new type of police training and a more open-minded criminal justice system presented as a means to resolve some of the tensions and behaviors presented in this book. The chapter concluded with some remedies for public redress, including the proposal of a national legal service run along similar lines to the NHS, for members of the public to gain protection from a police institution that often fails their interests.

Officers may argue that the sheer amount of horror seen and dealt with on a daily basis as part of the job numbs one to the facts, but, as this book has shown, there is no excuse for poor investigations or discrediting the public. Moreover, policing is not unique in dealing with tragedy, nor in seeing the more morose side of the human ego. Doctors, nurses, firefighters, and others all deal with gruesome incidents, and there are few accident and emergency rooms in British hospitals where beds are freely available.[3] While members of the public might not wish to see police discretion minimized, the very use of discretionary powers was never meant to legitimize uncontrollable use of a Taser or the killing of innocent civilians such as Jean-Charles de Menezes.

In the case of de Menezes, killed by officers on July 22, 2005, a host of mistakes occurred, which the gold commander, Cressida Dick, admitted would likely reoccur in future.[4] Surveillance officers mistook him for someone else; he was tailed as he took a bus and then followed into a London underground station, which he approached calmly, entering his ticket in the barrier and making his way to the train like any other commuter—an electrician on his way to work. Though the admission of mistakes has been accepted, it remains extraordinary to many that the person who ordered that de Menezes be stopped "at all costs" was later promoted to the most senior policing position in the United Kingdom.[5]

The death of de Menezes and the lack of promises that serious errors could be avoided in future continues to raise doubt about police intelligence. Though de Menezes may be the worst case scenario for British justice, this book has established that members of the public, who are not trained investigators, are nevertheless able to establish the truth of events, so a trained police force has little excuse. The constant refrain within the police service that "austerity" prevents officers from acting efficiently has to be weighed against the availability of time and effort put into discrediting individuals, for which resources can always be found to protect the institution. Given the number of innocent people being discredited by the police and the risk of bias when it comes to arrest, is it surprising if members of the public fail to cooperate with a police investigation, as happened on New Year's Eve 2018?[6] While officers remain defensive, incidents where innocent members of the public find themselves targeted by police instead of being treated like victims, innocent bystanders, bereaved family members, or simply those with an opinion to share shows an inability to accept responsibility by the policing institution. Worse still, such behavior encourages individual officers to avoid responsibility, with those working for the police even more likely to conceal corrupt practices than officers on duty.[7] For an institution that claims to work *with* the public *for* the public, such practices can no longer be overlooked and public trust can only be gained by recognizing that no one individual or group is, or should be, above the law, regarded as special or morally superior.

Notes

Preface

1. In 2014–2015, there were more than 34,000 complaints against police in England and Wales. See BBC News (2015), "Complaints against police reach a record high," at https://tinyurl.com/y7ye7toy (accessed July 29, 2018).

2. Steven Box and Ken Russell (1975), "The Politics of Discreditability: Disarming Complaints Against the Police," *Sociological Review*, Vol. 23(2): 315–46.

Chapter 1: Discrediting Victims and Complainants

1. For discretion among police officers in India see, J. Belur, N. Tilley, D. Osrin, N. Daruwalla, M. Kumar, & V. Tiwari (2014), "Police investigations: Discretion Denied Yet Undeniably Exercised," *Policing & Society*, Vol. 25(5): 439–62.

2. Phil Scraton (1985), *The State of the Police* (London: Pluto Press), 42.

3. See Fiona Hamilton (2017), "Lazy police fail to grasp law, says top prosecutor," *The Times*, July 17. A crown prosecutor states that many police officers are failing to understand the law and are only interested in charging offences. See also, Anna Lvovsky (2017), "The Judicial Presumption of Police Expertise," *Harvard Law Review*, Vol. 130(8): 1197–2081. Lvovsky argues that courts often defer to police judgments inflating police expertise of the experience of the judiciary and qualified lawyers.

4. Police Federation (2017), *The Office of Constable: The Bedrock of Modern Day British Policing*, at www.polfed.org.

5. Stuart Kirby (2013), *Effective Policing? Implementation in Theory and Practice* (Basingstoke, UK: Palgrave Macmillan), 46.

6. Mike Brogden and Graham Ellision (2013), *Policing in an Age of Austerity* (London: Routledge), 104.

7. College of Policing (2014), *Code of Ethics* section 9, at https://tinyurl.com/hxtzeqd (accessed July 3, 2018).

8. See CPS, "Misconduct in public office," at https://tinyurl.com/y8gbc5bk (accessed October 12, 2017).

9. Law Commission (2016), *Misconduct in Public Office: Issue Paper 1* sections 2.153 and 2.154, p. 42, at https://tinyurl.com/yazs2ecv (accessed July 3, 2018).

10. It should be noted that although one officer was convicted with regard to the infamous "Plebgate" scandal of 2012 (PC Keith Wallis in 2014), PC Wallis was prosecuted not for discrediting Andrew Mitchell MP but for lying (claiming he had been a witness to events and was just an ordinary member of the public). Mitchell had been embroiled in a spat with police officers as he was leaving Parliament. PC Toby Rowland reported that Mitchell had called the police "fucking plebs"—a comment which was published the next day in *The Sun* newspaper. This claim was denied by Mitchell who called PC Rowland a liar. Those officers who went to the newspapers faced internal disciplinary inquiries and were sacked but were not charged with misconduct because of lack of evidence. Mitchell lost the libel case taken by PC Rowland and supported by the Police Federation, on the basis of "probabilities" when the judge concerned "thought it unlikely the officer had invented the 'pleb' exchange because he seemingly did not have the imagination to do so." See, Peter Walker (2014), "Andrew Mitchell and the Plebgate affair explained for non-Brits," *The Guardian*, November 27; BBC News (2015), "Andrew Mitchell in £80,000 libel payout to 'plebgate,'" at https://tinyurl.com/yd8ndsjb (accessed July 3, 2018); Simon Carsons (2016), "Misconduct in Public Office," *Criminal Law & Justice Weekly*, March 18.

11. Box and Russell, "The Politics of Discreditability."

12. This is most commonly against victims of rape, sexual abuse, and domestic violence; see, for example, Melanie Newman (2014), Investigating rape: revealed. Why the police are failing most rape victims," *The Bureau of Investigative Journalism*, February 28, at https://tinyurl.com/y9bwkk3k (accessed July 3, 2018).

13. See for example, Jan Jordan (2004), "Beyond belief? Police, rape and women's credibility," *Criminal Justice*, Vol. 4(1): 25–29; Ashley Savage (2016), "Whistleblowing in the Police Service: developments and challenges," *European Journal of Current Legal Issues*, Vol. 22(1), at https://tinyurl.com/ycca89vy (accessed July 3, 2018).

14. Rob Mawby and Alan Wright (2005), "Police Accountability in the United Kingdom" (Commonwealth: Human Rights Initiative), at https://tinyurl.com/64eoy9x (accessed July 3, 2018); IPCC (2011), "Corruption in the Police Service in England and Wales—First Report" (London: IPCC); Tim Newburn (2015), "Literature Review: Police Integrity and Corruption" (London: HMIC).

15. David Barrett (2015), "Drunk or flirty rape victims often 'to blame' says survey," *The Telegraph*, February 12.

16. Keir Starmer (2013), "False allegations of rape and domestic violence are few and far between," *The Guardian*, March 13.

17. Ministry of Justice (2015), *Code of Practice for Victims of Crime* (London: Stationary Office); Department of Justice (2015), *Victim's Charter: A Charter for victims of crime* (Northern Ireland Assembly).

18. HMIC (2014), *State of Policing The Annual Assessment of Policing in England and Wales 2013/2014*, at https://tinyurl.com/yd99hf5f (accessed July 4, 2018).

19. Eugene McLaughlin and Anja Johanssen (2002), "A Force for Change? The Prospects for Applying Restorative Justice to Citizen Complaints against the Police in England and Wales," *British Journal of Criminology*, Vol. 42: 635–653; 635.

20. Ibid.

21. HMIC (2014), *State of Policing*, 2.71, p. 4.

22. An example is that of Sara Reedy. After reporting a sexual violation at gunpoint, Sara Reedy was accused of lying by a detective assigned to the case and was arrested and jailed. Though the perpetrator, Wilbur Brown, went on to attack more women, charges against Reedy were not dropped until the day before Brown's trial after he had already been caught and confessed. Reedy sued the police and was awarded $1.5 million in damages. See, Joanna Walters (2016), "'Breaking the shackles of shame': The rape survivors leading a new wave of activism," *The Guardian*, May 16.

23. Matthew Weaver (2016), "Met chief: police should not believe all sexual offence complainants," *The Guardian*, December 14.

24. An initial literature review conducted in 2015 at the University of Portsmouth revealed very little by searching for the term "discredit." Other terms yielded better results. These included: "lies," "defame," "smear," "false claims," "exploit," "tarnish," "destroy," "blacken character," "victimise," "intimidate," "disrespect," "demean," "denigrate," and "bully" with key terms: "complainants," "complaints," "victims," "whistleblowers," or just blank but including the key terms "police" or "policing." Overall, sixty papers were read in the academic literature and more than sixty media stories. Though not exclusive, the table is in order of the amount of literature connected. As can be seen, incidents of rape and abuse are high on the agenda with multiple accounts reported of women being discredited.

25. Sandra Laville (2015), "Rape victim falsely accused of lying by police wins £20,000 payout," *The Guardian*, May 22.

26. Joanna Walters (2015), "An 11-year-old reported being raped twice, wound up with a conviction," *The Washington Post*, March 12.

27. Ibid.

28. Aisha Gill (2008), "MPS 'could have done more' to prevent the murder of Banaz Mahmod," *Safe: The Domestic Abuse Quarterly*, Summer: 24–25.

29. Ibid.

30. Nick Britten (2008), "Police failed to heed pleas from honour victim," *The Telegraph*, April 24.

31. Gill, "MPS 'could have done more,'" 24.

32. Press Association (2015), "Police 'need urgent improvement to tackle honour crime,'" *Evening Express*, December 8.

33. Alexis Jay (2014), *Independent Inquiry into Child Sexual Exploitation in Rotherham, 1997–2013* (Rotherham, UK: Rotherham Metropolitan Borough Council), 29, 92.

34. Rachel Roberts (2017), "Teenager 'murdered by ex-boyfriend' after police fined her for wasting their time over her fears about him, court hears," *The Independent*, March 18, at https://tinyurl.com/y7z6smoa (accessed July 4, 2018); BBC News (2017), "Shana Grice murder trial: Teenager penalised by police," at https://tinyurl.com/kryf349 (accessed July 4, 2018).

35. Weaver (2016), "Met chief."

36. HMIC (2014) State of Policing.

37. Simon Hattenstone (2000), "A Dangerous Pursuit," *The Guardian*, March 25.

38. Ibid.

39. Ibid.

40. See Home Office (2016), "Determinations and Findings of the Hillsborough Inquest," April 27, at shorturl.at/crxMS (accessed August 23, 2019).

41. David Conn (2017), "Hillsborough disaster: Six people, including David Duckenfield, charged," *The Guardian*, June 28. See, Eleanor Barlow (2018), "Hillsborough match commander David Duckenfield pleads not guilty to manslaughter of 95 Liverpool fans," *Mirror*, September 10, at https://tinyurl.com/y8k6ym99 (accessed September 13, 2018).

42. The Hillsborough Independent Panel (2012) questioned the rationale behind Duckenfield's appointment. See Hillsborough Independent Panel (2012), *The Report of the Hillsborough Independent Panel* (London: The Stationary Office), 7 (2.13 and 2.15).

43. Phil Scraton (2016), *Hillsborough: The Truth* (Edinburgh, Scotland: Mainstream Publishing), 170.

44. Hillsborough Independent Panel (2012), *The Report*, 7; David Conn (2016), "Hillsborough inquests jury rules 96 victims were unlawfully killed," *The Guardian*, April 26; Liz Hull (2016), "Hillsborough police 'told to blame fans': Chief alleged to have briefed officers to 'to go away and gather evidence' so they could say drunken supporters were responsible," *Daily Mail*, March 5, 2015, at https://dailym.ai/2m6nRmD (accessed November 21, 2019).

45. Police Oracle (2018), "Judge gives the green light for David Duckenfield Hillsborough Trial," *Press Association*, June 29, Comments, at https://tinyurl.com/y8gockjg (accessed July 10, 2018).

46. After a ten-week trial followed by a retrial, Duckenfield was found not guilty of manslaughter; see David Conn (2019), "David Duckenfield found not guilty of manslaughter," *The Guardian*, November 28.

47. Scraton makes the point in *Hillsborough: The Truth*, 451.

48. Hillsborough Independent Panel (2012), *The Report*, Chapter 11 "Review and Alternation of Statements." See also Phil Noble (2016), "After 27 years, police blamed for Hillsborough tragedy," *Reuters*, April 26, at https://reut.rs/2XCOoGt (accessed November 21, 2019); David Conn (2015), "David Duckenfield: Why I lied about Hillsborough," *The Guardian*, March 13.

49. Hillsborough Independent Panel (2012), *The Report*, 326.

50. Ibid.

51. Ibid.

52. Ibid.

53. Ibid., pp. 8, 12, 326.

54. Phil Scraton (2013), "The Legacy of Hillsborough: Liberating Truth, Challenging Power," *Institute of Race Relations*, Vol. 55(2): 1–27; 4–5.

55. Ibid., p. 6.

56. Ibid., p. 16.

57. Information received from a Freedom of Information Request to the Metropolitan police by email on October 9, 2014.

58. Agencies (2014), "Black female officer discriminated against by Met Police, tribunal finds," *The Telegraph*, July 1; Lola Okolsie (2014), "I'm not shocked by the police's discrimination against Carol Howard," *The Guardian*, July 3.

59. Paul Peachy (2013), "Kevin Maxwell: 'I was meant to be the future. I ticked the boxes,'" *The Independent*, June 17.

60. Helen Pidd (2015), "Police poster boy cleared of fraud alleges smear campaign by own force," *The Guardian*, January 23.

61. Tom Harper (2015), "Officers menaced for exposing Yard binges," *The Sunday Times*, February 8.

62. India Pollock (2015), "'Poor' British Transport Police data 'risks safety,'" BBC News, January 19, at https://tinyurl.com/oymjpvc (accessed July 4, 2018).

63. John Scheerhout (2017), "Police boss was 'fitted up' and 'branded a liar and a criminal' by GMP for whistleblowing, tribunal hears," *Manchester Evening News*, January 10; John Scheerhout (2017), "Detective finds evidence of son's attacker missed by colleagues—but gets placed under investigation by bosses," *Manchester Evening News*, April 18; BBC (2015), "Transport police chief denies suspending whistleblowers," January 20, at https://tinyurl.com/ybvw92o6 (accessed July 4, 2018).

64. Yvonne Roberts (2013), "Trauma of autistic boy shackled by police," *The Observer*, February 17.

65. Brian Chapman (1970), *Police State* (London: Pall Mall), 97.

66. Paul Lewis, Paul Evans, and Vikram Dodd (2013), "National police unit monitors 9,000 'domestic extremists,'" *The Guardian*, June 26.

67. Box and Russell, "The Politics of Discreditability," 327.

68. Graham Smith (2004), "Rethinking Police Complaints," *British Journal of Criminology*, Vol. 44(1): 15–33; 19.

69. Vaughan Bell (2013), "You needn't be wrong to be called delusional," *The Guardian*, August 4.

70. Box and Russell (1975), "The Politics of Discreditability," 333–41.

71. The Crown Prosecution Service (CPS), *Legal Guidance: Misconduct in Public Office*, at https://tinyurl.com/y8gbc5bk (accessed October 12, 2017).

Chapter 2: The Meaning of Bias in Police Investigations

1. Tracey G. Gove (2011), "Implicit Bias and Law Enforcement," *The Police Chief*, (78) October: 44–56.

2. Police and Criminal Evidence Act (PACE; 1984), section 76, at https://tinyurl.com/y892n7t5 (accessed July 4, 2018).

3. Stuart Armstrong (2012), "Regulatory Interviews and the PEACE Model of Interviewing," at https://tinyurl.com/yaybc5qz (accessed October 12, 2017).

4. Vikram Dodd (2016), "Police officers must be aware of biases, says training college," *The Guardian*, October 27.

5. Project Implicit (2011), Harvard University, at https://tinyurl.com/6yyyc (accessed July 4, 2018).

6. Gregory Mitchell and Philip E. Tetlock (2017), "Popularity as a Poor Proxy for Utility: The Case of Implicit Prejudice," in *Psychological Science Under Scrutiny: Recent Challenges and Proposed Solutions*, edited by Scott O' Lilienfeld and Irwin D. Waldman (Oxford: Wiley), 166.

7. Ibid., 173.

8. For a criticism of implicit bias and the IAT testing methods, see Mitchell and Tetlock, "Popularity as a Poor Proxy for Utility." See also, BBC News Magazine (2017), "Implicit bias: Is everyone racist?" June 5, at https://tinyurl.com/y8hpfwtl (accessed September 13, 2017), and comments on Hillary Clinton, Daniel A. Yudkin, and Jay van Bavel (2016), "The Roots of Implicit Bias," *New York Times*, December 9. Project Implicit Inc., run by the same researchers who created the IAT tests at Harvard University, has received substantial federal grants and thousands of dollars from private corporations. The basis for their research is that everyone has implicit prejudices so the (highly lucrative) study can be accused of setting out to prove what it has already endorsed in the project itself, which argues that *implicit biases can predict behavior*. See Mitchell and Tetlock, "Popularity as a Poor Proxy for Utility," 171; Project Bias is thus telling people that they are biased even when people claim not to harbor any prejudices.

9. In Howard J. Ross (2014), *Everyday Bias: Identifying and Navigating Unconscious Judgements in Our Daily Lives* (Lanham, MD: Rowman & Littlefield), 4.

10. Ibid.

11. See, Equality and Human Rights Commission (2016), *Public Sector Duty*, at https://tinyurl.com/y9enm8at (accessed December 13, 2017).

12. The report into the death and behavior by police following the murder of the black teenager Stephen Lawrence on April 22, 1993 by white supremacists heralded a landmark recognition in the United Kingdom of racism within the police. The subsequent report determined that the Metropolitan Police were institutionally racist. Racism was thus neither implied nor implicit but a recognizable and explicit bias that existed within the organization. See William Macpherson (1999), *Report of the Stephen Lawrence Inquiry* (London: HMSO), at https://tinyurl.com/ngc8wje (accessed July 4, 2018).

13. For police officers' own accounts of sexist and racist bias, see Rob Mawby and Irene Zempi (2016), "'Every time it happens, you question continuing as an officer': The experiences of police workers as victims of hate crime," at https://tinyurl.com/ycslgq84 (accessed July 4, 2018), and Graham Smith, Harry Hagger Johnson, and Chris Roberts (2015), "Ethnic minority police officers and disproportionality in misconduct proceedings," *Policing and Society*, Vol. 25(6): 561–78.

14. Nigel Morris (2015), "Black people still far more likely to be stopped and searched by police than other ethnic groups," *Independent*, August 6, at https://tinyurl.com/y75de84w (accessed July 4, 2018).

15. Ibid.

16. L. Song Richardson (2012), "Cognitive Bias, Police Character, and the Fourth Amendment," *Arizona State Law Journal*, Vol. 44: 267–303; 285.

17. Lois James, Stephen M. James, and Bryan J. Vila (2016), "The Reverse Racism Effect: Are Cops More Hesitant to Shoot Black than White Suspects?" *Criminology and Public Policy*, Vol. 15(2): 457–79.

18. I have shown this in several papers, but see, Eccy de Jonge (2005), "A Philosophical Analysis into the Causes and Prevention of Deliberate Self Harm," *Practical Philosophy*, Autumn: 30–34.

19. David Barrett (2014), "Rotherham child sex scandal: watchdog says police tried to 'disprove' victims," *The Telegraph*, August 28.

20. See HMIC (2015), "The depths of dishonour: Hidden voices and shameful crimes," at https://tinyurl.com/ybrvrd42 (accessed July 4, 2018). Lopez argues that police targets ensure that the most vulnerable groups in society, black people, gay people, and other groups are targeted not because of implicit bias but as a result of the accessibility and ease at stopping the most vulnerable people in society. See German Lopez (2016), "Police officers explain how they're encouraged to act in racist ways," *Vox*, July 8, at https://tinyurl.com/yd7repr2 (accessed July 4, 2018).

21. Gove, "Implicit Bias and Law Enforcement," 44–56.

22. Richardson, "Cognitive Bias," 271.

23. Ibid., 272.

24. Katherine B. Spencer, Amanda K. Charbonneau, and Jack Glaser (2016), "Implicit Bias and Policing," *Social and Personality Psychology Compass*, Vol. 10(1): 50–63; 54.

25. Richardson, "Cognitive Bias," 286.

26. Lise Gotell (2002), "The Ideal Victim, the Hysterical Complainant, and the Disclosure of Confidential Records: The Implications of the Charter for Sexual Assault Law," *Osgoode Hall Law Journal*, Vol. 40(3.4): 251–95; Jordan, "Beyond belief," 25–59.

27. Lisa Frohmann (1991), "Discrediting Victims' Allegations of Sexual Assault: Prosecutorial Accounts of Case Rejections," *Social Problems*, Vol. 38(2): 213–26; 220.

28. Gotell, "The Ideal Victim," 260–62.

29. Jordan, "Beyond belief," 39.

30. Michael Scarce (1997), *Male on Male Rape: The Hidden Toll of Stigma and Shame* (New York: Plenum Press).

31. See Barrett, "Rotherham child sex scandal." In 2013 the HMIC reported that a quarter of all sex-related crimes were not being recorded, with a huge disparity in force statistics across the country. These figures reveal that many police forces are dismissing public reports of criminal behavior (including rape) as being simply unworthy of investigation. Channel 4 News (2014), "Which forces are best and worst at recording crime?" November 18, at https://tinyurl.com/yachgky7 (accessed February 12, 2015).

32. Dean Jones (2016), "Fatal Call: Getting Away with Murder," PhD Thesis, University of Portsmouth, England, at https://tinyurl.com/yae37hgg (accessed July 4, 2018), p. 129.

33. Ibid.

34. Clifford Scott and Hugo Gorringe (2014), "From Robert Peel to PLTs: Adapting to Liaison-Based Public Order Policing in England and Wales," in *The Future of Policing*, edited by Jennifer M. Brown (Abingdon: Routledge), 239–51; 239.

35. HMIC (2009), *Adapting to Protest* (London: HMIC), 6, at https://tinyurl.com/y9gfcj93 (accessed July 4, 2018).

36. Pete Walker and Jonathan Page (2010), "Student protests—as they happened," *The Guardian*, December 9.

37. Owen Bowcott (2017), "Met police chat forum was used to post insults aimed at Gypsies," *The Guardian*, September 21. See also, Richard Jinman (2015), "The Battle of the Beanfield: The violent new-age traveller clash with police at Stonehenge remembered 30 years on," *The Independent*, May 30.

38. In public order policing it is well-recognized that the way events are policed depends to a large extent on the way crowds are seen by the police; traditionally this has focused on a negative view of crowds as fundamentally irrational with the potential for violence. In miscarriages of justice, how someone is perceived determines to a large extent what happens to them. See David P. Waddington (2007), *Policing Public Disorder: Theory and Practice* (Cullompton, UK: Willian Publishing).

39. See Alistair Painter (2017), "Licence holder age group driving offences—Analysing the data," *LicenceLink*, at https://tinyurl.com/ydeo9kt6 (accessed July 4, 2018).

40. Renze Salet and Jan Terpstra (2013), "Critical Review in Criminal Investigation: Evaluation of a Measure to Prevent Tunnel Vision," *Policing*, Vol. 8(1): 43–50; 43.

41. Keith A. Findley (2009), "Tunnel Vision," *Legal Studies Research Paper Series No. 1116* (Madison: University of Wisconsin Law School), 1–2.

42. Ibid., 9.

43. Colin Wastell, Nicole Weeks, Alexander Wearing, and Piers Duncan (2012), "Identifying Hypothesis Confirmation Behaviors in a Simulated Murder Investigation: Implications for Practice," *Journal of Investigative Psychology and Offender Profiling*, Vol. 9: 184–98; 196.

44. See ACPO (2015), *Core Investigative Doctrine* (Wyboston, UK: NCPE); Dean Jones (2011), "Miscarriages of Justice: The Role of Homicide Review," *Medicine, Science and Law*, Vol 51: 63–67; Wastell et al., "Identifying Hypothesis Confirmation Behaviors," and Kim Rossmo (2014), "Case Rethinking: A Protocol for Reviewing Criminal Investigations," *Police Practice & Research*: 1–17.

45. Keith A. Findley and Michael S. Scott (2006), "The Multiple Dimensions of Tunnel Vision in Criminal Cases," *Wisconsin Law Review*, 291–397; 207.

46. Stephen P. Savage and Becky Milne (2007), "Miscarriages of Justice," in *Handbook of Criminal Investigation*, edited by Tim Newburn, Tom Williamson, and Alan Wright (Cullompton, UK: Willan), 610–27; 615.

47. Ibid.

48. D. Kim Rossmo (2006), "Criminal Investigative Failures: Avoiding the Pitfalls (Part Two)," *FBI Law Enforcement Bulletin*, Vol. 75(10): 12–19; 14.

49. See, Richardson, "Cognitive Bias."

50. Steven G. Brandl (2014), *Criminal Investigations* (Los Angeles: Sage), 11.

51. Becky O'Neill and Becky Milne (2014), "Success within Criminal Investigations: Is Communication Still a Key Component?" in *Investigative Interviewing*, edited by Ray Bull (New York: Springer), 124.

52. Barbara O'Brien (2009), "Prime Suspect: An Examination of Factors that Aggravate and Counteract Confirmation Bias in Criminal Investigations," *Psychology, Public Policy & Law*, Vol. 15(4): 315–34.

53. Mark Roycroft (2008), "Historical Analysis of Public Inquiries of Homicide Investigations," *The Journal of Homicide and Major Incident Investigation*, Vol. 4(2) 43–56; 46.

54. Dean Jones (2014), "The Relationship Between Homicide Rates and Forensic Post Mortem Examinations in England and Wales," *The Journal of Homicide and Major Incident Investigation*, Vol. 9(2): 58–68.

55. Ibid., 61.

56. Ibid., 70.

57. Jerome Taylor and Ayshea Buksh (2013), "Ricky Reel died after a racist attack 16 years ago. Now his family says a new witness could prove he was murdered," *The Independent*, March 12, at https://tinyurl.com/yclohk8d (accessed July 4, 2018).

58. See The Monitoring Group (2016). "Sukdhev Reel: Mother of Ricky," at https://tinyurl.com/y8rcul98 (accessed October 29, 2017).

59. Jones, "Fatal Call," 26.

60. Ibid., 147.

61. Ibid., 8.

62. Ibid., 15

63. Ibid., 17.

64. Ibid., 21.

65. Ibid., 119.

66. Ibid., 120.

67. Ronald P. Fisher, Rebecca Milne, and Ray Bull (2011), "Interviewing Cooperative Witnesses," *Current Directions in Psychological Science*, Vol. 20(1): 16–19.

68. For example, see Saul M. Kassin, Sara C. Appleby, and Jennifer Torkildson Perillo (2010), "Interviewing Suspects: Practice, Science, and Future Directions," *Legal and Criminal Psychology*, Vol. 15: 39–55; Karen Franklin (2014), "Storm Clouds Gathering over Reid Interrogation Method," *Psychology Today*, March 31, at https://tinyurl.com/y79ehn58 (accessed July 4, 2018); Buffie Brooke Merryman (2010), "Arguments Against Use of the Reid Technique for Juvenile Interrogations," *Communication Law Review*, Vol. 10(2), at https://tinyurl.com/yd8jwpxz (accessed July 4, 2018); CBC News (2003), "Widely used police interrogation technique can result in false confession: Disclosure," January 28, at https://tinyurl.com/yb2ycwyo (accessed July 4, 2018); Douglas Starr (2013), "Do police interrogation techniques produce false confessions?" *The New Yorker*, December 9, at https://tinyurl.com/y975voqd (accessed July 4, 2018); see "The Good Fight" Season 1, episode 2 in Chancellor Agard (2017), "The Good Fight Recap: First Week," *Entertainment*, at https://tinyurl.com/ychuya94 (accessed October 4, 2017).

69. Micah Schwartzbach (2017), "Is a confession alone enough to convict a defendant? Some states follow the corpus delicti rule, while others focus on the reliability

of the confession," *Legal Encyclopaedia*, at https://tinyurl.com/y9rkyf74 (accessed October 4, 2017).

70. Innocence Staff (2017), "Leading police consultancy group will no longer teach the Reid Technique," *Innocence Project*, August 3, at https://tinyurl.com/ybe555ya (accessed October 4, 2017).

71. Eli Hager (2017), "The seismic change in police interrogations: A major player in law enforcement says it will no longer use a method linked to false confessions," *The Marshall Project*, July 3, at https://tinyurl.com/y7jswdwg (accessed October 4, 2017).

72. Ibid.

73. Rebecca Milne and Ray Bull (1999), *Investigative Interviewing: Psychology and Practice* (Chichester, UK: John Wiley & Sons), 84–85.

74. Becky Milne, Gary Shaw, and Ray Bull (2007), "Investigative Interviewing: The Role of Research," in *Applying Psychology to Criminal Justice*, edited by David Carson, Becky Milne, Frances Pakes, Karen Shalev, and Andrea Shawyer (Chichester, UK: John Wiley & Sons), 65–80; 67.

75. College of Policing (2016), Investigative Interviewing, chapter 4, at https://tinyurl.com/y87nsm3g (accessed August 16, 2018).

76. Milne et al., "Investigative Interviewing," 67–68.

77. See Fisher et al., "Interviewing Cooperative Witnesses"; Carol Hill, Amina Memon, and Peter McGeorge (2008), "The role of confirmation bias in suspect interviews: A systematic evaluation," *Legal and Criminological Psychology*, Vol. 13(2): 357–71; Andrea Shawyer, Becky Milne, and Ray Bull (2009), "Investigative interviewing in the UK," in *International Developments in Investigative Interviewing*, edited by Tom Williamson, Becky Milne, and Stephen P. Savage (Cullompton, UK: Willan Publishing), 24–38, and Martine B. Powell, Carolyn H. Hughes-Scholes, and Stefanie J. Sharman (2012), "Skill in Interviewing Reduces Confirmation Bias," *Journal of Investigative Psychology & Offender Profiling*, Vol. 9(2): 126–34.

78. Aldert Vrij quoted in Shawyer et al., "Investigative Interviewing in the UK," 28.

79. Colin Clarke, Rebecca Milne, and Ray Bull (2011), "Interviewing Suspects of Crime: The Impact of PEACE Training, Supervision and the Presence of a Legal Advisor," *Journal of Investigative Psychology and Offender Profiling*, Vol 8: 149–62.

80. Leora C. Dahl, C. A. Elizabeth Brimacombe, and D. Stephen Lindsay (2009), "Investigating Investigators: How Presentation Order Influences Participant-Investigators. Interpretations of Eyewitness Identification and Alibi Evidence," *Law and Human Behaviour* Vol. 33: 368–80; 370.

81. Findley, "Tunnel Vision," 7, 12.

82. Findley and Scott, "The Multiple Dimensions," 335.

83. See Karl Ask, Anna Rebelius, and Anders Granhag (2008), "The 'Elasticity' of Criminal Evidence: A Moderator of Investigator Bias," *Applied Cognitive Psychology*, Vol. 22: 1245–59, and Wastell et al., "Identifying Hypothesis Confirmation Behaviors," 19.

84. Findley and Scott, "The Multiple Dimensions," 311.

85. For example, see Bradford T. Ulery, R. Austin Hicklin, JoAnn Buscaglia, and Maria Antonia Roberts (2011), "Accuracy and Reliability of Forensic Latent Fingerprint Decisions," *PNAS*, Vol. 108(19): 7733–38, at https://tinyurl.com/y8okb4mq (accessed July 5, 2018); Jennifer L. Mnookin (2003), "Fingerprints: Not a Gold Standard," *Issues in Science and Technology*, Vol. 2 (1), at https://tinyurl.com/gm6feom (accessed July 5, 2018); Sarah Lucy Cooper (2016), "Challenges to Fingerprint Identification Evidence: Why the Courts Need a New Approach to Finality," *Mitchell Hamline Law Review*, Vol. 42(2), at https://tinyurl.com/y74kxgaq (accessed July 5, 2018).

86. Carrie Sperling (2014), "When Finality and Innocence Collide," in *Controversies in Innocence Cases in America*, edited by Sarah Cooper (London: Routledge), 157.

87. ACPO, *Core Investigative Doctrine*; Findley and Scott (2006), "The Multiple Dimensions," 325.

88. Wastell et al., "Identifying Hypothesis Confirmation Behaviors," 186.

89. See Findley and Scott, "The Multiple Dimensions," 339; Jones, "Miscarriages of Justice," 66; Susan J. Lea and Nick Lynn (2012), "Dialogic Reverberations: Police, Domestic Abuse, and the Discontinuance of Cases," *Journal of Interpersonal Violence*, Vol. 27(15): 3091–114, 3109; Richardson, "Cognitive Bias"; Itiel E. Dror (2013), "Practical Solutions to Cognitive and Human Factor Challenges in Forensic Science," *Forensic Science Policy & Management,* Vol. 4(3–4): 105–13; Rossmo, "Case Rethinking," 6.

90. Savage and Milne, "Miscarriages of Justice," 624.

91. Findley and Scott, "The Multiple Dimensions," 296–97.

92. Brandl, *Criminal Investigations*, 11.

93. Travis Kirchner (2013), "David Camm Blog: Investigation Under Fire," *WDRB*, October 11, at https://tinyurl.com/yazkxka5 (accessed July 5, 2018).

94. Rossmo, "Case Rethinking," 12–13.

95. Ron Stodghill (2002), "The Confession of the Central Park Rapist," *Time*, December 9.

96. Elaine Cassell (2002), "The False Confessions in the Central Park Jogger Case," *Find Law*, December 17, at https://tinyurl.com/y8ny7uxe (accessed July 5, 2018).

97. Findley and Scott (2006), "The Multiple Dimensions," 305–07.

98. Ibid.

99. See, Innocence Project: Death Penalty Information Center, at https://tinyurl.com/yd3sldhk (accessed October 9, 2017).

100. Innocence Project, Death Row Penalty Information Centre: Case 88, at https://tinyurl.com/yd3sldhk (accessed October 9, 2017).

101. Karl Ask and Par Anders Granhag (2005), "Motivational Sources of Confirmation Bias in Criminal Investigations: The Need for Cognitive Closure," *Journal of Investigative Psychology and Offender Profiling*, Vol. 2: 43–63; 44.

102. Gwyn Topham (2013), "Wrongly jailed Victor Nealon spends first night as free man on streets," *The Guardian*, December 16.

103. Jon Robins (2015), "Sam Hallam: The man who spent over seven years in jail for a murder he did not commit," *Independent*, May 9, at https://tinyurl.com/ycfkjp9f (accessed July 5, 2018).

104. Ed Davey (2012), "Maguire Seven man's warning for freed Sam Hallam," *BBC News*, May 17, at https://tinyurl.com/y7jc9dad (accessed July 5, 2018).

105. Amaury Murgado (2014), "Dealing with Confirmation Bias," *Police: The Law Enforcement Magazine*, July 17, at https://tinyurl.com/y8o3t53b (accessed July 5, 2018).

106. Andrew Gilligan (2014), "Christopher Jefferies was treated disgracefully by the police—not just the press," *The Telegraph*, December 11.

107. Steven Morris (2013), "Christopher Jefferies wins apology over Joanna Yeates murder arrest," *The Guardian*, September 16.

108. Christopher Jefferies (2014), "How I Was Hounded," *BBC News*, January 10, at https://tinyurl.com/p4d93q4 (accessed July 5, 2018).

109. Interview with Georgina Halford-Hall in 2015 by author.

110. Ibid.

111. Police and Criminal Evidence Act (1984), C.60 part 2, at https://tinyurl.com/y7px2fdl (accessed July 5, 2018).

112. Ben Riley-Smith (2015), "My fear for being a whistle-blower," *The Telegraph*, June 26.

113. Camilla Turner (2017), "Ministry of Defence accused of attempting to cover up claims of abuse at top military boarding school," *The Telegraph*, March 17.

114. Peter J. Van Koppen (2008), "Blundering Justice—the Schiedam Park Murder," in *Serial Murder and the Psychology of Violent Crimes*, edited by Richard N. Kocsis (Totowa: Humana Press), 207–28.

115. Ibid.

116. Salet and Terpstra, "Critical Review in Criminal Investigation," 45; Eric Rassin, Anita Eerland, and Isle Kuijpers (2010), "Let's Find the Evidence: An Analogue Study of Confirmation Bias in Criminal Investigations," *Journal of Investigative Psychology and Offender Profiling*, Vol. 7: 231–46; p. 233.

117. See Savage et al., "Miscarriages of Justice," 625; The ACPO's *Core Investigative Doctrine* (now the College of Policing's APP on Investigations) encourages investigators to adopt "hypotheses testing," similar to that used by the Contrarians, 23, 72–73.

118. J. H. Kertsholt and A. R. Eikelbloom (2007), "Effects of Prior Interpretation on Situation Assessment in Crime Analysis" *Journal of Behavioral Decision Making*, Vol. 20(5): 455–65; 455.

119. Salet and Terpstra, "Critical Review in Criminal Investigation," 45.

120. Ibid., 46.

121. Ibid.

122. Ibid., 49.

123. Heather L. Price and Leora C. Dahl (2014), "Order and Strength Matter for Evaluation of Alibi and Eyewitness Evidence," *Applied Cognitive Psychology*, Vol. 28: 143–50; 48, Findley, "Tunnel Vision," 21.

124. Findley, " Tunnel Vision," 17.

125. Ibid., 22.

126. Rossmo, "Criminal Investigative Failures (Part Two)," 15; Salet and Terpstra, "Critical Review in Criminal Investigation," 48.

127. Keith, "Tunnel Vision," 21–22.

128. ACPO, *Core Investigative Doctrine*, 59–60.

129. Ibid., 59.

130. Ibid., 58–60.

131. Ibid., 62.

132. Jones, "Fatal Call," 116.

133. Ibid., 126.

134. Ibid., 13.

135. Ibid., 16.

136. Savage and Milne, "Miscarriages of Justice," 617.

137. Findley, "Tunnel Vision," 23.

138. D. Kim Rossmo (2006), "Criminal Investigative Failures: Avoiding the Pitfalls," *FBI Law Enforcement Bulletin*, Vol. 75(9): 1–8; 2.

139. Rossmo, "Case Rethinking," 6. For police bias toward domestic violence victims see Lea and Lynn (2012), "Dialogic Reverberations," 3109.

140. Richardson, "Cognitive Bias," 293.

141. Gove, "Implicit Bias and Law Enforcement," 52.

142. Ronan Farrow (2017), "From Aggressive Overtures to Sexual Assault: Harvey Weinstein's Accusers Tell Their Stories," *The New Yorker*, October 10.

143. Robin Bloom (2017), "Naming Crime Suspects in the News: 'Seek Truth and Report It' vs. 'Minimizing Harm,'" in *Media Law, Ethics, and Policy in the Digital Age*, edited by Nhamo A. Mhiripiri and Tendai Chari (Hershey, PA: IGI Global), 207–25; 216.

144. Milne et al., "Investigative Interviewing," 21.

145. Findley and Scott, "The Multiple Dimensions," 320.

146. Dahl et al., "Investigating Investigators," 368; Findley and Scott, "The Multiple Dimensions," 17; O'Brien, "Prime Suspect," 318; Rossmo, "Case Rethinking," 3–6.

147. Findley, "Tunnel Vision," 7.

148. Ask and Granhag, "Motivational Sources," 46.

149. Jeremy Bamber was convicted in 1986 for the murder of his adopted parents, sister, and her children. Essex Police hold evidence that might secure his innocence. Even though the Court of Appeal and a Judicial Review ordered Essex police to release this information, they have continually failed to do so even after thirty years. Simon Hattenstone and Eric Allison (2017), "Jeremy Bamber still waits for the evidence that might clear his name," *The Guardian*, March 24.

Chapter 3: Covert Policing

1. Art Buckwater (1983), *Surveillance & Undercover Investigation* (Woburn, MA: Butterworth), 2.

2. See Roger Billingsley, ed., (2009), *Covert Human Intelligence Sources* (London: Waterside Press).

3. James Sheptycki (2013), "To go beyond the cycle of intelligence-led policing," in *Understanding the Intelligence Cycle*, edited by Mark Phythian (Abingdon, UK: Routledge), 109.

4. BBC (2011), "Plain-clothes officers 'were deployed at G20 demo,'" January 19, at https://tinyurl.com/ycst7m36 (accessed August 28, 2018).

5. The Ecologist (2014), "Smiling spies: Police Liaison Officers exposed," *Ecologist*, June 18, at https://tinyurl.com/y8v5s3eq (accessed July 7, 2018); see also NETPOL (2013), "Police Liaison Officers," *The Network for Police Monitoring*, at https://tinyurl.com/y8f7p3xp (accessed July 7, 2018).

6. Serious Fraud Office (2012), *Covert Investigative Techniques* (last accessed January 17, 2017). It was originally obtained by the Serious Fraud Squad Office (UK) at http://bit.ly/1nCRGhT but has now been taken down and is no longer available from the Serious Fraud Office. See https://tinyurl.com/ycor2783 (accessed February 23, 2018).

7. Human Rights Act (1998), at https://tinyurl.com/yc7ploe4 (accessed August 28, 2018).

8. Jonathan Lennon (2009), "A Defence Perspective," in Billingsley, *Covert Human Intelligence Sources*, 30–31.

9. Serious Fraud Office, *Covert Investigative Techniques*.

10. MPS (2011), *Covert Policing Standards Policy*, Version 3 SCD, September, at https://tinyurl.com/ydeces6k (accessed August 29, 2018), p. 3.

11. Rob Evans (2017), "Sir John Mitting to Take Over Undercover Policing Inquiry," *The Guardian*, May 13, at https://tinyurl.com/yardhhhq (accessed February 15, 2018).

12. Undercover Policing Inquiry (2018), at https://www.ucpi.org.uk/ (accessed February 15, 2018).

13. Rob Evans (2014), "Special Demonstration Squad: unit which vanished into undercover world," *The Guardian*, July 24.

14. BBC (2013), "Police commission: Neighbourhood policing under threat," at https://tinyurl.com/k8mtj6s; BBC (2014), "Metropolitan Police gathered information on 18 family campaigns," July 24, at https://tinyurl.com/mtrc682; Press Association (2013), "Ex-West Yorkshire police chief referred to IPCC over Lawrence allegations," *The Guardian*, July 3.

15. Rob Evans, "Doreen Lawrence calls for undercover police who spied on family to be named," *The Guardian*, July 16.

16. Rob Evans and Paul Lewis (2014), *Undercover: The True Story of Britain's Secret Police* (London: Guardian Books and Faber & Faber), 275.

17. Ibid., 274.

18. Ibid., 277.

19. Ibid., 285.

20. Channel4 News (2011), "Undercover police officer was 'agent provocateur,'" July 20, at https://tinyurl.com/y992rnqb (accessed February 16, 2018).

21. Paul Lewis (2014), "How the scandal of Scotland Yard's secret spy unit emerged," *The Guardian*, March 6, at https://tinyurl.com/y8yd5oss (accessed August 30, 2018).

22. Nick Collins (2011), "What is the National Public Order Intelligence Unit?" *The Telegraph*, January 10, at https://tinyurl.com/2926dhe (accessed February 15, 2018).

23. Mick Creedon (2015), *Operation Herne: Report 1 - use of covert identities*, at https://tinyurl.com/y7cfwohw (accessed February 15, 2018), p. 1.

24. Ibid.

25. Rob Evans and Paul Lewis (2014), "Undercover whistleblower Peter Francis gives evidence to official inquiry," *The Guardian*, January 17, at https://tinyurl.com/ydxcpxru (accessed August 30, 2018).

26. June Kelly and Dominic Casciani (2014), "Met pays £425,000 to mother of undercover policeman's child," *BBC News*, October 24, at https://tinyurl.com/ogmoge6 (accessed August 30, 2018).

27. Rob Evans and Paul Lewis (2013), "Anatomy of a betrayal: the undercover officer accused of deceiving two women, fathering a child, then vanishing," *The Guardian*, February 21, at https://tinyurl.com/y8fhcs9z (accessed August 30, 2018).

28. Buckwater, *Surveillance & Undercover Investigation*, 127.

29. Chapman, *Police State*, 89.

30. Tom Barker (1996), *Police Ethics: Crisis in Law Enforcement* (Springfield, IL: Charles C Thomas), 49.

31. Ibid., 50.

32. Rob Evans (2017), "Probe into claim that police spy set fire to Debenhams could end by July," *The Guardian*, January 16, at https://tinyurl.com/jscn4zf (accessed August 30, 2018).

33. Hayley Dixon and Kate McCann (2017), "Exclusive: Special Branch monitored Jeremy Corbyn for 20 years amid fears he was 'undermining democracy,'" *The Telegraph*, June 7, at https://tinyurl.com/yc5svrl3 (accessed August 30, 2018).

34. Rob Evans and Vikram Dodd (2016), "Police anti-extremism unit monitoring senior Green party figures," *The Guardian*, April 28, at https://tinyurl.com/y9p7bvm2 (accessed August 30, 2018).

35. This chapter focuses almost exclusively on the situation in the UK. For information on the databases in the United States, particularly criminal background checking (which unlike the system in the UK is carried out by private agencies), see chapter 5 of James B. Jacobs (2015), *The Eternal Criminal Record* (Cambridge, MA: Harvard University Press).

36. Daniel Marshall and Terry Thomas describe other national police databases in further detail. See Marshall and Thomas (2017), *Privacy and Criminal Justice* (London: Palgrave Macmillan), chap. 5; the MPS is known to hold several covert databases; among these is MERLIN, advertised as a database for missing persons but containing information on those with mental health problems (including those diagnosed by the police themselves); in addition the MPS also hold a database on gang membership. "Amnesty has uncovered that 35% of the 3,600-odd people on the database have not committed 'serious crimes,' 75% have been victims of crime themselves and 80% are aged 12 to 24." See Steven Hopkins (2018), "Met Police Urged To Scrap 'Shady' Gang Database Amid Claims 35% Of Its Subjects Aren't Serious

Offenders," *Huffington Post*, January 2, at https://tinyurl.com/yb9bzm7t (accessed August 30, 2018).

37. Michael Bichard (2004), *The Bichard Inquiry: Report* (London: Stationery Office), at https://tinyurl.com/hgm9xbs (accessed August 30, 2018).

38. HMIC (2013), *Mistakes were made: HMIC's review into allegations and intelligence material concerning Jimmy Savile between 1964 and 2012*, at https://tinyurl.com/ybmvvfsy (accessed 5 February 2018), p. 34.

39. Duncan Campbell (1980), "Policing the Police," pp. 118–119 and 129, quoted in Marshall and Thomas (2017), *Privacy and Criminal Justice*, 105–6.

40. GeneWatchUK (2012), *Police National Computer*, at https://tinyurl.com/y9mjkp66 (accessed February 6, 2018).

41. MPS (2017), Information Rights Unit: Freedom of Information Request on Information about Accessing the Police National Database, at https://tinyurl.com/y7a2ttff (accessed February 5, 2018).

42. GeneWatch UK (2017), *The Police National DNA Database*, at https://tinyurl.com/6xmnp7t (accessed August 30, 2018).

43. Tessa Lambri (2013), "Modelling the implementation and acceptance of the Police National Database in UK police forces," PhD Thesis, Loughborough University, England, pp. 15 and 18.

44. HMIC, *Mistakes were made*, 34.

45. Ibid.

46. James Murdock (2016), "Mysterious UK surveillance system will store billions of records 'without parliamentary oversight,'" *International Business Times*, November 18, at https://tinyurl.com/yaosr9sd (accessed August 30, 2018).

47. Samuel Osborne (2017), "Liam Allan: Falsely accused student supports anonymity for rape suspects," *The Independent*, at https://tinyurl.com/yatxsu73 (accessed August 30, 2018).

48. National Union of Journalists (2016), "Journalists & John Catt challenge UK domestic extremism database," July 25, at https://tinyurl.com/y899vchl (accessed February 21, 2018).

49. Jason N. Parkinson (2016), "The Human Rights Act helps us hold power to account. We must defend it," *The Guardian*, July 26, at https://tinyurl.com/hv9r76z (accessed February 21, 2018).

50. Powerbase (2016), National Domestic Extremism Database (last modified April 25, 2016), at https://tinyurl.com/y8xchyjz (accessed February 13, 2018).

51. Email from Deborah Solomon, MPS, to the author, Freedom of Information Request Reference No: 2014070001191 (August 7, 2014).

52. Seaumus Miller and Ian A. Gordon (2014), *Investigative Ethics* (Chichester, UK: John Wiley & Sons), 90.

53. India Pollock (2015), "'Poor' British Transport Police data 'risks safety,'" *BBC News*, January 19, at https://tinyurl.com/oymjpvc (accessed September 5, 2018).

54. Care Quality Commission (CQC), Safeguarding People, at https://tinyurl.com/ycl5wbmw (accessed February 5, 2018).

55. European Court of Human Rights, Case of *M.M. v The United Kingdom*, November 13, 2012 section 40. (April 29, 2013).

56. Home Affairs Committee (2015), Oral Evidence: Police National Database, January 20, at https://tinyurl.com/y6v6z6eq (accessed September 5, 2018).

57. European Court of Human Rights, *Case of M.M. v The United Kingdom*, section 77, at https://tinyurl.com/y8pbz6cr (accessed September 5, 2018).

58. Ibid., 101/102.

59. Ibid., 207.

60. GeneWatch (2011), *Supreme Court Judgement*, at https://tinyurl.com/yc6gu6ra (accessed September 5, 2018).

61. Miller and Gordon, *Investigative Ethics*, 264.

62. Ibid., 286.

63. BBC News (2016), "Criminal record disclosure checks ruled 'unlawful,'" January 22, at https://tinyurl.com/y7vq6w7u (accessed September 5, 2018).

64. Metro Reporter (2011), "One in Four Britons on Police Database," *The Metro*, June 16, at https://tinyurl.com/y76pczjk, and Chris Greenwood (2011), "15 Million Britons—that's one in four of us—are listed on new national police database," *Daily Mail*, June 17, at https://tinyurl.com/y8ak4z69 (accessed September 5, 2018).

65. James Meikle (2012), "Police may have to destroy photos of innocent people after court ruling," *The Guardian*, June 22, at https://tinyurl.com/yczdr8gd (accessed September 5, 2018).

66. Alan Travis (2017), "Police told to delete on request millions of images of innocent people," *The Guardian*, February 24, at https://tinyurl.com/jknc4av (accessed September 5, 2018).

67. House of Lords (2017), Police National Database: Facial Images/Questions, March 2, at https://tinyurl.com/yab5tnr2 (accessed September 5, 2018).

68. Rob Evans and Owen Bowcott (2014), "Green party peer put on database of 'extremists' after police surveillance," *The Guardian*, June 15, at https://tinyurl.com/ybebz8dw (accessed September 5, 2018).

69. In the United States, the phrase "Community Liaison Officer" describes local police working within the community. The use of the term "liaison" here should not be confused with how it is inaugurated within UK policing. See, https://tinyurl.com/yazyu763 (accessed September 5, 2018).

70. College of Policing (2014), Authorised Professional Practice: Public order: Tactical Options: Police liaison teams, Section 3.3, at https://tinyurl.com/y8gc97f8 (accessed September 5, 2018).

71. Nicola Lester (2015), *Forces Support: Consultancy—Scoping Study* (Leeds: Leeds Beckett University); Ian K. Pepper and Helen Pepper (2008), *Key Words in Policing* (London: Open University Press).

72. Fraser Clarke (2016), "Family of missing Fife man Allan Bryant left 'disgusted' with police as they claim force are taking revenge for inquiry criticism," *Daily Record*, September 17, at https://tinyurl.com/ybvhqdtc (accessed September 5, 2018).

73. BBC News (2012). "European court says 'kettling' tactics in 2001 lawful," March 15, at https://tinyurl.com/jvmgncd; Vikram Dodd and Paul Lewis (2011), "Kettling of G20 protesters by police was illegal, high court rules," *The Guardian*, April 14, at https://tinyurl.com/yb9lsek4 (accessed September 5, 2018).

74. HMIC (2009), *Adapting to Protest: Nurturing the British Model of Policing* (London: HMIC), at https://www.justiceinspectorates.gov.uk/hmicfrs/media/adapting-to-protest-nurturing-the-british-model-of-policing-20091125.pdf (accessed July 4, 2018), p. 75.

75. Stott and Gorringe, "From Robert Peel to PLTs," 247.

76. The Ecologist, "Smiling Spies."

77. Netpol (2012), *The Intelligence Role of Police Liaison Officers*, September 7, at https://tinyurl.com/y9zxl89a (accessed September 5, 2018).

78. Jason N. Parkinson," Police Liaison Officers Accused of Harrassing Activist—Video," *The Guardian*, September 4, at https://tinyurl.com/ybcmxygd (accessed February 8, 2018).

79. See Ruth Hayhurst's Freedom of Information Request made to Sussex Police on May 16, 2012, at https://tinyurl.com/yauqdbgy; see also NetPol (2013), *Spies in Blue Bibs*, October 21, at https://tinyurl.com/ycc6hhml (accessed February 8, 2018).

80. HealthTalk (2015), *The Police Family Liaison Officer's Role*, at https://tinyurl.com/yd2rr9xt (accessed February 8, 2017).

81. MacPherson, *The Stephen Lawrence Inquiry*, section 1.3.

82. Ibid., section 13.21.

83. ACPO (2008), *Family Liaison Officer Guidance* (Wyboston, UK: NCPE), 6, at https://tinyurl.com/y8hcptd3; ACPO (2003), *Family Liaison Strategy Manual*, at https://tinyurl.com/ycczbq6m (accessed September 5, 2018), p. 12.

84. ACPO, *Family Liaison Officer Guidance*, 20.

85. Ibid., 21.

86. William Middleton (2014), "Wrongly Accused: The Role of the Family Liaison Officer," January 1; details of the Middleton case can be found at: https://tinyurl.com/ycxxwwvx (accessed September 5, 2018).

87. Mark Ellison (2014), *The Stephen Lawrence Independent Review* (London: House of Commons), March 6, section 4.2.1, at https://tinyurl.com/y9rmdh9a (accessed September 5, 2018).

88. IPCC (2006), *Report of the Review into the Events, Leading up to and Following the Death of Christopher Alder on 1st April 1998* (London: House of Commons), March 27, at https://tinyurl.com/y9x5hxcx; Rob Evans (2015), "Surveillance operation targeting sister of former paratrooper 'not properly authorised,'" *The Guardian*, November 26, https://tinyurl.com/y7qbrhro (accessed September 5, 2018).

89. BBC News (2017), "Humberside Police officers face misconduct hearings over Janet Alder surveillance," November 1, at https://tinyurl.com/ydgowsga (accessed September 5, 2018).

90. D. McGarry and Kevin Smith (2011), *Police Family Liaison* (Oxford: Oxford University Press), 7.

91. College of Policing (2017), "Family Liaison Officer Activities," in *Investigation: Working with Victims and Witnesses*, at June 12, https://tinyurl.com/y7g53ykn (accessed August 29, 2018).

92. Private documents in the author's possession.

93. Michael Chatterton (2008), *Losing the Detectives: Views from the Frontline* (Surbiton, UK: The Police Federation of England and Wales), 31.

94. ONS (2016), *Compendium: Homicide*, February 11, at https://tinyurl.com/yacca5ka (accessed August 28, 2018).

95. Private documentation in the author's possession.

96. Steve Woodward (2014), *The Long Short Walk: Diary of a Traffic Police Family Liaison Officer* (Aylesbury: ShieldCrest).

97. John Thomson, private email to author, July 17, 2014.

98. Vikram Dodd (2014), "Police want right to see Medical Records without Consent," *The Guardian*, August 10.

99. P. Duff (1997), "Diversion from Prosecution into Psychiatric Care: Who Controls the Gates?" *British Journal of Criminology*, Vol. 37(1): 15–34; 23.

100. Ibid., 19.

101. See, David Latham (2017), *Mental Health and a Fair Trial: A Report by Justice* (London: Justice), at https://tinyurl.com/y9tkvw77 (accessed September 5, 2018); Nina Lakhani (2009), "Legal System denies justice to 'mentally ill victims of crime,'" *The Independent*, January 25, at https://tinyurl.com/btb4na (accessed September 5, 2018).

102. Simon Mackay (2015), *Covert Policing: Law and Practice*, 2nd ed. (Clarendon, UK: Oxford University Press), Section p. 234, Section 7.88 Code of Practice para 4.21.

103. Dodd, "Police want right to see medical records."

104. Liberty (2012), *Keep Politics out of Policing*, at https://tinyurl.com/nl59udc (accessed February 16, 2018).

105. Chapman, *Police State*, 25–26.

Chapter 4: Road Deaths

1. Department for Transport (2016), *Reported Road Casualties in Great Britain: Main results 2015*, June 30, at http://bit.ly/296ivOW (accessed March 8, 2017), p. 35.

2. World Health Organisation (WHO) (2015), *Global Status Report on Road Safety*, at http://bit.ly/1MyiKf0 (accessed March 8, 2017).

3. House of Commons: Home Affairs Committee (2011), *New Landscape of Policing*, Fourteenth Report of Session 2010–12, Vol. 1: 21, Evidence, p. 168.

4. ACPO (2007), *Road Death Investigation Manual* (RDIM), at http://bit.ly/2n26mQb, and College of Policing (2013), *Road policing: Investigation of fatal and serious injury road collisions*, at http://bit.ly/2lAPCCF (accessed March 8, 2017).

5. ACPO, *Road Death Investigation Manual*, 10.

6. L. M. Pearce (2002), *Dangerous Driving and the Law: Road Safety Research Report* No. 26 (Crowthorne, UK: Transport Research Laboratory), 14.

7. ACPO, *Road Death Investigation Manual*, 40.

8. Ibid., 44.

9. Ibid., 68.

10. Ibid., 93.

11. Adam Elliot-Cooper (2014), "Doreen Lawrence, Police Spies and Institutional Racism," *Open Security*, January 14, at https://tinyurl.com/y9ozt9xz (accessed March 25, 2017).

12. College of Policing (2013), *Road Policing: Investigation of Fatal and Serious Injury Road Collisions*, at http://bit.ly/2lAPCCF (accessed March 25, 2017).

13. See Sussex Police (2014), *Road Traffic Collisions—Attendance, Recording, Investigating and Management*, at https://tinyurl.com/ybzsbhg6 (accessed March 25, 2017).

14. The Police and Criminal Evidence Act (PACE), 1984, details policing powers and procedures and includes archaic language (re: Part VIII: 77 "Confessions by mentally handicapped persons") and out-of-date details re: Part IX *The Police Complaints Authority* which no longer exists. There are, however, constant updates such as to the Revised PACE Code E, 2016, on audio recording with suspects. See https://tinyurl.com/y9a7t2wz (accessed September 7, 2018).

15. Fraser Sampson (2007), *Blackstone's Police Manual* (Clarendon, UK: Oxford University Press), 36.

16. Kate Cairns (2017), "Submission to the Inquiry into Cycling and the Justice System," *All-Party Parliamentary Group on Cycling*, February 7, at https://allparty-cycling.org/ (Papers submitted to the inquiry and to me in correspondence). Kate also sent me full and detailed documentation relating to meetings with police officers. In addition to the information in the main body of the text, the family were also equally unhappy with the FLO (who refused to speak to Kate or respond to any of her emails), the SIO who only visited the scene of death a day before the inquest and the forensic collisions investigator who was at that time under investigation for fraud for which he was later found not guilty but his wife charged instead.

17. Lydall Ross (2011), "Sisters fury at coroner's failure to prevent more cyclist HGV deaths," *Evening Standard* (blogs), at https://tinyurl.com/y7ebs3a2 (accessed March 22, 2017).

18. Richard Hartley-Parkinson (2012), "Short-sighted lorry driver killed pedestrian, 97, while ignoring warnings to wear glasses after causing death of cyclist two years ago," *Daily Mail*, August 6, at https://tinyurl.com/ybroesjg (accessed March 22, 2017) and Martic Porter (2012), "Joao Lopes Sentence," *The Cycling Lawyer*, at https://tinyurl.com/arq7yhr (accessed March 22, 2017).

19. Ruth Lawson (2013), "Eilidh Cairns death crash driver escapes driving ban," *The Journal*, June 25, at https://tinyurl.com/y788ubte (accessed March 22, 2017).

20. Cairns, "Submission to the Inquiry."

21. Michael Marsh (2015), "Parents of Durham lorry crash victim Jake Thompson bid to reduce road tragedies," *Chronicle Live*, November 1, at https://tinyurl.com/y9eagfdu (accessed March 30, 2017); BBC (2014), "Jake Thompson death lorry driver 'drove through red light,'" at https://tinyurl.com/ybrwkp7h (accessed March 30, 2017).

22. See Rob Evans and Leila Haddou (2014), "Police investigated woman after she questioned handling of mother's death," *The Guardian*, October 30.

23. Simon Hattenstone (2000), "A Dangerous Pursuit," *The Guardian*, March 25.

24. Maria Docking, Tom Bucke, Kerry Grace, and Helen Dady (2007), *Police Road Traffic Incidents: A Study of Cases Involving Serious and Fatal Injuries* (London: Independent Police Complaints Commission), vi.

25. The same PC Morris was charged with gross misconduct in 2017 for using excessive force while a man was in his custody. He was given a caution and remains on active duty. See https://tinyurl.com/ya3fye8w (accessed July 30, 2018).

26. Hastings and St Leonard's Observer (2015), "Police driver involved in fatal Hastings collision defends actions," May 19, at https://tinyurl.com/ydyu6qeh (accessed March 13, 2017).

27. APPCG (2017), "Police Investigation and Initiatives," (Audio Feed from the House of Lords Select Committee, Session 3), at https://tinyurl.com/y9obp8ak (accessed March 31, 2017).

28. See, for instance, Chris Marshall-Bell (2017), "Several police forces look at introducing 'close pass' scheme after success in West Midlands," *Cycling Weekly*, at http://bit.ly/2nCXkK3, and BBC (2016), "West Midlands Police Target Drivers Too Close to Cyclists," at https://tinyurl.com/zda9gav (accessed March 31, 2017).

29. WMP (2017), "Close Pass Update" (West Midlands Police—Traffic Unit—Blog), January 2017, at https://tinyurl.com/y8txf74c (accessed September 7, 2018).

30. London Cycling Campaign, "Cycle Superhighways," at https://tinyurl.com/y7b4cszr (accessed March 14, 2017); BBC (2017), "London coroner urges 'slippery' cycle superhighway review," March 13, at https://tinyurl.com/y7uafeeh; Francesca Gillett (2016), "Hair-raising moment cyclists are thrown off bikes in central London cycle-superhighway pile-up," October 12, at http://bit.ly/2oGlRNI (accessed March 14, 2017).

31. Eccy de Jonge (2016), *Report on Cycle Casualties in Torrington/Tavistock Place, 1999–2015*, Bloomsbury Residents Action Group (unpublished).

32. Njoki Nicole Coleman (2017), "Cyclist dies in Tower Hamlets on cycle superhighway 2," *East London Lines*, February 8, at https://tinyurl.com/ya8bv9y5 (accessed March 14, 2017).

33. Jamie Bullen (2017), "Cyclists 'falling like skittles' on 'greasy' Cycle Superhighway in Stockwell," *London Evening Standard*, January 7.

34. CPS (ND), "Code for Crown Prosecutors," at http://bit.ly/2oheorU (accessed March 31, 2017).

35. See P. J. Hewson (2005), "Cycle helmets and road casualties in the UK," *Traffic Injury Prevention* Vol. 6(2):127–34; A. Erke and R. Elvik (2007), "Making Vision Zero real: Preventing pedestrian accidents and making them less severe," *TOI, Norwegian Centre for Transport Research Report* 889; F. T. Möllman, B. Rieger, and H. Wassmann (2004), "Specific patterns of bicycle accident injuries—An analysis of correlation between level of head trauma and trauma mechanism," DGNC Köln.

36. M. C. Dix and A. D. Layzell (1983), *Road Users and the Police* (London: Croom Helm and the Policing Foundation, University of Oxford), 91.

37. Terence Morris (1999), "Full speech from opening speaker," in Victim Support, *Inter-Agency Seminar on Death on the Road*, Occasional Paper 2 (1999), 17.

38. Road Share (2014), "Why Presumed Liability?" at https://tinyurl.com/y9szhd8e (accessed March 31, 2016).

Chapter 5: Police Support Networks

1. The tragic case of Sally Clark, convicted of killing her two baby boys, who died eighteen months apart, has become notorious is British miscarriages of justice cases, as her conviction rested on false statistical evidence provided by the paediatrician Roy Meadows and the failure to disclose medical evidence by the forensic pathologist, Alan Williams. See R. Clark, v [2003] EWCA Crim 1020 (April 11, 2003), at https://tinyurl.com/6uj64cy (accessed March 23, 2018).

2. Alys Harte and Clive Coleman (2018), "Evidence not being disclosed on a daily basis, lawyers say in survey," *BBC News*, at https://tinyurl.com/ydfjm4lp (accessed March 5, 2018).

3. Sophie Garrod (2018), "Solicitors frustrated with disclosure failings," *Police Oracle*, March 5, at https://tinyurl.com/yb8c59hd (accessed September 11, 2018).

4. Owen Bowcott (2019), "Rape cases 'could fail' if victims refuse to give police access to phones," *The Guardian*, April 29.

5. J. Lammers and I. Van Beest (2014), "The Effects of Power on Immorality," in *Power, Politics, and Paranoia: Why People Are Suspicious of Their Leaders*, edited by J.-W. Van Prooijen and P. A. M. Van Lange (Cambridge, UK: Cambridge University Press), 17–32; 24.

6. The Coroners Inquest Rules (2013), Section 27, p. 6, at https://tinyurl.com/y73goszb (accessed September 11, 2018).

7. Ibid., 19.

8. Phil Scraton and Kathryn Chadwick (1987), *In the Arms of the Law: Coroners' Inquests and Deaths in Custody* (London: Pluto Press), 17; Official guidelines by the British government state that, "In some areas the local police force employs the coroner's officers. However the officers' work is always carried out under the authority of the coroner who works independently from both the local authority and the local police." This is misleading since coroners rely entirely on the police for evidence gathering and witnesses. See Ministry of Justice, *Guide to Coroner Services*, at https://tinyurl.com/ycjhsrlf (accessed September 11, 2018).

9. Mike Redmayne (2007), "Rethinking the Privilege Against Self-Incrimination," *Oxford Journal of Legal Studies*, Vol. 27(2): 209–32; 209.

10. Ibid., 7.

11. Alan Craze, coroner to next-of-kin, email dated March 13, 2014.

12. Alan Craze (coroner) to PC Kelly Newton, email, April 15, 2014 (revealed in Subject Access Request).

13. Sergeant Melanie Doyle, "Minutes of a Case Conference held on 20 January 2014" (revealed in Subject Access Request).

14. Communication from Sussex Police and Crime Commissioner dated April 15, 2014.

15. John Fenwick (1980), "Misadventures of the Coroners' Inquest," *New Law Journal*, Vol. 130 (5980) December 11: 1164–65.

16. Ibid.

17. Ministry of Justice (2011), *Your Jury Service in the Coroner's Court*, at https://tinyurl.com/y8w6uz58 (accessed March 2, 2018), p. 5.

18. Ibid.

19. Anthony Morris, quoted in Scraton and Chadwick, *In the Arms of the Law*, 60.

20. Coroners' Juries Bill (1983), *Hansard*, Vol. 442, May 10: 434–35, at https://tinyurl.com/ybrd9dp9 (accessed September 11, 2018).

21. The chief coroner also specified that "if the original jury was discharged, a new jury must be summoned," (Paragraph 11 of Schedule 1 section 4(a)). Chief Coroner (2013), Guide to the Coroner's and Justice Act 2009, at https://tinyurl.com/j5dj4g9 (accessed March 21, 2018).

22. Hastings & St Leonards Observer (2015), "Cleaner was electrocuted at train depot," April 14, at https://tinyurl.com/ya68gqds (accessed September 11, 2018).

23. Gwyn Topham (2017), "Southeastern rail and contractor fined £3.6m over cleaner's death," *The Guardian*, November 17.

24. Scraton and Chadwick, *In the Arms of the Law*, 11.

25. JR Claim No: CO/4969/2010 in the High Court of Justice. Witness Statement: Shirley Radcliffe, October 27, 2010 Exhibit SR1 (documents provided to the author),

26. Conn, "Hillsborough inquests jury rules 96 victims were unlawfully killed,"

27. Scraton and Chadwick, *In the Arms of the Law*, 12.

28. Jones, "Fatal Call," 162–63.

29. Fenwick, "Misadventures of the Coroners' Inquest," 1165.

30. Andrew Sanders, Richard Young, and Mandy Burton (2010), *Criminal Justice*, 4th ed. (Oxford: Oxford University Press), 668.

31. Scraton and Chadwick, *In the Arms of the Law*, 16.

32. Ibid., 19.

33. This was commented on in the early 1980s by the coroner of Yorkshire, Anthony Morris, quoted in Scraton and Chadwick, *In the Arms of the Law*, 60. It is also duly noted in Ministry of Justice (2014), *Guide to Coroner Services*, 4.

34. GM Complaint [report] dated August 8, 2014 [private correspondence].

35. Jones, "Fatal Call," 167.

36. For a detailed account, see Radley Balko (2017), "Federal court rejects appeal of man convicted by absurd 'death mask' testimony," *Washington Post*, February 27.

37. Ibid.

38. Ibid.

39. Sanders et al. (2010), *Criminal Justice*, 371.

40. Ibid., 427.

41. APPCG (2017), "Police Investigation and Initiatives" (Audio Feed from the House of Lords Select Committee, Session 3), at https://tinyurl.com/y9obp8ak (accessed March 31, 2017). The Threshold Test is provided at https://tinyurl.com/ya7jrbp8 (accessed April 4, 2018).

42. Sanders et al., *Criminal Justice*, 372.

43. Ibid.

44. Ibid., 377.

45. Ibid., 380.

46. London Cycling Campaign (2009), Cyclists demonstrate against CPS and driver apathy, July 2, at https://tinyurl.com/ydh8ledl (February 28, 2018).

47. Harte and Coleman, "Evidence not being disclosed."

48. Hannah Quirk (2006), "The Significance of Culture in Criminal Procedure Reform: Why the Revised Disclosure Scheme Cannot Work," *The International Journal of Evidence & Proof*, Vol. 10(1): 42–59; 47.

49. Ibid., 51.

50. Ibid., 52.

51. Criminal Procedure and Investigations Act 1996 (CPIA), Part 1: Disclosure, at https://tinyurl.com/y9m48ofp (accessed March 9, 2018).

52. BBC, Radio 4 [radio] "File on 4: Disclosing the Truth," February 27, 20.00.

53. Harte and Coleman, "Evidence not being disclosed."

54. Sanders et al., *Criminal Justice*, 427–28.

55. See, Marshall Edmonds McMahon, Victims' Right to Review—How effective is the right? at https://tinyurl.com/ybb2khdy (accessed March 12, 2018).

56. CPS (2013), "Victims' Right to Review (VRR)," at https://tinyurl.com/yc9hedes (accessed March 13, 2018).

57. Pseudonyms have been allocated for each member of this case.

58. CPS (2013), *The Code for Crown Prosecutors*, at https://tinyurl.com/yayf3bgj (accessed April 13, 2018).

59. Maeve McClenaghan (2013), "New figures reveal the CPS has lost more than 20% of its legal teams," *Bureau of Investigative Journalism*, July 27, at https://www.thebureauinvestigates.com/stories/2013-07-27/new-figures-reveal-the-cps-has-lost-more-than-20-of-its-legal-teams (accessed March 12, 2018).

60. Ministry of Justice (2016), "Efficiency in the Criminal Justice System," *National Audit Office*, March 1, section 10.

61. Ibid., section 13.

62. Duncan Cambell (2018), "Why the secret handshake between police and Freemasons should worry us," *The Guardian*, January 2; Vikram Dodd (2017), "Freemasons are blocking reform, says Police Federation leader," *The Guardian*, December 31.

63. Rebecca Broadbent (2013), "Challenging the decision to charge," *The Student Lawyer*, June 21, at https://tinyurl.com/y6wwzm4p (accessed March 13, 2018). Even the British Citizen's Advice Bureau get this wrong, stating on one site that "the Crown Prosecution Service (CPS) . . . make the decision whether a suspect should be charged with an offence or not." The CPS make the decision to *prosecute* where a suspect has *already been charged*. See Citizens Advice, "Child Abuse: How the police investigate allegations," at https://tinyurl.com/yd829jdb (accessed March 13, 2018).

Chapter 6: Accountability: A Gray Area

1. Cressida Dick, the Commissioner for the MPS, has stated that the word "corruption" is "associated with officers taking illegal payments," in "Met chief 'confident' in professional standards department amid watchdog probe," *Police Oracle*, August 2, 2018, at https://tinyurl.com/ya9ohmdk (accessed August 3, 2018); see also Tim Prenzler (2013), *Ethics and Accountability in Criminal Justice*, 2nd ed. (Toowong, QLD: Australian Academic Press), 45; Tim Newburn (2015), *Literature Review*; see IPCC (2012), *Corruption in the Police Service in England and Wales—Second Report* (London: IPCC), 4.

2. Ibid., 57.

3. Louise Westmarland (2013), "Ethics and Policing," in *The Future of Policing*, 466.

4. Ian Waters and Katie Brown (2000), "Police Complaints and the Complainants' Experience," *The British Journal of Criminology*, Vol. 40(4) 1: 617–38; 617.

5. Tamar Hopkins (2011), "When Police Complaint Mechanisms Fail: The Use of Civil Litigation," *Alternative Law Journal*, Vol. 36(2): 99–103; 100.

6. Sanders et al., *Criminal Justice*, 686, see also fn96.

7. IPCC (2014), *Focus: Statutory Guidance*, Section 5, August at https://tinyurl.com/yd3rgzsa (accessed July 19, 2018).

8. Kevin Stenson and Dan Silverston (2014), "Making Police Accountable: Governance and Legitimacy," in *The Future of Policing*, 429–45; p. 435.

9. Smith, "Rethinking Police Complaints," 17.

10. Sanders, et al., *Criminal Justice*, 680, 681 (see also fn78).

11. Nick Davies (2008), "Crisis at Police Watchdog as Lawyers Resign," *The Guardian*, February 25, at https://tinyurl.com/y85c9ymz (accessed April 30, 2018).

12. Sanders et al., *Criminal Justice*, 689.

13. Tim Prenzler (2009), *Police Corruption: Preventing Misconduct and Maintaining Integrity* (Boca Raton: CRC Press), 100.

14. HM Courts & Tribunals Service (2017), Vexatious Litigants, at https://tinyurl.com/ya58g6t9 (accessed July 30, 2018).

15. ICO (2000), Dealing with Vexatious Requests, Section 14 *Freedom of Information Act*, at https://tinyurl.com/ycw567z3 (accessed July 30, 2018), p. 6.

16. The newly formed IOPC uses the IPCCs definition of vexatious in its dictionary form. See IPCC (2017), *Vexatious Complaints and Persistent Complainants—Complaints Handling and Managing Complainants' Needs*, at https://tinyurl.com/ycrzgqhv (accessed July 30, 2018).

17. Kevin Donoghue (2015), Five Ways to Cut Police Complaints, February 4, at https://tinyurl.com/ydxcdqzp (accessed May 1, 2018).

18. In a subsidiary case where the complainant wrote directly to the Chief Constable of Cleveland Police for a breach of confidence by the then ACPO lead for Roads Policing, the Assistant Chief Constable formally apologised.

19. Westmarland, "Ethics and Policing," 465.

20. Timothy Brain (2013), *A Future for Policing in England and Wales* (Oxford: Oxford University Press), 205.

21. Steve Bird (2018), "Police furious as crowd cheers fleeing suspect," *The Sunday Times*, August 19.

22. The College of Policing make clear that "officers should provide the subject with a clear warning of their intention to use a CED [TASER]." See https://tinyurl.com/yc4v6bjw (accessed July 17, 2018).

23. Axon, The new Taser—the Taser X2 now has four propelled darts allowing police officers to taser people twice or to "try again" if they miss. See https://tinyurl.com/y85eq2l7 (accessed April 24, 2018).

24. Tess Owen (2015) ,"'This instrument can kill': Tasers are not as harmless as previously thought," *Vice News*, at https://tinyurl.com/nrkmn4q (accessed June 18, 2018).

25. Drive stun mode is documented in the use of Taser in the Approved Guidelines, see *Armed policing: Conducted energy devices (Taser)*, at https://tinyurl.com/yc4v6bjw (accessed July 17, 2018).

26. CBS News (2007), "U.N.: Tasers are a form of torture," November 25, at https://tinyurl.com/y9fzwwtc (accessed June 19, 2018); Amnesty International USA (2007), Amnesty International's concerns about Taser use: Statement to the US Justice Department inquiry into deaths in custody, October 1, at https://tinyurl.com/yb8ka3al (accessed July 7, 2018).

27. Mark Lefty (2016), "United Nations warns UK Government to stop tasering children," *Independent*, at https://tinyurl.com/yd9awhek (accessed July 17, 2018).

28. The duration of the initial discharge and any subsequent discharge must be proportionate, lawful, accountable, and absolutely necessary. College of Policing (2018), *Armed Policing: Conducted Energy Devices*, at https://tinyurl.com/yc4v6bjw (accessed September 11, 2018).

29. Alexandra Topping (2014), "Met police helicopter service accused of encouraging Twitter abuse of critics," *The Guardian*, July 11.

30. Lucy Moreton (2018), "Opinion: unfair criticism of Home Office staff over Windrush deflects blame from cuts," *Civil Service World*, April 23, at https://tinyurl.com/ydz8hwvs (accessed April 24, 2018).

31. BFI: The COI Collection Volume One: *Police and Thieves*, at https://tinyurl.com/y8nyen95 (accessed July 7, 2018). See also BFI Player: *Police Annual Inspection at Birchfields Park* (1901), at https://tinyurl.com/ybpj2cug (accessed July 7, 2018) and BFI Player: *Evidence* (1935), at https://tinyurl.com/y9chcrnf (accessed July 7, 2018); Katy McGahan (2015), "1930s hidden-camera footage is first film used as evidence in UK courts," at https://tinyurl.com/y7g6z3q7 (accessed July 7, 2018).

32. Murray Lee and Alyce McGovern (2014), *Policing and Media: Public Relations, Simulations and Communications* (Abingdon, UK: Routledge), 146.

33. Channel 4 (2018), *24 Hours in Police Custody*, Series 6: Ep 1 SO6E01 "Sex and Corruption." First aired on 20 February; dir. Tom Barrow.

34. Luton Today (2018), "Bedfordshire Police 'overwhelmed' by viewers' reaction after story of corrupt detective featured on documentary," at https://tinyurl.com/y8p75asx (accessed July 7, 2018).

35. Elizabeth Monk-Turner, Homer Martinez, Jason Holbrook, and Nathan Harvey (2007), "Are reality TV crime shows continuing to perpetuate crime myths?" *Internet Journal of Criminology*, at https://tinyurl.com/y7h3ukmg (accessed July 16, 2018).

36. Phillip Chong Ho Shon and Bruce A. Arrigo (2006), "Reality-based television and police-citizen encounters," *Punishment and Society*, Vol. 8(1) January: 59–85; 65.

37. Ibid., 64.

38. Ibid.

39. Jessica M. Fishman (1999), "The Populace and the Police: Models of Social Control in Reality-Based Crime Television," *Critical Studies in Mass Communications*, Vol. 16 (3): 268–88; 268–69.

40. Ibid., 274.
41. Chapman, *Police State*, 101.
42. See Jones, "Fatal Call," chapter 4.
43. Personal communication: the man in question was the author's neighbor.
44. Robert D. Storch (1976), "The Policeman as Domestic Missionary: Urban Discipline and Popular Culture in Northern England, 1850–1880," *Journal of Social History*, Vol. 9(4): 481–502; 481.
45. Ibid., 482.
46. Ibid., 485.
47. Chapman, *Police State*, 104.
48. At current estimates, police officers make up just 0.2 percent of the population in England & Wales.
49. Satnam Choongh (1998), "Policing the Dross: A Social Disciplinary Model of Policing," *The British Journal of Criminology*, Vol. 38(4): 623–34; 623.
50. Ibid.
51. See James Q. Wilson and Richard J. Hernstein (1985), *Crime and Human Nature* (New York: The Free Press).
52. Thomas Hobbes (1973), *Leviathan* (London: JM Dent & Sons), 63–90.
53. For a more detailed discussion on this topic, see Eccy de Jonge (2018), "Thinking Ecologically: A post-Enlightenment Perspective," in *Deep Philosophy, Deep Ecology*, edited by Mary-Ann Crumplin (Lydney, UK: Prometheus Trust), 167–85.
54. Joseph Rankin and Roger Kern (2001), "Social Control Theory," *The Sage Dictionary of Criminology* (London: Sage), 270.
55. Mike McConville and Chester Mirsky (1995), "Guilty Pleas Courts: A Social Disciplinary Model of Criminal Justice," *Social Problems* Vol. 42(2): pp. 216–34.
56. Owen Bowcott (2017), "'Global epidemic' of US-style plea bargaining prompts miscarriage warning," *The Guardian*, April 27; Mike McConville and Luke Marsh (2014), *Criminal Judges: Legitimacy, Courts and State-Induced Guilty Pleas in Britain* (Cheltenham and Northampton: Edward Elgar), 63.
57. Personal communication, Mike McConville, email, August 16, 2018.
58. Choongh, "Policing the dross," 625–26.
59. Ibid., 627.
60. Ibid.
61. Ibid., 629.
62. Ibid.
63. Ibid., 630.
64. Ibid., 632.
65. See de Jonge, "Thinking Ecologically," 167.
66. Samuel Vincent Jones (2018), "Police, Heroes, and Child Trafficking: Who Cries When Her Attacker Wears Blue," *Nevada Law Journal*, Vol. 18(3): 1007–58.
67. Ibid., 1014.
68. Ibid., 1023.
69. Jamie Grierson, Vikram Dodd, Sarah Marsh, and Kevin Rawlinson (2018), "Parliament Crash: Man Arrested on Suspicion of Terrorism," *The Guardian*, August 15.
70. Police Federation, *The Office of Constable*.

71. Anna Kopec-Massey (2017), "Exploring the Role of Empathy in Social Enterprise," PhD thesis, University of Northampton, England, p. 11.

72. Ibid., 19.

73. Ibid., 27.

74. Kopec-Massey, "Exploring the Role of Empathy," 30.

75. Ibid., 31.

76. See HMIC (2009), *Adapting to Protest*, and HMIC (2009), *Adapting to Protest: Nurturing the British Model of Policing*, at https://tinyurl.com/ycjjymph (accessed July 12, 2018); HMIC (2011), *The Rules of Engagement: A Review of the 2011 Disorders*, December 20, at https://tinyurl.com/yahocx7d (accessed July 12, 2018); ACPO (2010), *Manual of Guidance on Keeping the Peace* (Wyboston, UK: Specialist Operations Centre), at https://tinyurl.com/y6wavtng (accessed July 12, 2018).

77. Stenson and Silverston, "Making Police Accountable," 430.

78. This is seen particularly in the case of crowds with police regarding anyone within a crowd as being fundamentally irrational with the potential for violence. Waddington, *Policing Public Disorder*, 40.

79. Raeka Prasad (2011), "English riots were 'a sort of revenge' against the police," *The Guardian*, December 5.

80. This view is the basis for the philosophical position known as deep ecology. See Eccy de Jonge (2004), *Spinoza and Deep Ecology* (London: Routledge).

81. Prasad, "English riots."

82. College of Policing (2014), The effects of problem-oriented policing on crime and disorder: What Works Briefing, at https://tinyurl.com/ybtetaou (accessed September 11, 2018).

83. Brogden and Ellison, *Policing in an Age of Austerity*, 134–35.

84. Jones, "Police, Heroes, and Child Trafficking," 1023.

85. The National Audit Office reported that the new government initiative of changing welfare benefits to one Universal Credit was causing great hardship and poverty, forcing people to use food banks. In response, the Work and Pensions Minister Alok Sharma spoke on BBC Radio 4s *Today Programme* denying there was any problem. See BBC (2018), *Today*, June 15, and Hannah Richardson (2018), "Universal Credit 'could cost more than current benefits system'" *BBC News Education*, at https://tinyurl.com/y92b8gv6 (accessed July 12, 2018); Patrick Butler (2018), "Universal credit savaged by public watchdog," *The Guardian*, June 15.

86. McConville and Marsh, *Criminal Judges*, 27.

87. See Cyril Dixon (2018), "Police solve less than 3% of burglaries," *Express*, June 18, and Ryan Wilkinson (2018), "Just 5 per cent of UK burglaries and robberies are being solved by police," *The Independent*, June 17, at https://tinyurl.com/yc3cm2fh (accessed July 12, 2018).

Conclusion

1. Home Office (2008), Circular 025/2008 *The Taylor Reforms—Police conduct, Performance and Associated Regulation* (London: HMSO).

2. Rob Evans (2018), "Undercover police whistleblower joins boycott of inquiry," *The Guardian*, May 9.

3. The King's Fund (2018), "What's going on with A&E waiting times?" at https://tinyurl.com/ksbttxq (accessed July 10, 2018).

4. See Mark Hughes (2008), "Seven mistakes that cost De Menezes his life," *Independent*, December 13.

5. Hayden Smith (2017), "Appointment of Cressida Dick as first woman Met Police Commissioner sparks criticism," February 22, at https://tinyurl.com/y7usxdt8 (accessed June 24, 2018).

6. Press Association (2019), "Hammersmith stabbing: 39 people under investigation," *The Guardian*, January 1, at https://tinyurl.com/ybtzq256 (accessed January 3, 2019).

7. Barry Wright (2010), "Civilianising the 'Blue Code?' An Examination of Attitudes to Misconduct in the Police Extended Family," *International Journal of Police Science & Management*, Vol. 12(3): 339–56.

Selected Bibliography

ACPO. (2005). *Core Investigative Doctrine.* Wyboston, UK: NCPE.

———. (2008). *Family Liaison Officer Guidance.* Wyboston, UL: NCPE. Available at: https://tinyurl.com/y8hcptd3 (accessed September 5, 2018).

———. (2010). *Manual of Guidance on Keeping the Peace, Specialist Operations Centre.* Available at: https://tinyurl.com/y6wavtng (accessed July 12, 2018).

Barker, Tom. (1996). *Police Ethics: Crisis in Law Enforcement.* Springfield, IL: Charles C Thomas.

Bichard, Michael. (2004). *The Bichard Inquiry: Report.* London: Stationery Office. Available at: https://tinyurl.com/hgm9xbs (accessed August 30, 2018).

Billingsley, Roger, ed. (2009). *Covert Human Intelligence Sources.* London: Waterside Press.

Box, Steven, and Ken Russell. (1975). "The Politics of Discreditability: Disarming Complaints Against the Police." *Sociological Review,* Vol. 23(2): 315–46.

Brain, Timothy. (2013). *A Future for Policing in England and Wales.* Oxford: Oxford University Press.

Brandl, Steven, G. (2014). *Criminal Investigations.* Los Angeles: Sage.

Brogden, Mike, and Graham Ellison. (2013). *Policing in an Age of Austerity.* London: Routledge.

Buckwater, Art. (1983). *Surveillance & Undercover Investigation.* Woburn, MA: Butterworth.

Carsons, Simon. (2016). "Misconduct in Public Office." *Criminal Law & Justice Weekly.* March 18.

Chapman, Brian. (1970). *Police State.* London: Pall Mall.

Chatterton, Michael. (2008). *Losing the Detectives: Views from the Frontline.* Surbiton, UK: The Police Federation of England and Wales.

Choongh, Satnam. (1998). "Policing the Dross: A Social Disciplinary Model of Policing." *The British Journal of Criminology,* Vol. 38(4): 623–34.

College of Policing. (2014). *Code of Ethics.* Available at: https://tinyurl.com/hxtzeqd (accessed July 3, 2018).

Davidson, Julia, and Petter Gottschalk. (2014). *Police Deviance and Criminality: Managing Integrity and Accountability.* New York: Novinka.

de Jonge, Eccy. (2005). "A Philosophical Analysis into the Causes and Prevention of Deliberate Self Harm." *Practical Philosophy,* Autumn: 30–34.

———. (2015). "Literature Review: Confirmation Bias in Policing Investigations." Unpublished masters paper: Portsmouth University, England.

———. (2016). *Spinoza and Deep Ecology*. London: Routledge.

———. (2018). "Thinking Ecologically: A Post-Enlightenment Perspective." In Mary-Ann Crumplin, ed., *Deep Philosophy, Deep Ecology* (pp. 167–85). Lydney: Prometheus Trust.

Dix, M. C., and A. D. Layzell. (1983). *Road Users and the Police.* London: Croom Helm and the Policing Foundation, University of Oxford.

Docking, Maria, Tom Bucke, Kerry Grace, and Helen Dady. (2007). *Police Road Traffic Incidents: A Study of Cases Involving Serious and Fatal Injuries.* London: Independent Police Complaints Commission.

Ellison, Mark. (2014). *The Stephen Lawrence Independent Review*. London: House of Commons: March 6, section 4.2.1. Available at: https://tinyurl.com/y9rmdh9a (accessed September 5, 2018).

Evans, Rob, and Paul Lewis. (2014). *Undercover: The True Story of Britain's Secret Police* London: Guardian Books and Faber & Faber.

Hillsborough Independent Panel. (2012). *The Report of the Hillsborough Independent Panel.* London: The Stationery Office.

HMIC. (2009). *Adapting to Protest.* London: HMIC. Available at: https://tinyurl.com/y9gfcj93 (accessed July 4, 2018).

———. (2009). *Adapting to Protest: Nurturing the British Model of Policing.* Available at: https://tinyurl.com/ycjjymph (accessed July 12, 2018).

———. (2011). The Rules of Engagement: A Review of the 2011 Disorders. Available at: https://tinyurl.com/yahocx7d (accessed July 12, 2018).

———. (2013). Mistakes were made: HMIC's review into allegations and intelligence material concerning Jimmy Saville between 1964 and 2012. Available at: https://tinyurl.com/ybmvvfsy (accessed February 5, 2018).

———. (2014). *State of Policing: The Annual Assessment of Policing in England and Wales 2013/2014*. Available at: https://tinyurl.com/yd99hf5f (accessed July 4, 2018).

———. (2015). "The depths of dishonour: Hidden voices and shameful crimes." Available at: https://tinyurl.com/ybrvrd42 (accessed July 4, 2018).

Hobbes, Thomas. (1973). *Leviathan.* London: JM Dent & Sons.

Hopkins, Tamar. (2011). "When Police Complaint Mechanisms Fail: The Use of Civil Litigation." *Alternative Law Journal*, Vol. 36(2): 99–103.

House of Commons. (2018). *Gosport War Memorial Hospital The Report of the Gosport Independent Panel.* London: OGL.

IPCC. (2006). *Report of the Review into the events, leading up to and following the death of Christopher Alder on 1st April 1998.* London: House of Commons. Available at: https://tinyurl.com/y9x5hxcx (accessed September 5, 2018).

———. (2011). *Corruption in the Police Service in England and Wales—First Report.* London: IPCC.

———. (2012). *Corruption in the Police Service in England and Wales—Second Report.* London: IPCC.

———. (2012). *The Abuse of Police Powers to Perpetrate Sexual Violence.* London: IPCC.

———. (2014). *Focus: Statutory Guidance* Section 5. Available at: https://tinyurl.com/yd3rgzsa (accessed July 19, 2018).

———. (2017). *Vexatious Complaints and Persistent Complainants—Complaints Handling and Managing Complainants' Needs.* Available at: https://tinyurl.com/ycrzgqhv (accessed July 30, 2018).

Jacobs, James B. (2015). *The Eternal Criminal Record.* Cambridge, MA: Harvard Press.

Jay, Alexis. (2014). *Independent Inquiry into Child Sexual Exploitation in Rotherham, 1997–2013.* Rotherham, UK: Rotherham Metropolitan Borough Council.

Jones, Dean. (2011). "Miscarriages of Justice: The Role of Homicide Review." *Medicine, Science and Law,* Vol 51: 63–67.

———. (2014). "The Relationship Between Homicide Rates and Forensic Post Mortem Examinations in England and Wales." *The Journal of Homicide and Major Incident Investigation,* Vol. 9(2): 58–68.

———. (2016). "Fatal Call: Getting Away with Murder." PhD thesis, University of Portsmouth, England. Available at: https://tinyurl.com/yae37hgg (accessed July 4, 2018).

Kirby, Stuart. (2013). *Effective Policing? Implementation in Theory and Practice.* Basingstoke, UK: Palgrave Macmillan.

Kopec-Massey, Anna. (2017). "Exploring the Role of Empathy in Social Enterprise." PhD thesis, University of Northampton, England.

Lambri, Tessa. (2013). "Modelling the Implementation and Acceptance of the Police National Database in UK Police Forces." PhD thesis, Loughborough University, England.

Latham, David. (2017). *Mental Health and a Fair Trial: A Report by Justice.* London: Justice. Available at: https://tinyurl.com/y9tkvw77 (accessed September 5, 2015).

Law Commission. (2016). *Misconduct in Public Office: Issue Paper 1.* Available at: https://tinyurl.com/yazs2ecv (accessed July 3, 2018).

Lee, Murray, and Alyce McGovern. (2014). *Policing and Media: Public Relations, Simulations and Communications.* Abingdon, UK: Routledge.

McConville, Mike, and Chester Mirsky. (1995). "Guilty Pleas Courts: A Social Disciplinary Model of Criminal Justice." *Social Problems,* Vol. 42(2): 216–34.

McConville, Mike, and Luke Marsh. (2014). *Criminal Judges: Legitimacy, Courts and State-Induced Guilty Pleas in Britain.* Cheltenham, UK: Edward Elgar.

Mackay, Simon. (2015). *Covert Policing: Law and Practice*, 2nd ed. Clarendon, UK: Oxford University Press.

McLaughlin, Eugene, and Anja Johanssen. (2002). "A Force for Change? The Prospects for Applying Restorative Justice to Citizen Complaints against the Police in England and Wales." *British Journal of Criminology,* Vol. 42: 635–53.

MacPherson, William. (1999). *The Stephen Lawrence Enquiry*. London: HMSO. Available at: https://tinyurl.com/ngc8wje (accessed July 4, 2018).
Marshall, Daniel, and Terry Thomas. (2017). *Privacy and Criminal Justice.* London: Palgrave Macmillan.
Mawby, Rob, and Alan Wright. (2005). *Police Accountability in the United Kingdom.* Available at: https://tinyurl.com/64eoy9x (accessed July 3, 2018).
Mawby, Rob, and Irene Zempi. (2016). *"Every Time It Happens, You Question Continuing as an Officer": The Experiences of Police Workers as Victims of Hate Crime.* Available at: https://tinyurl.com/ycslgq84 (accessed July 4, 2018).
Miller, Seaumus, and Ian A. Gordon. (2014). *Investigative Ethics.* Chichester, UK: John Wiley & Sons.
Milne, Rebecca, and Ray Bull. (1999). *Investigative Interviewing: Psychology and Practice.* Chichester, UK: John Wiley & Sons Ltd.
Ministry of Justice. (2015). *Code of Practice for Victims of Crime.* London: Stationery Office.
Newburn, Tim. (2015). *Literature Review: Police Integrity and Corruption.* London: HMIC.
Prenzler, Tim. (2009). *Police Corruption: Preventing Misconduct and Maintaining Integrity.* Boca Raton, FL: CRC Press.
———. (2013). *Ethics and Accountability in Criminal Justice: Towards a Universal Standard*, 2nd ed. Toowong QLD: Australian Academic Press.
Punch, Maurice. (2009). *Police Corruption: Deviance, Accountability and Reform in Policing.* Cullompton, UK: Willan.
Ross, Howard, J. (2014). *Everyday Bias: Identifying and Navigating Unconscious Judgments in Our Daily Lives.* Lanham, MD: Rowman & Littlefield.
Rossmo, D. Kim. (2006). "Criminal Investigative Failures: Avoiding the Pitfalls (Part Two)." *FBI Law Enforcement Bulletin,* Vol. 75(10): 12–19.
———. (2006). "Criminal Investigative Failures: Avoiding the Pitfalls." *FBI Law Enforcement Bulletin,* Vol 75(9): 1–8.
Sampson, Fraser. (2007). *Blackstone's Police Manual.* Clarendon, UK: Oxford University Press.
Sanders, Andrew, Richard Young, and Mandy Burton. (2010). *Criminal Justice,* 4th ed. Oxford: Oxford University Press.
Scarce, Michael. (1997). *Male on Male Rape: The Hidden Toll of Stigma and Shame.* New York: Plenum Press.
Schneider, Stephen. (2010). *Crime Prevention: Theory and Practice.* Boca Raton, FL: CRC Press.
Scraton, Phil. (1985). *The State of the Police.* London: Pluto Press.
———. (2016). *Hillsborough: The Truth.* Edinburgh: Mainstream Publishing.
Sherman, Lawrence. (2013). *The Rise of Evidence-Based Policing: Targeting, Testing and Tracking.* Chicago: University of Chicago.
Souryal, Sam S. (1992). *Ethics in Criminal Justice.* Cincinnati: Anderson Publishing.

Van Koppen, Peter J. (2008). "Blundering Justice—The Schiedam Park Murder." In Richard N. Kocsis, ed., *Serial Murder and the Psychology of Violent Crimes.* Totowa: Humana Press.

Waddington, David, P. (2007). *Policing Public Disorder: Theory and Practice.* Collumpton, UK: Willan.

Wilson, James Q., and Richard J. Hernstein. (1985). *Crime and Human Nature.* New York: The Free Press.

Wolf, Jonathan. (2011). *Ethics and Public Policy: A Philosophical Enquiry.* Abingdon, UK: Routledge.

Woodward, Steve. (2014). *The Long Short Walk: Diary of a Traffic Police Family Liaison Officer.* Aylesbury: ShieldCrest.

Index

About the Author

Eccy de Jonge, PhD, is a British philosopher, author, and artist. She holds a PhD in philosophy from the University of Essex and a postgraduate certificate in policing, policy, and leadership from the University of Portsmouth. The author of *Spinoza and Deep Ecology* and *Reinstating the Infinite*, she has published numerous articles in books and journals on metaphysics, applied ethics, and mental health. She has appeared on national radio and presented papers at international conferences. A keen birder and hiker, she has recently completed a memoir, set on the Shetland islands, exploring the nature of grief. *On St Ninian's Isle: A Search for Solace* is forthcoming.